The Philosophy of Camus

The Philosophy of Camus

Through a Kierkegaardian Lens

ANTHONY RUDD

OXFORD
UNIVERSITY PRESS

OXFORD
UNIVERSITY PRESS

Great Clarendon Street, Oxford, OX2 6DP,
United Kingdom

Oxford University Press is a department of the University of Oxford.
It furthers the University's objective of excellence in research, scholarship,
and education by publishing worldwide. Oxford is a registered trade mark of
Oxford University Press in the UK and in certain other countries

© Anthony Rudd 2024

The moral rights of the author have been asserted

All rights reserved. No part of this publication may be reproduced, stored in
a retrieval system, or transmitted, in any form or by any means, without the
prior permission in writing of Oxford University Press, or as expressly permitted
by law, by licence or under terms agreed with the appropriate reprographics
rights organization. Enquiries concerning reproduction outside the scope of the
above should be sent to the Rights Department, Oxford University Press, at the
address above

You must not circulate this work in any other form
and you must impose this same condition on any acquirer

Published in the United States of America by Oxford University Press
198 Madison Avenue, New York, NY 10016, United States of America

British Library Cataloguing in Publication Data
Data available

Library of Congress Control Number: 2024940120

ISBN 9780198924838

DOI: 10.1093/9780198924869.001.0001

Printed and bound by
CPI Group (UK) Ltd, Croydon, CR0 4YY

Links to third party websites are provided by Oxford in good faith and
for information only. Oxford disclaims any responsibility for the materials
contained in any third party website referenced in this work.

To Jeanine

Contents

Preface	viii
Note on References	ix

Introduction	1
I Pseudonymity, Indirect Communication, Appropriation	4
II Stages and Cycles	10
III The Self as Synthesis	17
IV The Religious	18

1. The Absurd	23
I Absurd Epistemology: Truths and the Truth	23
II Absurdity as Absence of Meaning	30
III Is Absurdism Consistent?	40
IV Absurdism and Value	50
V Conclusion to Chapter 1	57

2. Rebellion	59
I Rebellion as Revelation of Value	60
II Metaphysical Rebellion	67
III Refusing to Be a God	78
IV Applications: Camus's Politics	92
V Conclusion to Chapter 2: Some Kierkegaardian Questions	99

3. Nemesis	104
I Beyond the Ethical	105
II Back to the Greeks: Human Nature and Virtue Ethics	108
III Back to the Greeks: A Metaphysics of Limit	116
IV Beyond Disenchantment: 'A Sense of the Sacred'	123
V Affirmation and Denial: Camus's Tragic Sense of Life	134
VI Finding a Language	146
VII Radical Evil? Reading *The Fall*	151

Conclusion	167
Bibliography	169
Index	177

Preface

The idea for this book came from a course I taught on various occasions at St Olaf College, Minnesota, called 'Kierkegaard and Existentialism'. The title suggested that, although mostly about Kierkegaard, the course should also include some comparative and contrastive material on other thinkers in the broadly existentialist tradition. I chose Camus as my main foil to Kierkegaard and, as I continued to teach the course, I found that the dialogue that it set up between Kierkegaard and Camus—in which they featured in part as antagonists, but also in part as complementary to one another—proved rather enlightening. In particular, it helped me to see that Camus was a richer and more complex thinker than I had started by assuming. This gave me the idea of writing an article comparing Kierkegaard and Camus, using Kierkegaard's dialectic of the 'stages of life'—the aesthetic, the ethical, and the religious—as a template for understanding Camus's philosophical development. When, after toying with that idea for some time, I finally started work on it, I found that the writing I was doing kept expanding, until I realized that I needed to write a book, not just an article. Here it is. It is a book about Camus, rather than about Kierkegaard, but I hope that the 'Kierkegaardian lens' through which I look at Camus will help to bring his philosophical achievement into sharper focus. There are, of course, many ways in which one might approach the interpretation of Camus's thought, but I found that the comparison with Kierkegaard was very helpful to me in coming to understand Camus better—and appreciate him more—as a philosopher. I hope that others, too, will find this a helpful way to approach a thinker whose philosophical merits are still, I think, insufficiently recognized.

I am grateful to my students in the 'Kierkegaard and Existentialism' course over the years for taking up the challenge of reading these two thinkers together, and, by so doing, helping to assure me that it was a worthwhile enterprise to do so. My thanks to Steven DeLay for his interest in this project, and for inviting me to present some of this material to a seminar in Woolf University's 'Post-Kantian Philosophy' seminar series. I am grateful to the Danish Royal Library in Copenhagen for permission to use the image of Kierkegaard with a spyglass (taken from a letter by Kierkegaard to his fiancée, Regine Olsen) on the cover. Many thanks to Matt Vinton for his work compiling the index. As always, my greatest debt is to my wife, Jeanine Grenberg, for her encouragement as I worked on this project during a time of big transition in our lives. I am afraid that the book still does not include as many commas as she would like, however.

Note on References

Works by Camus and by Kierkegaard are referred to throughout the book by abbreviations (e.g., MS, SUD, etc.) which are explained at the start of the Bibliography. Where I quote frequently from certain works by Camus, these abbreviations are given in the main text; otherwise in footnotes.

Introduction

This book is an attempt to take Camus seriously as a philosopher. Many commentators, while recognizing Camus's importance as a literary figure, or his historical significance as a participant in political controversies in mid-twentieth-century France, still see him as a philosophical lightweight, or not 'really' a philosopher at all. For instance, his biographer, Olivier Todd claims: 'In terms of philosophy, Camus cannot be placed in the Plato, Jean-Paul Sartre or Wittgenstein league. Camus kept repeating that he was no philosopher ... but evidently he did not insist enough.'[1] Perhaps things are starting to change; some valuable studies have appeared arguing in detail for the importance of Camus's philosophical agenda, and for the seriousness and tenacity with which he pursued it.[2] However, the editors of a recent collection of essays, dedicated to taking Camus seriously as a philosopher, still feel the need to begin their Introduction with the acknowledgement that

> it has become customary that scholarly works devoted to the study of Camus' philosophical thought begin with an apology ... The wealth of articles, chapters and book-length volumes dedicated to one of the most important and widely-read thinkers of the [the] 20th Century have not yet succeeded in overcoming Sartre et al's paternalistic dismissal of Camus as an amateur in philosophy ...[3]

Clearly Camus was not a technical, academic philosopher; if one's paradigm of a philosopher is someone like Frege or Quine, he would hardly count. But the concept of philosophy as it is actually used is far more expansive than that, and I shall be arguing here that Camus's work is a serious, carefully argued meditation on what are recognizable as central philosophical themes. The approach I am taking is comparative, for it is often helpful in exploring what sort of thinker someone was, to consider his or her affinities to (and differences from) other

---

[1] Todd, *Albert Camus*, 418. This passage, of course, involves a highly dubious inference from Camus not being one of the very greatest philosophers to his not being a philosopher at all. Todd does go on to concede—rather patronizingly—that 'not being a philosopher did not prevent him from being a stimulating thinker' (Todd, *Albert Camus*, 418).

[2] See, especially, Srigley, *Camus' Critique of Modernity*, and Sharpe, *Camus, Philosophe*.

[3] Sharpe, Kaluza, and Francev, 'Introduction', in Sharpe, Kaluza, and Francev (eds), *Brill's Companion to Camus*, 1. (They do, of course, dissent from that Sartrean dismissal, insisting that 'the issue today is not whether Camus was a philosopher but what kind of philosophy he proposed for our consideration' (*Brill's Companion to Camus*, 1).)

The Philosophy of Camus. Anthony Rudd, Oxford University Press. © Anthony Rudd (2024).
DOI: 10.1093/9780198924869.003.0001

2   THE PHILOSOPHY OF CAMUS

thinkers. For instance, Ronald Srigley has interpreted Camus as basically hostile to the philosophies of modernity and as being concerned most deeply to return us to the outlook of ancient Greek thinking. And Matthew Sharpe, while recognizing the importance of Camus's classical sources, has suggested that he should be primarily aligned with the early modern French *philosophes* and *moralistes* from Montaigne to Diderot.[4] While I think these comparisons do indeed shed a good deal of light on Camus, I am going to proceed by making a different comparison: between Camus and Søren Kierkegaard. I will try to show that Camus was, in important ways, pursuing a philosophical project parallel to Kierkegaard's, and that, accordingly, some of Kierkegaard's main ideas can be used to provide an interpretative framework for a comprehensive overview of Camus's philosophical work.

I should emphasize that this is a hermeneutical experiment—I hope to show that looking at Camus through this 'Kierkegaardian lens', as I am calling it, can help to make perspicuous the seriousness and integrity of Camus's intellectual itinerary. My aims are not primarily biographical/historical ones. I am not centrally concerned here to establish what books by Kierkegaard Camus had read, or when; nor am I even attempting to argue that Kierkegaard was in fact a major influence on Camus.[5] We know that Camus did read a number of Kierkegaard's works and that he admired (while also criticizing) him; but I do not think that there is sufficient evidence to show that Kierkegaard was a constant dialogue partner for Camus, someone he was always arguing with in his own mind, in the way that I think both Dostoevsky and Nietzsche certainly were.[6] Nevertheless, I will try to show that it is illuminating to read Camus *as if* he were in such a dialogue with Kierkegaard. I should emphasize that my main concern is with understanding Camus; the references to Kierkegaard are intended to serve this purpose, so this is not a full-blown comparative study in which each author gets equal billing, as it were (although I hope it can indicate the possibility and desirability of such a detailed comparative study). Accordingly, although I presuppose a general familiarity with Camus's works, I try not to presuppose a comparable familiarity with Kierkegaard. That is why this Introduction will include an overview of those aspects of Kierkegaard's thinking that I believe are particularly helpful for understanding Camus; I ask the reader to bear in mind that this is the limited purpose that these discussions of Kierkegaard are intended to serve.

One initial worry that should be mentioned about interpreting Camus through a comparison with Kierkegaard is that it might threaten to take us back to reading

---

[4] See Srigley, *Camus' Critique*, and Sharpe, *Camus, Philosophe*; see also Sharpe's review essay on Srigley's book: 'Restoring Camus as *Philosophe*'.

[5] Two useful survey essays that consider the extent and timing of Camus's knowledge of Kierkegaard, the translations that would have been available to him, etc., are Stan, 'Albert Camus: Walled within God', and Berg, 'Albert Camus and Soren Kierkegaard'.

[6] It is strikingly fitting that the two books found in Camus's briefcase after the car accident in which he died were Dostoevsky's *Demons* and Nietzsche's *The Gay Science*.

INTRODUCTION 3

Camus as an 'Existentialist'—an interpretative frame that determined much of the initial reception of his works, and that more sophisticated later treatments have been keen to repudiate.[7] Camus himself protested early on against being labelled an 'existentialist':

> No, I am not an existentialist. Sartre and I are always surprised to see our names linked. We have even thought of publishing a short statement in which the under-signed declare that they have nothing in common with one another and refuse to be held responsible for the debts they might respectively incur. It's a joke, actually ...When we did get to know each other, it was to realize how much we differed.[8]

Of course, Camus is here distinguishing his position from Sartre's, which was itself very different from Kierkegaard's. Furthermore, much Kierkegaard scholarship has protested that to label *Kierkegaard* as an existentialist, or as 'the Father of Existentialism', is simplistic and may be distorting. In a later interview Camus was more nuanced: 'If the premises of existentialism are found, as I believe they are, in Pascal, Nietzsche, Kierkegaard or Chestov, then I agree with them. If its conclusions are those of our existentialists [i.e. Sartre and his disciples] I do not agree, because they are contradictory to the premises.'[9] Here he aligns himself with one kind of 'existentialism' against another, and it is significant that the thinkers he identifies as his precursors are all deliberately anti-systematic and literary in their approach.[10] But, whether or not we use the term 'existentialism', I do think that the affinities that Camus himself recognized between his kind and style of thinking and Kierkegaard's are important for understanding Camus as a philosopher, and what sort of philosopher he was.

There are many different kinds of philosophical question. Some philosophers are primarily concerned with issues raised by mathematics or the natural sciences; others by socio-political problems. For both Kierkegaard and Camus, the most basic philosophical issue is the meaning of human existence; what it can mean to exist, not just as a stone or a chair, or even a cat, exists, but as a self-aware person. This shared fundamental concern leads both of them to investigate the various possible ways in which people try—implicitly or explicitly—to make sense of their lives, of what their existence means to them. But neither Kierkegaard nor Camus proceeds with the neutral objectivity of a scientific psychologist or sociologist; their shared approach is both first-personal and normative. The basic question

---

[7] See, again, Srigley, *Camus' Critique*, and Sharpe, *Camus, Philosophe*.
[8] Camus, 'No, I am not an existentialist' (1945), from 'Three Interviews', in *LCE* 345.
[9] *OC* iv. 663. Quoted in Hefferman, 'Camus and Husserl', 196.
[10] Of course, Sartre was a 'literary' thinker in that he explored ideas in his novels and plays. But his central philosophical work, *Being and Nothingness*, is a systematic treatise in the grand style, very different from the kinds of philosophical writing we find in Kierkegaard or Nietzsche.

4   THE PHILOSOPHY OF CAMUS

with which they are concerned has to be asked first-personally, as 'what (if any-thing) does my life, my existence, mean to me?' But this question is disturbing enough that we tend to repress or evade it. Kierkegaard (speaking through his pseudonym, Johannes Climacus) expresses his concern to act as a corrective in a culture where 'people ... have forgotten what it means to exist and what inward-ness is.'[11] And Camus insists that, although we often try to evade it, the only 'truly serious' philosophical question is 'whether life is or is not worth living' (MS 3)—and, if it is, how, or on what basis. But, although each of us has to ask this question first-personally, for him- or herself, the question is universal, and both thinkers are looking for generally valid answers. And, for both, the basic issue is normative, in that it is, inescapably, about the possibilities for *better* or *worse* ways of living. Hence, it can also be expressed as the question, 'how should I live?'[12]

Given this basic commonality of philosophical concern between Kierkegaard and Camus, there are four main aspects of Kierkegard's authorship that will con-stitute the 'Kierkegaardian lens' through which, I will argue, we can see Camus's philosophical project more clearly. These are: (1) his literary methodology—including Pseudonymity, Indirect Communication, and Appropriation; (2) his account of the 'Stages of Life'; (3) his understanding of the self as a synthesis; and (4) his central concern with religious issues. In the remainder of this Introduc-tion, I will discuss these four themes in turn, and will try to show in a preliminary way that comparisons with Camus under those headings can help us to appreciate key aspects of Camus's philosophical work. The detailed case for their usefulness, though, will be made by their application in the main body of the book that follows.

I Pseudonymity, Indirect Communication, Appropriation

Some may think it a bit quixotic to make a case for Camus's philosophical respectability by appealing to Kierkegaard, since plenty of doubts have been raised about whether Kierkegaard is a 'real philosopher'. (Too religious! Too literary! Too unsystematic! Too ironic!) Such complaints seem to me to presuppose an unduly narrow conception of philosophy (as well as tending to ignore plenty of argument and analysis in Kierkegaard's work, which is quite unproblematically philosoph-ical, even in a narrow academic sense).[13] But one obvious similarity between

[11] CUP i. 249. 'Inwardness' here means precisely this first-personal concern with the meaning of one's own life.

[12] Both Kierkegaard and Camus start by considering attitudes to life—Kierkegaard's 'aestheticism', Camus's Absurdism—that, on the face of it, repudiate that question, by responding 'there is no way you *should* live' or 'live however you like!' But to repudiate a question is still, in a way, to give an answer to it. And both the aesthetic and Absurdism, as we shall see, do in fact have their own normative (even if one does not want to say *ethical*) dimensions.

[13] For studies that address the question of Kierkegaard as philosopher, and that show that there is plenty of philosophical meat to chew on in his corpus, see Evans, *Kierkegaard on Faith and the Self*; Hannay, *Kierkegaard* and *Kierkegaard and Philosophy*; Pattison, *The Philosophy of Kierkegaard*.

Kierkegaard and Camus is that they do both combine what is recognizable as 'straight' philosophy with more literary forms of writing, and neither sees himself shifting to a radically different kind of activity in doing so. Kierkegaard did not see a contradiction (though perhaps a paradox) in subtitling one of his works a 'dialectical lyric',[14] nor did Camus think it inappropriate to make important philosophical moves in his 'Lyrical Essays'.

It was part of Kierkegaard's literary methodology that many of his works were ascribed to pseudonyms. This was not done to conceal his identity, but he used the pseudonyms for a variety of purposes. Some of them (such as 'A' and Judge William in *Either/Or*) are fictional characters, stating views with which Kierkegaard himself did not necessarily (or fully) agree. Others explore the Christian beliefs that Kierkegaard did hold, but from outside of them, in order to 'defamiliarize' what Kierkegaard felt had become so familiar in his culture that it was not properly noticed.[15] Others still articulate ideals that Kierkegaard accepted but did not feel that he personally had succeeded in living up to.[16] Kierkegaard created these pseudonyms in large part because of his concern with subjectivity. He is committed to philosophizing in a first-personal way, but this, for him, has little to do with the spectre of solipsism that was raised by Descartes, and that has haunted subsequent philosophy. On the contrary, Kierkegaard's commitment to the first-personal is what led him to multiply perspectives and to speak in voices other than his own.

A 'subjective' approach, for Kierkegaard, is one that is concerned, not merely with understanding certain principles in the abstract, but with what it might mean to live by (or in the absence of) them. 'Truth has always had many loud proclaimers, but the question is whether a person will in the deepest sense acknowledge the truth, will allow it to permeate his whole being, will accept all its consequences.'[17] One of Kierkegaard's major philosophical achievements was to bring this question of *acknowledgement* or *appropriation* to the fore; to shift our attention from the propositional content of what one believes, or the epistemological justification for it, to what it means for an individual to live in terms of those beliefs, to make them part of his or her own existence.[18] Hence his effort (via the pseudonyms) to explore from the inside what it is to inhabit (or to repudiate) an outlook, a world view, rather than simply reporting, objectively, on the

---

[14] This is the subtitle of *FT*.

[15] These include Johannes *de silentio* in *FT*, who repeatedly denies having faith, and Johannes Climacus in *PF* and *CUP*, who denies being a Christian.

[16] Principally 'Anti-Climacus', in *SUD* and *PC*.

[17] *CA* 138. (*The Concept of Anxiety* is a pseudonymous work, but Kierkegaard had not written it with that intention and added the pseudonym only just before publication. I do not think there is any problem with taking its contents to represent Kierkegaard's own thinking.)

[18] This concern is central to Kierkegaard's whole *oeuvre* but is most explicitly thematized in *CUP*, especially the chapters 'Becoming Subjective' and 'Truth is Subjectivity' (*CUP* i. 129–300)

6   THE PHILOSOPHY OF CAMUS

content of such a view. This is what he means by 'indirect communication'.[19] For instance, rather than (or in addition to) examining and criticizing amoralism from an outside perspective,[20] he writes, in works like 'The Seducer's Diary',[21] from the perspective of an amoralist. Of course, he does so with an agenda; he is not just exploring with a neutral curiosity the various attitudes to life that people might have. He is trying to bring out what is wrong with an amoral existence; not, however, by directly stating it, but by making the defects of an amoral life manifest through an honest, non-caricaturing presentation of what such a life might actually be like, how it might be lived.

Camus does something similar in his novels and plays where he explores ideas through showing them embodied in the characters and actions of his protagonists. Early on, in 1935, he wrote in his *Notebooks*: 'People can think only in images. If you want to be a philosopher, write novels'.[22] But the point of this remark is that to write novels may itself be a way of philosophizing. And it is true both that his literary works are highly philosophical *and* that his (explicitly) philosophical works have a sophisticated literary form and style. Another *Notebook* entry runs: 'Why am I an artist and not a philosopher? Because I think according to words, and not according to ideas'.[23] Here he is accepting (perhaps just ironically, or for the sake of argument) a dichotomy too strict to apply helpfully to his work, but to think 'in words' (or in images) is still to *think*, albeit in a way that is not simply reducible to abstract conceptual thinking. (I will have a little more to say in Chapter 3 about the specifically philosophical reasons Camus had for adopting a literary approach to philosophizing—one that is connected not only to his own particular interests and talents, but also to his reading of ancient Greek philosophy.)

That Camus explored philosophical ideas in his fictional works is clear enough. However, he did not do so simply by creating fictional characters to serve as his mouthpieces; one should not assume that one can identify his own views with those of his characters. (Certainly not with those of Caligula, or Martha from *The Misunderstanding*, but also not with those of Meursault in *The Outsider*, or even perhaps Dr Rieux from *The Plague*; and not with those of *The Fall*'s Jean-Baptiste Clamance, either.[24]) It can, I think, be helpful to regard these characters as akin to Kierkegaardian pseudonyms, deployed by Camus in order to explore and articulate certain views of life from the inside. This should not, indeed, be a terribly controversial view, though the point is still worth making, given the tendency of some readers to take *The Outsider* and *The Plague* in particular as more direct

[19] See, e.g., *CUP* i. 242–50.
[20] And even this 'outside' critique is not made from a 'view from nowhere' but from the perspective of an existing ethically committed individual, such as Judge William.
[21] In *E/O* i. 301–445.
[22] *NB I*, 10.
[23] *NB II*, 113.
[24] It does not, of course, follow from this that he rejects all his characters' views, or that he is not closer to some than to others.

statements of Camus's own views than I think they were intended to be. I will not, in fact, be spending very much time on most of Camus's fictional works in what follows, although I will mention or allude to them from time to time. (The only one I will consider in any detail is *The Fall*—the reasons for this exception will appear in Chapter 3). My focus will instead be on Camus's discursive, non-fictional works (*The Myth of Sisyphus* and *The Rebel*, but also some of his other essays and sometimes his *Notebooks*). This is partly to keep this book succinct, but also because it is generally agreed that Camus was a significant philosophical novelist and the secondary literature on his fictional work is already very substantial. Less has been written to show that Camus's non-fictional works should be taken seriously as philosophy, and that is my concern here.

This does not, however, mean that we should ignore the literary qualities of these works, or treat them simply as 'direct' communications. In particular, I think it is important to ask whether we can assume that Camus himself believed, or fully believed, everything that he wrote under his own name, in his non-fictional works. Might even they have some similarity to Kierkegard's pseudonymous writings? In the prefatory note to *The Myth of Sisyphus* Camus states that 'there will be found here merely the description, in the pure state, of an intellectual malady. No metaphysic, no belief is involved in it for the moment' (*MS* 2). Reading the book itself, it is hard not to get the impression that its author is advocating for an Absurdist outlook. But that prefatory note might suggest that 'Albert Camus', as the authorial voice of *The Myth*, functions a bit like a Kierkegaardian pseudonym, expressing and exploring a world view that its ultimate author did not necessarily or fully share.[25] In a later essay Camus seems to confirm this, stating that all he did in *The Myth* was 'to set it [the idea of the absurd] far enough from me to analyse it and decide on its logic'.[26] One might still wonder whether this—and the rather brilliant comparison of Absurdism to Descartes's methodological doubt, which one passes through, but only to get beyond it[27]—was a retrospective reinterpretation by Camus of what he was doing in *The Myth*. That this was the case might be suggested by another retrospective reflection, where he describes himself as 'having lived for a long time without morality ... and having actually advocated nihilism, though not always knowingly'.[28] The qualification is interesting; but, if ever Camus

---

[25] John Cruickshank seems to have been the first to suggest that the *Myth* was not an expression of Camus's own considered views; see his *Albert Camus and the Literature of Revolt*, 42–3. Joseph McBride criticizes Cruickshank for this, insisting that Camus is speaking for himself in the *Myth*; see McBride, *Albert Camus: Philosopher and Litterateur*, 71–3. Srigley argues that Camus cannot be identified with the first-personal narrative voice of the *Myth* (*Camus' Critique*, 24), though I think he is too confident in postulating a clear difference between them. None of these authors mentions Kierkegaard and his pseudonyms in this connection.

[26] Camus, 'The Enigma', in *SEN* 144 (*LCE* 158).

[27] Camus, 'The Enigma', *SEN* 145 (*LCE* 158): 'Cartesian doubt ... is not enough to make Descartes into a sceptic.' Cf. also *R.* 10.

[28] *DR* 207. (This essay was probably written in 1952 following his bitter public controversy with Sartre in that year, but was not published in Camus's lifetime.)

8   THE PHILOSOPHY OF CAMUS

did *knowingly* advocate nihilism (as the remark does imply), it was surely in *The Myth* (along with the other roughly contemporaneous works exploring the idea of the Absurd: *The Outsider, Caligula,* and *The Misunderstanding*).

A *Notebook* entry from 1943, shortly after *The Myth* was published, sheds interesting light on the question. There Camus makes a distinction

> between a philosophy of evidence and a philosophy of preference ... one can end up with a philosophy distasteful to the mind and the heart *but which commands respect.* Thus my philosophy of evidence is the absurd. But that doesn't keep me from having (or more precisely from *knowing*) a philosophy of preference, Ex: a fair balance between the mind and the world, harmony, plenitude.[29]

One could read this passage as saying that Camus wanted to get beyond Absurdism, but could not at the time see how to do so in an intellectually honest way. (The 'evidence' was against him.) But he does say that he finds Absurdism distasteful to his 'mind' as well as to his 'heart'. It seems clear that Camus was personally conflicted: both drawn to and repelled by Absurdism, but nevertheless feeling that it needed to be given as thorough and sympathetic a statement as he could manage. For philosophical, as opposed to strictly biographical, purposes, we do not really need to know whether Camus first believed in Absurdism, and then moved away from it, or whether he only ever entertained it in a hypothetical sense. In either case, I think it is helpful to see *The Myth* as doing something similar to what Kierkegaard did in some of his pseudonymous works—that is, to confront his readers (and himself) with a powerful articulation *as if* from the inside, of a view of life in order to challenge them (himself) to consider what its merits or weaknesses might be. And it matters that this articulation is 'subjective' in Kierkegaard's sense of the word. Camus, in *The Myth*, is not primarily concerned to argue (metaphysically) that life is absurd, or even (epistemologically) that it is reasonable to suppose that it is (although he comes closer to that); but rather to explore what it is like to experience life as absurd, and whether or not it is possible to live with that perception.

Is this parallel with the Kierkegaardian pseudonymous works true only of *The Myth*, or can we say something similar about Camus's later essays, and, in particular, *The Rebel*? There is an interesting remark from the *Notebooks* (1948 or 1949) that is relevant here: 'From my first books (*Nuptials*) to *La Corde* and *The Rebel*, my whole effort has been in reality to depersonalize myself (each time in a different tone). Later on, I shall be able to speak in my own name.'[30] A little later he

---

[29] *NB II*, 62.
[30] *NB II*, 210. *La Corde* ('The Rope') was the working title for the play that was eventually published and produced as *Les Justes* ('The Just').

writes: 'After *The Rebel*, free creation.'[31] So is he not, in *The Rebel*, writing freely, or in his own name? Perhaps he just means that he felt obligated to write that book in order to analyse the intellectual roots of the political horrors of his day, but after that he hopes to be able to turn to more deeply personal topics. That is, he felt a responsibility to write *The Rebel*, as a sincere expression of his own views; but it was not a free creative act in which he expressed himself as an artist. I think this is at least part of what he means. But we should note that he includes even his early lyrical essays (*Nuptials*), which seem very personal, as belonging to this 'depersonalized' writing. Perhaps even the 'Albert Camus' who signed these apparently very autobiographical reflections was a little bit like a Kierkegaardian pseudonym, giving expression to a view of life that its own ultimate author may not have shared?

'May not', of course, is not the same as 'did not'; it does not follow from the comparison with Kierkegaard that Camus himself would have simply rejected the outlook expressed in *Nuptials*. Kierkegaard's pseudonyms differ considerably in their distance from or closeness to Kierkegaard himself, and many of them, I think, do express views that Kierkegaard himself held. But even the closer ones do not fully express Kierkegaard's own views.[32] Returning to *The Rebel*, we should note that its interpretation is complicated by the fact that Camus was, at some points in the earlier parts of the book, articulating the stance of the 'Metaphysical Rebel', about which, it becomes clear as the book continues, he was at best highly ambivalent. (As with Absurdism, he was both genuinely drawn to the attitude of the Metaphysical Rebel, and disturbed by it.) One problem with reading *The Rebel* is that Camus does not clearly demarcate where he is expressing his own considered opinion and where he is speaking in the voice of the Metaphysical Rebel. (I will say more about this in Chapter 2.) But it does seem to me helpful in interpreting the book to think of it as having been *in part* authored by a pseudonym in the Kierkegaardian sense. As for the final position that is arrived at in *The Rebel*, with its critical assessment of both the importance and the dangers of rebellion, I do not think there is any evidence to suggest that Camus held that view at arm's-length, or that he articulated it only hypothetically. But the political ethics of *The Rebel* certainly did not represent Camus's full or final outlook. It was something that needed to be stated—and not just so it could be transcended or left behind—but in it he was trying to articulate a universal political outlook, rather than speaking fully for himself, entirely and simply in his own name. But the question of where Camus himself stood in relation to his writings will be one that I will continue to explore in the following chapters.

---

[31] *NB II*, 254.
[32] Except, I think, Vigilius Haufniensis in *CA* and also Anti-Climacus (*SUD* and *PC*).

10   THE PHILOSOPHY OF CAMUS

II Stages and Cycles

Kierkegaard's explorations 'from the inside' of the possible ways in which people can live and understand their lives led him to distinguish three main options: the aesthetic, the ethical, and the religious (though there are many subdivisions within each kind). He calls these, variously, the 'spheres of existence' or the 'stages of life'. The latter term suggests a developmental account, and Kierkegaard does think that we start with the aesthetic (all children are 'aesthetes' in his sense, although of a distinctive kind) and that the ethical and the religious are progressively more adequate ways to cope with the problems that arise through living in purely aesthetic terms. The account is thus normatively developmental; each stage represents an advance on its predecessor(s).[33] However, Kierkegaard does not think that there is any inevitability to the progression; if made at all, it is made by the free choice of each individual. The three 'stages' for Kierkegaard are not primarily doctrines or theories, but ways of living—though they certainly involve ways of thinking as well. But there may well be a disconnect between someone's 'official', explicit beliefs, and the way that person lives and experiences things (including, crucially, him- or herself).

It seems to me that Kierkegaard's account of the stages of life can serve rather well as a sort of model or template for understanding Camus's philosophical work. Not only is it true in general terms that Camus was concerned with the various ways in which people try (explicitly or implicitly) to make sense of their lives and the values that they live by, but there are also real parallels between the specific attitudes that he and Kierkegaard distinguished. I will try to show, accordingly, that it is illuminating to map the various stages of Camus's thought onto Kierkegaard's schema. I will say more shortly in order to give a preliminary justification for this claim (again, the full justification can consist only in using this interpretative model and seeing how it works in detail); but first, as I do not want to presuppose a substantial knowledge of Kierkegaard, it might be helpful for me to give a brief overview of his account of the stages.

By the 'aesthetic' life Kierkegaard does not necessarily mean one that is devoted to the pursuit of beauty or the arts (though an aesthete may pursue those things); it is, rather, the default position of someone who has not made a serious ethical or religious commitment. The aesthete is someone who acts on desires or inclinations—which may be of all sorts, and which may include altruistic and sympathetic ones. Kierkegaard—or his pseudonyms—distinguish various forms of aesthetic life. One is simple unreflective sensuality, the outlook of someone

---

[33] This is, at least, the standard, or orthodox, interpretation of Kierkegaard. I think it is correct and will be assuming its correctness in what follows. It has, however, been questioned—especially as far as the relationship of the aesthetic and the ethical is concerned. See, e.g., Carlsson, 'The Ethical Life of Aesthetes'; also Lippitt, 'Getting the Story Straight'. It would take me too far afield to respond to these arguments here, though see my comments on Lippitt in Rudd, 'Reason in Ethics Revisited', 189–90.

who judges life in terms of the physical pleasure and displeasures that it offers or threatens. Kierkegaard, who, like Camus, tended to think in images, sees this outlook most completely embodied in the mythical figure of Don Juan, especially as presented in Mozart's opera *Don Giovanni*.[34] But there are other kinds of unreflective aestheticism, including the attitude of the social conformist, who simply goes along with the standards and mores of his or her society, or lives in the way that 'all the others' live. (Such persons may well, of course, believe themselves to be highly ethical and/or religious.) But unreflective aesthetes are not necessarily unintellectual ones. Someone may be a brilliant thinker—perhaps a scientist who knows all about some specialized field—but still lack any reflectiveness about his or her own life. And even a speculative philosopher who is no mere specialist but can survey and synthesize all areas of objective knowledge may still be utterly lacking in *self*-knowledge.[35]

But an aesthete need not be lacking in self-reflection in this way, and an aesthetic life can be self-consciously inhabited. Kierkegaard's main fictional or pseudonymous aesthete (from *Either/Or*), known simply as 'A', is not only highly intelligent and well educated, but intensely introspective; indeed, he often seems paralysed by his reflectiveness, by his awareness of all the options that he could choose while finding himself lacking any decisive reason for preferring any of them to any other.[36] To the extent he does develop any positive rule of life for himself, it is to take advantage, as it were, of this indecisiveness. Rather than living for pleasure, he will live for 'the interesting' and to avoid boredom.[37] (An admixture of the unpleasant may precisely serve to keep life interesting.) To this end, he makes no long-term plans, no deep or binding commitments. What matters more than the particular situation he finds himself in, though, is the attitude he can take to it, his ability to find in it something, however tangential to the apparently obvious meaning of the situation, that can pique his interest. What is insignificant becomes, for him (temporarily) crucial; what seems central becomes marginal. In the end his aim is to live so as to maximize his freedom and his sense of being in control of whatever situation he contrives, or finds himself in.

By contrast, Kierkegaard's main ethical pseudonym, Judge William, admonishes 'A' in a series of personal letters to give up what he sees as a self-destructive lifestyle; as 'A' bounces from one short-term project to another, he risks losing any real sense of his own identity. Refusing—or trying to refuse—to care deeply about anyone or

---

[34] See 'The Immediate Erotic Stages', in *E/O* i. 47–135. Don Juan was an important archetypal figure for Camus also; see, especially, *MS* 69–77.

[35] This is indeed a recurrent theme in Kierkegaard: how objective knowledge can (though it need not) blind people to the crucial existential question of what their own lives mean to them. 'A thinker erects a huge building ... a system embracing the whole of existence, world history etc, and if his personal life is considered ... the appalling and ludicrous discovery is made that he himself does not live in this huge domed palace, but in a shed alongside it, or in a doghouse ...' (SUD 43–4).

[36] See, in particular, the section 'Diapsalmata', in *E/O* i. 19–43.

[37] See 'Rotation of Crops', in *E/O* i. 285–300.

12 THE PHILOSOPHY OF CAMUS

anything, he risks losing the sense of self that goes with such commitments and cares. Judge William warns him:

> I have seen people in life who have deceived others for such a long time that eventually they are unable to show their true nature ... can you think of anything more appalling than having it all end with the disintegration of your essence into a multiplicity ... thus you would have lost what is most inward and holy in a human being, the binding power of the personality?[38]

One might think that Judge William is urging 'A' to pull himself together by committing to some particular relationship or cause—some 'ground project', as Bernard Williams put it[39]—in pursuit of which he could unify himself and find a meaning for his life. The Judge *is* urging that, but he is urging more than that. A life unified by commitment to a chosen project could still be an aesthetic life. The Judge imagines someone saying: 'I have a natural capacity to be a Don Juan, a Faust, a robber chief. I will now train this natural capacity, for esthetic [sic] earnestness demands that I become something specific.'[40] But, for the ethical, the point is not simply to become unified, but to become unified around the Good. Indeed, for Kierkegaard there really is no other way to become unified. To try to make myself on my own terms, without reference to standards of good and evil, accepted as authoritative and binding, is an essentially arbitrary exercise.[41] The life that the 'earnest' aesthete has chosen has no claim on him or her except that he or she has chosen it; and what is established by arbitrary choice can equally well be torn down by a further arbitrary choice:

> The self is its own master, absolutely its own master ... On closer examination, however, it is easy to see that this absolute ruler is a king without a country ... his sovereignty is subject to the dialectic that rebellion is legitimate at any moment ... Consequently, the self in despair is only building castles in the air ...[42]

In the ethical sphere, by contrast to the aesthetic, self-choice is constrained by moral demands. Judge William is very Kantian in arguing that morality depends on principle rather than inclination, and that real autonomy consists in acting according to principle, rather than being driven by my passing whims and desires.

---

[38] *E/O* ii. 160.

[39] See Williams, 'Persons, Character and Morality'.

[40] *E/O* ii. 225.

[41] See the long discourse 'On the Occasion of a Confession: Purity of Heart is to Will One Thing' in *UDVS* 5–154. Camus notes the connection that Kierkegaard makes between 'unity and the good' in this work, and comments: 'I am far from the good and I thirst for unity. That is irreparable' (*NB II*, 55).

[42] *SUD* 69. The pseudonymous author of this work, 'Anti-Climacus', is certainly speaking for Kierkegaard here (and throughout) and is making a point that Judge William would certainly agree with also.

INTRODUCTION   13

For, although moral principles exercise genuine authority over the self, they do not simply stand over against the self as heteronomous standards, but are deeply rooted in its own nature.[43] And, like the ancient Greek ethicists, Judge William sees ethics as being about human flourishing, the pursuit of what is good for human beings. This is why the ethical does not abolish or replace the aesthetic—the sphere of desire and fulfilment—but relativizes or 'dethrones' it. (It is not wrong to pursue the pleasurable or the interesting, but they should not be pursued at the expense of doing what is right.) However, what constitutes human flourishing is not simply up to each individual to decide for him- or herself; it is constrained by certain basic facts about human nature. We are temporal beings and, as such, we need to pursue long-term projects that will knit our lives together across time. And, as essentially social beings, we need these projects to be, at least in part, cooperative, social projects, which involve binding commitments to others. Hence the ethical person needs 'civic' as well as 'personal' virtues.[44] Judge William interestingly combines the Hegelian stress on social morality (*Sittlichkiet*)—the importance of constructively engaging with the social and political world in which one finds oneself—with the Kantian emphasis on acting autonomously according to principle.

What, though, about the religious stage? It is not defined simply by belief in God. Aesthetes and ethicists may believe in God; what matters for Kierkegaard, indeed, is whether one's belief in God is essentially aesthetic,[45] or ethical—or genuinely religious. Judge William is, by his own lights, a religious man; a serious believer, not just a Sunday-morning conformist or hypocrite. However, he does not probe as deeply as Kierkegaard would like into the difference that a serious religious outlook would make to one's view of the world. The religious does not abolish the ethical, any more than the ethical abolishes the aesthetic. But, from a religious perspective, Kierkegaard has two major concerns about the *merely* ethical, these being most forcefully expressed by his pseudonym Johannes *de silentio* in *Fear and Trembling*. The first is that an ethical world view, even if notionally still religious, will tend to reduce the religious element to the ethical, until it becomes so thinned out as to fade away:

The ethical is the universal and as such is also the divine. Thus it is proper to say that every duty is essentially duty to God, but if no more can be said than this, then it is also said that I actually have no duty to God ... 'God' in a totally abstract sense is here understood as the divine—that is the universal, that is duty. The whole existence of the human race rounds itself off as a perfect self-contained

[43] *E/O* ii. 253–7.
[44] *E/O* ii. 262–3.
[45] As may be the case, not only with the easily caricatured 'conventional churchgoers' but also with born-again enthusiasts, whose 'faith' Kierkegaard suspects may often really be a mixture of superficial emotional excitement and cozy in-group feeling.

14   THE PHILOSOPHY OF CAMUS

sphere ... God comes to be an invisible vanishing point, an impotent thought; his power is only in the ethical which fills all of existence.[46]

Not only does God—considered as transcendent and personal—fade away on such a nominally religious ethical outlook, but so does human individuality. There is nothing higher than the ethical—that is, the universal; and it becomes the task of the individual simply to conform to these universal ethical demands.[47] Johannes does not accuse this ethical outlook of being inconsistent per se. But, if there is a personal and transcendent God, and if there is something irreducibly individual in each of us that needs the relation to God in order fully to become itself; then the purely ethical sphere will be experienced as stifling by someone who is not engaged in self-deception, even if he or she may not be able to articulate clearly what is being stifled. There is, at any rate, Johannes argues, conceptual space for one to consider an alternative to the purely ethical: 'The paradox of faith, then, is this: that the single individual is higher than the universal; that the single individual ... determines his relation to the universal [ethics] by his relation to the absolute [God], not his relation to the absolute by his relation to the universal.'[48] And this, Johannes notoriously argues, creates space for at least the *possibility* that God might 'teleologically suspend' the ethical—that is, temporarily set it aside for the sake of a higher purpose.[49]

The second problem that Johannes notes does pose a more direct challenge to the coherence of the ethical or, rather, to the possibility of living a satisfactory life on purely ethical terms. This is the observable fact that people do not seem to be able to live up to ethical demands—and the more seriously one takes those demands, and the more rigorously one scrutinizes one's motives and desires, the more painfully apparent this becomes. We can call this condition 'sin' or 'radical evil' but, in any case, 'it is a contradiction on the part of the universal to want to demand itself from the person who lacks the *conditio sine qua non* [indispensable condition] ... An ethics that ignore sin is a completely futile discipline, but if it affirms sin, then it has *eo ipso* [thereby] exceeded itself.'[50] If we stick with the ethical, we are condemned to a hopeless cycle of guilt and repentance; and we might then be tempted, citing the dictum 'ought implies can!', to shrug off the ethical demands as unfulfillable, and return to the aesthetic. Hence the need for the religious, and indeed, for Kierkegaard, the need to go beyond the generically religious (what one of his pseudonyms calls 'Religiousness A'[51]) to the specifically Christian: the recognition of one's inability to do right by one's own efforts and the turn, not

---

[46] *FT* 68.
[47] See *FT* 54. It should be noted that Johannes *de silentio* seems to have in mind a more rigorist conception of ethics than the one Judge William defends in *Either/Or*.
[48] *FT* 70.
[49] See *FT*, Problema I (54–67). Note that such suspension does not abolish the ethical.
[50] *FT* 98–9. See also *CA* 15–20.
[51] Johannes Climacus, at *CUP* i. 555.

INTRODUCTION   15

to an abstract first principle, but to a personal God of forgiveness and grace.[52] Only on that basis can we return to ethics—a 'second ethics' that presupposes the reality of sin and forgiveness.[53]

I have taken some time to outline this Kierkegaardian schema because I think it can serve as a useful framework for considering Camus's work. Camus devised his own schema for organizing his writings, that of the 'cycles', and I shall argue that there are significant parallels to be found between these cycles and Kierkegaard's stages. Each of Camus's cycles deals with a large theme—such as absurdity or revolt—and explores that theme through a novel, two plays, and a philosophical essay. (Other writings of his—lyrical and critical essays, journalism, commentaries on contemporary events—fall outside this schema.) He completed two cycles—that of the Absurd (*The Outsider, Caligula, The Misunderstanding,* and *The Myth of Sisyphus*) and that of Revolt (*The Plague, State of Siege, The Just,* and *The Rebel*)—and he certainly planned more. A note from 1947 proposes a total of five cycles or 'series', including the Absurd and Revolt (the last series, he self-mockingly declares, will be called 'The System' and consist of 'big novel + great meditation + unplayable play').[54] A later note (from 1950) sketches a more modest and shorter-range plan: 'I: The Myth of Sisyphus (absurd)—II. The Myth of Prometheus (revolt)—III. The Myth of Nemesis.'[55] The theme of Nemesis had already emerged at the end of *The Rebel* and in 'Helen's Exile' from 1948 (as the theme of Revolt had already emerged towards the end of *The Myth*), but Camus made little progress on this third cycle during what remained of his life. A 1956 *Notebook* entry identifies what became his novel *The Fall* and his short-story collection, *Exile and the Kingdom,* as constituting a sort of interlude, 'before the third stage', dealing with 'themes of judgement and exile'.[56] But he was still planning the Nemesis cycle, and in the same note he gives a little more detail: 'the third stage is love: The First Man, Don Faust, the Myth of Nemesis.'[57] *The First Man* was the autobiographical novel on which he was working when he died. *Don Faust* was a projected play, merging the legends of Faust and Don Juan, for which he made various notes.[58] 'The Myth of Nemesis' must now refer to the projected essay, rather than to the proposed cycle as a whole, but there are only a few enigmatic hints towards what the content of that essay might have been.[59] Clearly the projected third cycle was underway with

---

[52] See *CUP* i. 561–86, on sin and its forgiveness as the crucial distinction between Religiousness A and 'Religiousness B' (Christianity).

[53] See *CA* 20–4.

[54] *NB II,* 158. The ironic reference to the System might well be a tip of the hat to Kierkegaard's mockery of the Hegelian 'System'; in a slightly earlier remark, Camus jokes with himself: 'Title for the future: System (1,500 pp)' (*NB II,* 151). If Sartre had written that, it would not have been a joke.

[55] *NB II,* 257.

[56] *NB III,* 172.

[57] *NB III,* 172.

[58] See, e.g., *NB III,* 95–6, 134, 135, 171, 195.

[59] See, e.g., *NB III,* 65, 67, 255.

16   THE PHILOSOPHY OF CAMUS

the work he had started on *The First Man*, but we cannot of course know how the rest of it might have turned out.

It is in any case interesting to note that Kierkegaard and Camus, as Eric Berg says, 'both seem to adhere to a set of three'.[60] Berg does not really develop the suggestion, but I think there are clear parallels between Camus's notion of the Absurd and Kierkegaard's aesthetic stage, while, in the cycle of Revolt, Camus develops an explicitly ethical philosophy. However appealing it might be for the sake of symmetry, one cannot, of course, assume that Camus's projected third cycle would have had any substantive similarity to Kierkegaard's religious stage. Some readers of Camus might indeed be inclined to rule out that suggestion from the start, on the grounds that Camus was, after all, a radically non- or even anti-religious thinker. I think that this (widespread) impression is at best a serious oversimplification. I shall argue that Camus in his later writings was looking for a way of thinking and being that would go beyond the ethical, without simply reverting to the Absurdism of his early work. In that sense we can say that he was, in contemplating his third cycle, searching for something that would at least have been *structurally* analogous to Kierkegaard's notion of the religious. (I will consider in a moment whether we can say more than that.) That Camus's 'cycles can to a considerable extent be mapped onto Kierkegaard's 'stages' provides me with the central organizing principle of this book, although it should be emphasized that it is a framework that allows substantive differences as well as similarities between Camus and Kierkegaard to become apparent. (That they were in many ways very different—personally, temperamentally, culturally, as well as in terms of their explicit beliefs—I do not deny for a moment.) Hence, I will be devoting a chapter to each of Camus's cycles—the third chapter being the longest precisely because we have no definitive statement of Camus's later thinking and therefore have to work at reconstructing it from the fragmentary evidence that we do have.[61]

My detailed justification for the claim that there are significant parallels between Kierkegaard's stages and Camus's cycles will be made in the discussions of the three cycles that follow, but I do want to emphasize here that these parallels are not simply static, as it were. Camus, like Kierkegaard, is offering a developmental account. Just as Kierkegaard articulates the positive ethical outlook through a critique of the aesthetic, so Camus begins *The Rebel* with a discussion of Absurdism, and the need to move beyond it. And, as I noted above, I shall argue that the intended third cycle was an attempt, not to repudiate, but to go beyond the ethical. So, like Kierkegaard, Camus does not just set out different views of life, but argues for the need to move from one to the other. (Although, also like Kierkegaard, he does not think there is any historical or psychological necessity that would compel such a movement.)

---

[60] Berg, 'Albert Camus and Soren Kierkegaard', 133.
[61] Given this set-up, I will not be looking systematically or in much detail at Camus's earliest works, prior to the cycle of the Absurd, though I will be referring to them at various points.

Hence the overall coherence of Camus's philosophical work is the coherence of a narrative recounting a journey, not the atemporal coherence of a fixed system of thought. We can only properly understand Camus's various works as descriptions of stopping places en route (or 'stages on life's way'). We should not expect that formulations in his earlier works will necessarily be consistent with those in his later works; nor should we assume that such differences necessarily reflect changes of mind on Camus's part. This is not to say that Camus had the whole trajectory of a planned life's work already formed in his mind when he started it (although, as noted above, he certainly did have a *penchant* for long-term literary planning); the 'journey' was no doubt a genuine journey of discovery for him. But this is true for Kierkegaard and his work too.[62]

III The Self as Synthesis

Towards the end of his active writing career, Kierkegaard summed up, in *The Sickness unto Death*, the understanding of selfhood that had emerged from his previous writings.[63] There he describes a human being as 'a synthesis of the infinite and the finite, of the temporal and the eternal, of freedom and necessity; in short, a synthesis'. And then he notes: 'Considered in this way, a human being is still not a self.'[64] To be a self involves more than simply being a human being (even a human being with normal mental abilities, a capacity for self-reflection, and so on). Selfhood is, beyond that, an ideal of coherence and integration; the failure to become, or fully to become, a self constitutes despair in Kierkegaard's sense (which is to be distinguished from conscious feelings of sadness and depression). The factors to be integrated (the elements in the 'synthesis') are given as three polarities, but I think one can see these three as aspects of one more basic polarity. Necessity, finitude, and temporality stand for our limitations; possibility, infinitude, and eternity for our capacity to transcend those limitations. One can call this basic polarity that of immanence and transcendence. Both factors are essential to us. We are limited in all sorts of ways—by the time and place we were born into, by our bodily constitution—but we also have the capacity, as other animals do not, to think and imagine beyond those limits. We as human persons are defined by the tension between our finite given natures and our capacities to project beyond them. To

---

[62] See Kierkegaard's discussion of his own authorship in 'The Point of View for my Work as an Author' in *PV*, in which he himself seems ambivalent about the question of whether or to what extent the whole trajectory from the aesthetic to the religious was all worked out from the beginning.

[63] This is, as noted above, technically a pseudonymous work, ascribed to 'Anti-Climacus'. But Kierkegaard added the pseudonym between writing and publishing the work; it was intended to acknowledge that Kierkegaard personally did not live up to the stringent ideals presented in the book but does not indicate any disagreement with its contents.

[64] *SUD* 13. For a more detailed account of Kierkegaard's view of selfhood, see Rudd. 'Kierkegaard on the Self'.

18   THE PHILOSOPHY OF CAMUS

be a 'self', then, is to succeed in actively holding these factors of transcendence and immanence together in a properly *creative* tension. And, according to Kierkegaard, this is possible only if the self as a whole relates properly to God—'the power that established it'.[65]

Camus nowhere sets out a systematic account of the self (or of the nature of human beings). But his crucial move away from the Absurdism of *The Myth* to the ethical philosophy of *The Rebel* turns on his recognition that, 'contrary to the postulates of contemporary thought' (he has in mind here primarily Sartrean existentialism) and in line with ancient Greek philosophy, 'a [normatively relevant] human nature does exist (*R.* 16). And, although he does not go into much explicit detail about this human nature, I will argue that he does develop, at least implicitly, an understanding of the self as a balance or synthesis between contrasting factors of immanence and transcendence that is close in important ways to Kierkegaard's account of selfhood. This, I will argue, underlies his critique of other philosophers, such as Marx, Nietzsche, and Sartre, and is also at the heart of his positive conception of moderation (*measure*), which is really the key to his mature thought. If we spell out the conception of selfhood that is presupposed in Camus's middle and later period works, I think we end up with something close to Kierkegaard's view. Looking at what Kierkegaard explicitly says about the self is thus helpful in articulating Camus's largely implicit understanding of selfhood. One large difference, of course, is that Camus does not accept Kierkegaard's claim that a relationship with God is necessary to achieve the synthesis of the potentially conflicting aspects of selfhood. And this brings us back to the question of whether an explicitly religious thinker like Kierkegaard can really serve as an appropriate model for understanding Camus.

IV The Religious

That Kierkegaard was a fundamentally and essentially religious thinker seems clear enough. His non-pseudonymous works are nearly all explicitly religious in character, and even most of the pseudonymous ones are constantly circling around religious questions. This does not mean that one cannot make illuminating comparisons between Kierkegaard and a non-religious thinker; for one thing, comparisons can include contrasts. But, more positively, I think that the comparison with Kierkegaard can help to bring out the sense in which Camus was, throughout his career, preoccupied with religious issues. Some have indeed argued that Camus was in fact a religious thinker *malgré lui*, or that he was turning specifically to Christianity towards the end of his life.[66] The latter claim, at

---

[65] *SUD* 14.
[66] See Mumma, *Albert Camus and the Minister.*

INTRODUCTION   19

least, seems quite questionable, but it needs to be remembered in this context that the religious is a broader category than the Christian. It is in any case very clear that Camus was a thinker for whom religion was a live issue. He was certainly not a comfortable secularist who could regard it as a historical curiosity. Religion in general (and Christianity in particular) was a topic at which he kept worrying away throughout both his fiction (from Meursault's confrontation with the prison chaplain at the end of *The Outsider*, to Father Paneloux's changing attitudes to human suffering in *The Plague*, to the Christian imagery that saturates *The Fall* from its title onwards) and in his theoretical work (from his early dissertation on *Christian Metaphysics and Neoplatonism* to his discussion of Christianity and capital punishment in 'Reflections on the Guillotine'.[67]) In *The Myth of Sisyphus*, as I will try to show in Chapter 1, Absurdism is essentially defined as the negation of a religious outlook; and in *The Rebel* the discussion of 'Historical Rebellion' is framed by that of 'Metaphysical Rebellion'—the rejection of the idea of a divine order in the universe. Fundamental to Camus's account of modern revolutionary politics—both its promise and its catastrophic outcomes—is his understanding of it as an essentially religious (or para-religious) phenomenon. These discussions of religion in general and of Christianity in particular are, of course, predominantly negative in character. But I think the basic contours of Camus's first two cycles are generated by a continual circling around that which they reject. Like a ring or a bowl, their shape is determined by the negation that lies at their centre. However, I will be going beyond this negative point and arguing not only that Camus's elusive third cycle would have been *structurally* analogous to Kierkegaard's religious stage, but that its central conception of love/nemesis had characteristics that could themselves properly be called religious. (And, indeed, that this was something that Camus himself acknowledged.)

Camus's concern with religious issues can be brought out by considering the crucial tension that runs throughout his work between affirmation and denial of the world (what he calls at one point 'that essential fluctuation from assent to refusal (*MS*, p. v)). On the one hand, he is strongly inclined to affirm life, the world, in all its contingency and pain—an attitude that is at first strongly influenced by Nietzsche's 'yea-saying' but which in his later works is underpinned more by a sense of the world as an ultimately harmonious cosmos, which he draws from ancient Greek thinking. But this stands in tension with a stance of rebellion; a quasi-Gnostic revulsion from a meaningless world, full of suffering and constantly shadowed by death. This is the world that he experiences as 'absurd' in his early work, but then embraces despite or in its absurdity. It is the world that, in *The Rebel*, 'Metaphysical Rebellion' repudiates, and that 'Historical Rebellion' tries to reconstruct. The complex dialectic between affirmation and rebellion runs through Camus's whole work; but (as I will argue) both these attitudes are

---

[67] In *RRD* 175–234.

essentially religious—or at least quasi-religious—ones. For a consistent atheistic naturalist there can be no sense in taking up an evaluative stance to reality as a whole. It is what it is; some aspects of it are favourable to human life and flourishing, other are unfavourable. Camus, though, is not a conventional atheistic naturalist; he is torn between a quasi-pantheistic acceptance of the world and life as having a normative significance for us, and a quasi-Gnostic rebellion against them, based on the equally normative sense that the suffering and death that pervade them ought not to be. This conflict, I shall argue, is never fully resolved in Camus's work, although the terms of it shift and develop. But it will be an important part of my thesis both that this tension is basic to Camus's thought, and that it is a fundamentally religious conflict. (And this does mean that even Camus's versions of, or parallels to, the aesthetic and ethical stages are themselves in a sense religious; that there is a religious quality even to his repudiation of the religious—certainly of Christianity—in the more obvious sense.) It is, in any case, clear that Camus remained throughout his career close enough to the issues that preoccupied Kierkegaard to make a dialogue between them both possible and valuable.

These, then, are the four Kierkegardian themes that provide me with the framework that I will use in interpreting Camus's philosophy. Thinking of Camus with these themes in mind can help us to recognize (1) his central concern with what it is to *live* a certain understanding of life and its significance; (2) the developmental and provisional nature of his thinking (which can free us from supposing that he necessarily endorsed all the ideas he explored) and the trajectory of that thinking, from a zero-point of Absurdism or nihilism towards the ethical and beyond it; (3) the importance of an understanding of selfhood in terms of limit and balance, which is presupposed in his mature thinking but never developed systematically; and (4) his persistent concern, negative and positive, with religious questions. I am not claiming that comparison with Kierkegaard is the only way that these aspects of Camus's thinking could be made perspicuous; but I do think it is one way, and one I have found particularly helpful. I have tried in this Introduction to show why I have used this particular interpretative frame or (to vary metaphors) lens for understanding Camus, but it can be properly justified only through making use of it in the detailed interpretative work that follows. I shall, as I continue, make some more detailed and specific comparisons between Kierkegaard and Camus, but only insofar as they seem to illuminate Camus's thinking on specific topics.

Although my main concern is to give a perspicuous overview of Camus's philosophical thinking, I do also engage in evaluation of it, defending Camus at some points, and raising criticisms at others. (It is not, in any case, really possible strictly to separate out exegesis/interpretation from critical evaluation of a thinker.) And at various points I develop my own lines of argument in order to defend or expand on Camus's stated positions, with an eye to showing them to be more defensible than some might suppose. I do not, however, try to offer a comprehensive exploration of these issues, but only an indication of how the arguments might be developed. And I make no attempt to consider all the criticisms that could be or have been made of Camus's philosophy. I have chosen to proceed mainly through a close focus on particular texts (or parts of texts) by Camus, and, although I do refer to the secondary literature, I have tried to avoid engaging in detailed exegetical arguments with other commentators. This is not because I have not found those commentators valuable; on the contrary, I have learned a lot from the secondary literature, even (or especially) when I have disagreed with it. (This is particularly true of the important books by Ronald Srigley and Matthew Sharpe I have already referenced; I engage in a running dialogue with them to a significantly greater extent than appears on the surface.) But, in the interests of keeping my own line of thought perspicuous, I have tried to avoid detailed interpretative disputes, or extended comparisons with other readings of Camus's work. I have aimed throughout at brevity and clarity, not at comprehensiveness.[68]

One self-imposed limitation I have mentioned already is that I shall not be discussing Camus's fictional works (except *The Fall*) in much detail. I should also mention that I shall not be saying much about the particular political stances that Camus took in his own lifetime, although I will be saying *something* about them— particularly his anti-Communism and his famous quarrel with Sartre, which I discuss in Chapter 2.[69] Camus is one of the paradigms of a politically engaged intellectual, but this is somewhat ironic, for, although he felt called on to take political positions, his philosophy (which is what I am concerned with here) is not primarily a political one. The ethical philosophy most fully articulated in *The Rebel*, though it has important political implications, does so precisely because it is intended to set limits to politics, to keep it in its proper place. What Camus wants is to prevent politics from masquerading as religion by purporting to offer a solution to all the problems of human life. We need, he argues, to

> put politics, wherever possible, back in its proper place, which is a secondary one. It is not actually a matter of giving this world a gospel, or a political or moral catechism ... The great misfortune of our time is precisely that politics claims to

---

[68] I have also tried to avoid referring much to the secondary literature on Kierkegaard. I have written quite extensively on Kierkegaard elsewhere and have given references to some of that work for those who are interested in seeing more detailed justifications for the interpretations of Kierkegaard that I largely assume here.

[69] In particular, I will not be discussing his attitude to the Algerian War of Independence, for which he has been attacked by various 'postcolonial' critics. (He condemned the violence of both sides, while attempting—unsuccessfully—to articulate a compromise solution.) I will just say that I think Camus was, whatever one might think about the detailed positions he took, absolutely right to see the Algerian situation as a *tragedy*, not as the real-life equivalent of a simple morality play in which the forces of good face off against those of evil. For a detailed reading of Camus's relation to the tortured politics of his homeland, see Caroll, *Albert Camus the Algerian*. See also Zaretsky, *Albert Camus*, ch. 4, and Foley, *Albert Camus*, ch. 6, for sympathetic and sensitive readings of his anguished and complex response to the war.

furnish us ... with a catechism, a complete philosophy ... But the role of politics is to do the housework, not to settle our domestic problems.[70]

That I do not discuss Camus's specifically political thinking at length does not mean that I think it is unimportant or is only of historical interest. On the contrary. Like him, we live now in a time of competing fanaticisms, of shrill, self-righteous partisanship; of brutal power politics and political violence; of people everywhere trying to feel good about themselves by demonizing the 'other'—whether that 'other' be defined in cultural, religious, racial, or political terms. And, in our time as in his, clarity of thought and openness of dialogue are in short supply, and much of the intelligentsia seems set on making matters worse rather than better in this respect. We need, more than ever, to listen to the simple honesty and humanity of Camus's political thinking, whether or not we agree with all the particular conclusions he came to in his own time, and whatever particular conclusions we might reach in trying to approach the issues of our day in his spirit. For he offered us no ideological master key, no algorithm to grind out automatic answers to complex specific political problems. It is up to us to try and take inspiration from his humane and sceptical outlook, as we try to think flexibly for ourselves about the particular issues we face. But I shall not be attempting either to make those applications to our own times here, or to provide a detailed commentary on Camus's own particular political interventions.

[70] Camus, 'The Crisis of Man', in *SO* 29.

1

The Absurd

Camus's investigation into the ways people make sense of, or try to find meanings in, their lives starts with a consideration of absurdity, the perception that life *has* no sense or meaning.[1] It may indeed seem that this is the most logical starting point for such an investigation; to begin with as little as possible and see if that is, nevertheless, enough for us to live by. But, however that may be, the sense of the absurd was in any case for Camus personally, historically, and sociologically unavoidable as a starting point. Whether or not he ever *fully* shared the perception of life as meaningless himself, he considered it to be characteristic of his generation, one that 'believed in nothing and lived in rebellion.'[2] To start with that perception was to start from where he was—even if not happily or comfortably. So the absurd is the central theme of Camus's first 'cycle', evoked or exemplified in *The Outsider*, *Caligula*, and *The Misunderstanding*, and explicitly analysed in *The Myth of Sisyphus*. Though it would be interesting to look in detail at the more literary treatments (which as I have insisted above, are also philosophical), I will concentrate in this chapter on the explicit philosophical analysis in *The Myth*. And, having raised in the Introduction the issue of whether Camus can be identified fully with the authorial voice we hear in *The Myth*, I will start by (mostly) setting it aside, so as to listen to that authorial voice itself. (I will return to the issue as we go on, however.) The work has its own integrity, and we need to understand what it is saying before we can speculate about what Camus himself intended in writing it, or the place it occupies in the development of his thought. I will mostly just refer to 'Camus' in what follows, since constantly using phrases like 'the authorial voice of *The Myth*' would be tiresome, but this should not be taken to indicate that I do fully identify Camus himself with that authorial voice.

I Absurd Epistemology: Truths and the Truth

What, then, is the absurd for Camus? Correcting a 'too hasty' initial formulation, he insists that the world itself is not absurd; it simply 'is not reasonable, that is all that can be said'. But 'what is absurd is the confrontation of this irrational and the

---

[1] I use 'absurd', 'absurdity', etc., with a lower-case 'a', to refer to the concept (as in, e.g., 'experiencing the world as absurd'); I use 'Absurdism', with an upper-case 'A', to refer to the doctrine according to which the world is without meaning, and 'Absurdist' to refer to someone who holds that doctrine.

[2] Camus, 'The Crisis of Man', in *SO* 19.

The Philosophy of Camus. Anthony Rudd, Oxford University Press. © Anthony Rudd (2024).
DOI: 10.1093/9780198924869.003.0002

24   THE PHILOSOPHY OF CAMUS

wild longing for clarity whose call echoes in the human heart (MS 21). And a little
later: 'The absurd is born of this confrontation between the human need and the
unreasonable silence of the world' (MS 28). But what exactly is this 'wild longing',
this 'human need'? John Foley claims that 'the absurd ... as conceived by Camus,
is fundamentally an epistemological claim addressing an ontological need, that
is, a claim regarding the knowledge we can have of the world'.[3] In other words;
we have a deep desire for knowledge, for a fullness and clarity of understanding;
but the world does not offer it to us. Camus does talk about 'the intellectual joy'
we would have if we could discover 'in the shimmering mirrors of phenomena
eternal relations capable of summing them up and summing themselves up in a
single principle' (MS 17), but then goes on to deny that science can give us such
unification: 'if, through science, I can seize phenomena and enumerate them, I
cannot, for all that, apprehend the world' (MS 20).

    The point is not a total scepticism. Despite his mention of science providing
us with knowledge merely of 'phenomena' I do not think there is any reason to
suppose that Camus was a phenomenalist, restricting us to knowledge of private
sense-data. Indeed, sensing the brute, indifferent reality of the natural world, apart
from all our conceptualizations of it, is for him an important part of the experience
of the absurd (see MS 14). He allows that I can know 'this heart within me [that]
I can feel' and 'the world [that] I can touch' (MS 19).[4] And, beyond these gener-
alities, Camus is happy to accept that both science and everyday experience can
provide us with knowledge about many particular matters of fact. His scepticism is
not so much about whether there is any reality beyond our subjective experience,
but about whether we are able, even in principle, to grasp what is real in a systematic, intellectually satisfying way. Nothing, he insists, allows us to arrange all the
particular things we may know in a single cohesive scheme. Even when it comes
to my own experience of myself, I can know 'aspects' of my psyche, 'but aspects
cannot be added up. This very heart which is mine will remain forever indefinable
to me' (MS 19). Camus sums up his view with a memorable aphorism: 'There are
truths but no truth' (MS 19). But, although this formula is striking, it is ambiguous,
for it can be taken either ontologically or epistemologically. Is Camus saying that
there is no rational order to reality; that there is such an order, but that we cannot
know it; or that we cannot know whether or not there is such an order?

---

    [3] Foley, Albert Camus, 8.
    [4] These being roughly equivalent to Sartre's 'Being for itself' (Etre pour soi) and 'Being in itself' (Etre
en soi) respectively. See Sartre, Being and Nothingness, introduction and passim. (I am not suggesting
that Camus was influenced by this work, which was not published until shortly after The Myth.) Interestingly, Camus does not mention here my knowledge of other minds (a topic that much occupied and
troubled Sartre in Being and Nothingness —see Pt three, in particular). Camus does note in passing that
'it is probably true that a man remains forever unknown to us ... But practically I know men and recognize them by their behavior ...' (MS 11). But other people play little role in The Myth; it is essentially
the drama of a solitary consciousness confronting a 'silent' physical world.

THE ABSURD   25

A comparison with Kierkegaard can be useful here. Kierkegaard distinguishes sharply between the empirical and the logical—substantive (empirical) claims are always uncertain, and formal (logical) truths purchase their certainty by their lack of content. Accordingly, as his most epistemologically oriented pseudonym, Johannes Climacus (but here I think clearly speaking for Kierkegaard himself), argues, 'a logical system can be given, but ... a system of existence cannot be given.'[5] There are lots of things we can know, but we cannot arrange them all in a grand explanatory system that would make complete sense of why they are as they are. And Hegel's attempt to develop a logic that would at the same time be an ontology 'simply confuses logic.'[6] However, Climacus continues: 'A system of existence cannot be given. Is there not, then, such a system? That is not at all the case. Neither is this implied in what has been said. Existence itself is a system—for God, but it cannot be a system for any existing spirit.'[7] Reality in itself (as created and known by God) is a coherent and reasonable system; but it is a mark of our finitude that we cannot grasp this system fully; and it is a mark of a properly religious humility that we acknowledge that limitation. Hence, Climacus would accept Camus's formula in one sense, but not in another. There is, ontologically, a 'truth' of things, but it is not epistemologically accessible to us.[8]

Daniel Berthold claims that both Kierkegaard and Camus take as a starting point Kant's assertion that 'human reason ... is burdened by questions which, as prescribed by the very notion of reason itself, it is not able to ignore, but which, as transcending all its powers, it is also not able to answer.'[9] Kierkegaard leaves us to trust that there are answers to the questions we cannot help asking about the ultimate Truth of things, without aspiring to know them, or, at any rate, to know them fully and completely. (From now on I will capitalize 'Truth' when referring to absolute, metaphysical Truth, so as to distinguish it from more modest empirical 'truths'.) But what of Camus? Does he allow that there may be some overall Truth of things, a coherent and even meaningful way things are, even if it is beyond our ability to grasp? He does, as we have seen, claim that the world is 'not reasonable', which might be taken as a denial of ontological Truth. But such a denial would itself seem to be a metaphysical assertion, and therefore at risk of self-refutation. (It is True there is no Truth.[10]) Camus is in fact aware of the danger of anti-metaphysical

[5] *CUP* i. 109. For a clear and comprehensive account of Kierkegaard's epistemology, see Piety, *Ways of Knowing*.
[6] *CUP* i. 109.
[7] *CUP* i. 118.
[8] It is, of course, knowable for God, so this is not simply a distinction between epistemology and ontology as such.
[9] Kant, *Critique of Pure Reason*, A vii. Quoted in Berthold, 'Kierkegaard and Camus: Either/Or?', 140.
[10] Note that it cannot simply be a truth that there is no Truth—the impossibility of metaphysical knowledge cannot itself be one more modest empirical truth. It would have to have an absolute, metaphysical status itself, which is why the problem of self-refutation arises for any would-be anti-metaphysical outlook.

26   THE PHILOSOPHY OF CAMUS

dogmatism,[11] and we should probably not read too much into his denial of the 'reasonableness' of the world.[12] His position does seem to be a cautious, agnostic one: 'I don't know whether this world has a meaning that transcends it. But I do know that I do not know that meaning' (MS 51). He does not reject out of hand the idea that reality might be systematically intelligible to a higher being with a greater perspective, but still 'the perspective of an angel or a god has no meaning for me. The geometrical spot where divine reason ratifies mine will always be incomprehensible to me' (MS 46). In the end, it seems, it does not really matter to him whether there is a deep Truth about reality as a whole, which is, however, inaccessible to us; or whether there simply is no such Truth. That too is, in the end, something we can probably never know. The important point is that we have a deep yearning to make sense of reality; and we are unable to do so.

Some commentators have compared Camus's attitude to that of Poststructuralists, such as Derrida, Foucault, and Lyotard. According to Sharpe,

> Camus anticipates many of the epistemic, ontological and political claims of later 'poststructuralist' theorizing. Like the poststructuralists' his work contains a strong critique of rationalistic modern philosophies ...Camus' thought is founded on a profound skepticism towards claims people make to have discovered absolute Truth ...The philosophy of the absurd, no less than Derrida's account of *différance* or Lyotard's 'incredulity towards metanarratives' is founded on the claim that such Truth is unavailable to us.[13]

Sharpe does, however, go on to note that 'the foundations of [Camus's] thinking, and its normative directions differ markedly from the later Parisian *maitres penseurs*' and that his criticism of hubristic rationalism 'never gives way to a total criticism of reason per se'.[14] So what is his relation to these later thinkers? I think that what is most characteristic of Poststructuralist thought (at least in its more radical forms) can be summed up as the conjunction of the three following claims: (*a*) that (absolute, metaphysical) Truth is not only inaccessible to us, but non-existent; (*b*) that the non-existence of Truth justifies us in a sceptical attitude towards even more modest empirical truths;[15] and (*c*) that to recognize this is liberating (both

---

[11] As he nicely puts it: 'Even the most rigorous epistemologies imply metaphysics. And to such a degree that the metaphysics of many contemporary thinkers consists in having nothing but an epistemology' (MS 44n.).

[12] He could simply be referring to the world as we experience it.

[13] Sharpe, Camus, Philosophe, 16. Sharpe references Lyotard's The Postmodern Condition for his 'incredulity'.

[14] Sharpe, Camus, Philosophe, 17.

[15] Sharpe mentions Postmodern Theory's tendency to a 'deep scepticism about ... claims to have established, through philosophy or the sciences any context-transcendent Truth about the world, or viable ethicopolitical norms. Progress in science, as in politics and ethics is another ideological or "metanarratival" illusion, alongside that of the transcendental Cartesian subject ... Students educated in the humanities over the last 20 years will be familiar with the claim that there is no knowable Truth.

THE ABSURD 27

personally and politically).[16] With respect to (*a*), Camus in *The Myth* seems, as I have suggested above, to be agnostic as to whether there might be Truth, though he is clear that it is not accessible to us. (As I also noted above, though, he certainly rejects the ontological idealism or anti-realism associated with more radical forms of Poststructuralism. At no point in his career would he have had any patience with the claim that nature is merely a social construction, or anything along those lines.) As for (*b*), he nowhere suggests that the absence of metaphysical Truth undermines everyday empirical or scientific truth-claims, which we can take as warranted in a pragmatic/contextual way. He does, however, explicitly make the move from no Truth to no truths as far as ethical/normative claims are concerned. (I will say more about that below.) About (*c*)—whether the absurd is a bleak or a liberating insight—I think Camus was conflicted (more about that, too, below), though *The Myth* as a whole is concerned with seeing how it could be experienced positively.

Critics have noted the contradictions that seem to afflict Poststructuralism— asserting the Truth that there is no Truth; eagerly proclaiming the liberatory message that all normative stances are illusory, and so on. Such problems of self-refutation have been raised for sceptical or relativistic philosophies since ancient times. It is interesting to note that Kierkegaard provides a partial defence of the ancient Greek Sceptics against such charges. Those who were rash enough to make claims such as 'there is no knowledge' or 'no truth-claims can be justified' would indeed refute themselves. But, as Kierkegaard stressed, classical scepticism was not really concerned to produce such theoretical (even if negative) pronouncements. It was essentially a practice—of countering arguments with contradicting argu-ments, so as to induce a suspension of judgement. Underlying this practice was an attitude, an existential stance: a passion for detachment, for a peace of mind (*ataraxia*) consequent on refusing to make intellectual commitments.[17] Hence, as Kierkegaard (Climacus) says, 'the doubter ... has no results, not even negative ones (for this would mean the acknowledgement of knowledge) but by the power of the

---

Granting this hyper-sceptical premise, it must follow that all claims by people to *have* established some "truth" or other can only exemplify so many instances of self-misunderstanding. These validity claims can then themselves be studied, at the second order, as so many claims to cultural or political power' (Sharpe, *Camus, Philosophe*, 13–14). Sharpe is clearly ascribing to the Poststructuralists a denial of truths in science and ethics, as well as—and following from—their denial of Truth in metaphysics.

[16] 'The Poststructuralist', defined as holding all those views, can be considered as an ideal type to whom the various canonical authors usually classified as Poststructuralists may correspond more or less fully. Deleuze, on the face of it, makes metaphysical claims of his own—about monism and the univocity of being, for instance; and Derrida, though his early writings contributed powerfully to giving claims (*a*) to (*c*) above the wide influence they gained, seems in his later writings at least, to be more of a Kantian than a Poststructuralist. In those later works, he seems to find notions of the ideal or absolute (absolute forgiveness, the absolute gift, etc.) to be at any rate regulative ideas, which we are unable to do without, even though we are unable ever to experience them as fully embodied.

[17] I interpret the Greek Sceptics as being, at least, primarily, concerned to reject metaphysical Truth, while accepting, non-dogmatically, everyday common-sense truth-claims but without commitment to any deeper account of what their truth amounted to or consisted in. See Rudd, 'The Skeptics', 166–70.

28   THE PHILOSOPHY OF CAMUS

will he decides to restrain himself'.[18] So a proper critique of scepticism would have to confront it, not just theoretically, but as an existential stance; it would need to show that it was unlivable, or resulted in a diminished form of life. (Which was precisely what Kierkegaard tried to do in his early, unfinished narrative, *Johannes Climacus, or, De omnibus Dubitandum Est*.[19])

I do not think that Poststructuralism can avail itself of this line of defence to the charge of self-refutation, since it tends to glory in its status as 'Theory', and seems to have little interest in the question of how an 'existing individual' might live by its teachings.[20] I do, however, think that Camus could appeal to something at least rather similar to Kierkegaard's defence of scepticism if questioned about the consistency of his formula that there are truths but no Truth.[21] As I have noted above, he tries to avoid the worry that it is a (self-stultifying) metaphysical assertion of the impossibility of metaphysics by presenting it in a cautious, agnostic tone, merely reporting that no claim to have found such Truth appears convincing. But even this is not primarily an epistemological verdict, but an expression of the *experience* of Truth's absence. Whether or not Camus can be fully identified with the Absurdist authorial voice of *The Myth*, his primary concern there is to investigate a way of experiencing the world in which a unifying Truth is not present, and to consider the question of whether one can live without such Truth. If he is not on the same side as Kierkegaard here, he is at any rate opposing him on the same—practical and experiential—ground. However, although the Greek sceptics—and Camus following them—could plausibly escape the charge of theoretical self-refutation, it seems harder for them to avoid the charge that they were, inconsistently, recommending sceptical *ataraxia* as the best way of life and suspension of judgement as preferable to the making of intellectual commitments, while at the same time repudiating any normative claims about the good life.[22] And it seems that Camus also (or at least The Absurdist of *The Myth*) does fall into inconsistency by both rejecting any normative outlook *and* arguing that life is lived better if it is recognized as having no meaning (*MS* 53).[23] (I will have more to say about this later in the chapter.)

Kierkegaard's claim that the Truth about things is the way it appears to God is important for him religiously, of course; but is it important epistemologically,

---

[18] *PF* 84–5. Climacus seems to me to be quite correct in his interpretation of the classical skeptics here; see Rudd, 'The Skeptics', 166–7.

[19] See *Johannes* Climacus, in *PF, passim*.

[20] Indeed, much of Poststructuralism tends to regard the existing individual, 'the Subject', etc., as an illusion anyway, although I think in fact it covertly presupposes a radical, unsituated subjectivity, which it is trying to liberate from the oppressive burdens of Truth.

[21] I am, of course, capitalizing (absolute) Truth, which Camus did not, but this is intended to bring out his meaning, rather than to impose mine on his formula.

[22] They did try to avoid this charge, though their attempts are more ingenious than convincing. See Sextus Empiricus, *Outlines of Pyrrhonism*, book one, sect. 12 (trans. B. Mates as *The Skeptic Way*, 92–3).

[23] Much the same is true of the Poststructuralists, who, despite their radical scepticism about the normative, do have a definite normative agenda—based, despite their theoretical denial of 'the Subject', on the maximizing of individual freedom. On this, see, e.g., C. Taylor, *Sources of the Self*, 487–90.

THE ABSURD   29

given that we cannot (and should not aspire to) share God's perspective? Does it matter, Camus would ask, that the world is a system for God, if it can never be one for us? I think Kierkegaard would reply that it does matter, because this is what underwrites the conviction that there is a way things are, which our reason and experience do give us some access to, however partial and perspectival it may be. Perhaps that conviction could be maintained on a non-theistic basis, but if we were to take away the conviction itself—that there is a (rationally ordered) reality on which our perspectives *are* perspectives—we would seem to be left with the highly paradoxical conclusion to which Nietzsche was at least sometimes drawn: a perspectivism without any common reality that is apprehended in the various perspectives.[24] Camus does not discuss either Kierkegaard or Nietzsche in this epistemological section of *The Myth*, but he does say something about Karl Jaspers (himself deeply influenced by both Kierkegaard and Nietzsche). Jaspers rejects all attempts to grasp reality intellectually as a rationally ordered system, and Camus approvingly notes that 'Jaspers despairs of any ontology because he knows we have lost "naivete". He knows that we can achieve nothing that can transcend the fatal game of appearances' (*MS* 24–5). But he then goes on to complain that Jaspers 'without justification ... suddenly all at once asserts the transcendent, the essence of experience and the superhuman significance of life ... Nothing logically prepares this reasoning. I can call it a leap' (*MS* 32–3). Jaspers would have rejected the claim that he was 'leaping' here. Although he does not think there is a strict deductive argument from the experienced world to a metaphysical ground of it (as in, for example, the traditional cosmological argument for God), he does argue that the limited knowledge we *can* get points us to a 'transcendence' that we can never fully or even consistently articulate, but that is presupposed implicitly by the knowledge that we do have. A consistent Nietzschean perspectivism—if that is even possible—would ultimately undercut even empirical truth-claims. So, according to this argument, if we do have some—however partial and elusive—knowledge of truths (which we do), then there must be Truth.[25]

Camus seems to come closest to dealing directly with this argument in a review essay he wrote in 1943 (the same year *The Myth* was published) of a book on the philosophy of language by Brice Parein. There he confronts the concern, fundamental to Poststructuralism, that determinate linguistic meaning may not be possible. 'For the problem is to know whether our most accurate expressions ... are not in fact empty of all meaning ... If language is meaningless, then everything

---

[24] For a sympathetic but rigorous account of Nietzsche's perspectivism and the difficulties it entails, see Richardson *Nietzsche's System*, ch. 4.

[25] This argument is really central to Jaspers' work as a whole. But see, for instance: 'We always live and think within a horizon. But the very fact that it is a horizon indicates something further which again surrounds the given horizon ...The Encompassing is not a horizon within which every determinate mode of Being and truth emerges for us, but rather that within which every particular horizon is enclosed as in something absolutely comprehensive which is no longer visible as a horizon at all' (Jaspers, *Reason and Existenz*, 52).

30 THE PHILOSOPHY OF CAMUS

is meaningless and the world becomes absurd.'[26] He poses a dilemma: 'Either, in fact, our words translate only our impressions and, partaking of their contingency, are deprived of any precise meaning; or else our words represent some ideal and essential truth, and consequently have no contact with tangible reality ...'[27] He notes Plato's solution: 'For words to have meaning, their meaning must come from somewhere else than the tangible world, so fleeting and so changeable.'[28] In other words: there can be no truths because (even more fundamentally) there are no meanings, unless there is Truth (Meaning). But, in order to avoid the second horn of the dilemma, this ideal Truth must somehow become embodied in this empirical world. Hegel's philosophy is concerned, precisely, with how *Geist* (Spirit) expresses itself in and through the 'tangible' world. But Camus notes, with apparent approval, Parein's response to Hegel: 'that we cannot conceive of a truth ... that participates at one and the same time in the physical and the universal.'[29] Since we cannot really understand how universal meanings can apply to particulars (the old Nominalist–Realist dispute), we either have to take the existence of linguistic meaning in a way on faith (which includes belief in some trans-empirical Truth) or give up on determinate meaning altogether. Hence, we are faced with a Pascalian choice between 'miracles or absurdity.'[30] Camus reports that Parein 'does feel, in spite of everything,' that language 'yields the elements of a hierarchy. It does not provide us with being, but it allows us to suspect that being exists.'[31] Camus does not commit himself to a solution here, but he does seem to endorse the claim that miracle and absurdity 'form the only possible choice.'[32] He thus excludes a third option—that our 'fleeting and changeable' impressions of the tangible world are nonetheless stable and consistent enough for meaning (and truths) to be established for practical purposes of communication, even without any metaphysical grounding. But it is only this third option, it would seem, that could allow for the 'truths but no Truth' formula.[33]

II Absurdity as Absence of Meaning

Camus at least raises important questions in epistemology and philosophy of language, though it cannot be pretended that he deals with them in enough detail to make much positive contribution to the important debates about the relation

[26] Camus, 'On a Philosophy of Expression by Brice Parein', in *LCE* 229–30.
[27] Camus, 'On a Philosophy of Expression', in *LCE* 230.
[28] Camus, 'On a Philosophy of Expression', in *LCE* 233.
[29] Camus, 'On a Philosophy of Expression', in *LCE* 236.
[30] Camus, 'On a Philosophy of Expression', in *LCE* 234, 238.
[31] Camus, 'On a Philosophy of Expression', in *LCE* 237.
[32] Camus, 'On a Philosophy of Expression', in *LCE* 238.
[33] Did Camus, perhaps under Parein's influence, change his mind in between writing *The Myth* and writing this essay? Or does the view he takes (however tentatively) in this essay give us further reason to think that he never fully endorsed the position taken in *The Myth*?

THE ABSURD   31

of empirical truths to metaphysical Truth in subsequent philosophy.[34] But it is not in any case clear that these epistemological discussions have really got us to the heart of what is troubling Camus. *The Myth of Sisyphus* is about whether the perception of the absurd ought to drive us to suicide. But, if the issue is a basically epistemological one, it is hard to see why it might even be supposed to have such drastic consequences. Someone longing for deeper certainties or more comprehensive explanations may be disappointed if they are not available to us, but would they really be driven to contemplate suicide? Plenty of people seem content to live with 'truths but no Truth'—whether in the spirit of a modest pragmatic empiricism or of Kierkegaard's religiously based epistemic humility. Conversely, even if physics did come up with a 'theory of everything', an equation that somehow explained the whole universe, it is hard to suppose that would assuage the 'wild longing' of which Camus writes. The issue for him, then, is not primarily an epistemological one, or, if it is, then it is a very particular kind of epistemology—one might say, the epistemology of value. In a 1946 lecture he describes a radical nominalism as part of the nihilistic or Absurdist attitude of his generation: the view that 'there was no truth, but only phenomena ... there might be Mr Smith, Monsieur Durand and Herr Vogel, but there could be nothing in common between these specific phenomena.'[35] But I do not think what he is referring to here is the implausible denial that, for example, anatomy can describe common features of the human bodily structure. What the Absurdist generation was denying was that there is a meaningful or normatively significant essence of humanity.[36]

Camus does say that 'the mind's deepest desire ... is an insistence on familiarity, an appetite for clarity. Understanding the world for a man is reducing it to the human, stamping it with his seal ... the mind that aims to understand reality can consider itself satisfied only by reducing it to terms of thought' (*MS* 17).

---

[34] Those who suppose (in either a positive or a negative sense) that there is a necessary link between truths and Truth are a disparate group. They include the Poststructuralists, who conclude that, since there is no Truth, there cannot really be truths either (at least, not in anything more than the most provisional and context-bound sense). But the principle that there cannot be truths without Truth has also been maintained by many philosophers who have argued, on the contrary, that, since there *are* truths, there must be Truth. This group includes, not only classical Rationalists, but also many contemporary naturalistic or materialist thinkers. These latter suppose that natural science is our attempt at least to approximate to an 'absolute point of view', and that its endeavours are intelligible only if we assume the validity of that notion. (For a particularly influential formulation of this claim, see Williams, *Descartes*, 236–49.) And several distinguished recent philosophers not only have argued that truths presuppose Truth (a rationally intelligible order in the nature of things, whether or not we can fully grasp it), but have also argued for the Kierkegaardian claim that this Truth must have a theistic basis. (See Kolakowski, *Religion*, ch. 2; Dummett, *Thought and Reality*, chs 7, 8; MacIntyre, 'First Principles', 'Philosophy Recalled to its Tasks', and 'Truth as a Good', all in MacIntyre, *The Tasks of Philosophy*. Other philosophers defend the idea of truths without Truth, holding that a pragmatic, contextual notion of truth can be robust enough to rescue us from Poststructuralist relativism while also avoiding Williams's 'absolutist' scientism. See, e.g., Putnam, *Reason, Truth and History* and *Renewing Philosophy*, chs 4–6.
[35] Camus, 'The Crisis of Man', in *SO* 20.
[36] This is the sense in which Sartre famously denied a human essence in his *Existentialism and Humanism*.

32 THE PHILOSOPHY OF CAMUS

(Which is why he can find no comfort in the idea that God, or an angel, might understand the world in terms that are incomprehensible to us.) This remark does suggest that, in the end, what Camus's 'absurd man' wants is not so much 'understanding' in a purely intellectual sense, but to feel at home in the world, to feel that it has meaning (significance, value) for us. As, indeed, he says at the beginning of *The Myth*, 'the meaning of life is the most urgent of questions' (*MS* 4).[37] Much of the time, he suggests, we do feel at home in the world, simply because we live in terms of routine, and these routines do give us a sense of 'familiarity'. But there come moments when the routines that make sense of our lives, or keep us from thinking about whether they really make sense, get called into question:

> It happens that the stage sets collapse. Rising, streetcar, four hours in the office or the factory, meal, streetcar, four hours of work, meal, sleep and Monday Tuesday Wednesday Thursday Friday and Saturday according to the same rhythm— this path is easily followed most of the time. But one day the 'why' arises and everything begins in that weariness tinged with amazement. (*MS* 12–13)

The 'why?' here is a normative question: what is the point in continuing with all these activities that normally structure my days and hours? If the answer is that I need to have a job so I can make money, so I can eat and go on living, one can ask why I think it is worthwhile to go on living. (Again, the question with which Camus opens *The Myth* is that of suicide.) There may be, as it were, localized experiences of absurdity—perhaps my job really is ridiculous, a waste of my time and effort—that may be overcome by changing my life and doing something I find more worthwhile. But what generates the sense of global absurdity is the sense that all the particular, local meanings I might find in my life are undercut by the lack of any ultimate or overall Meaning.[38] The absurd arises from the confrontation between the desire that the world not be indifferent to human values, needs, and aspirations, and the sense that the world is not such as to accommodate that desire.

Ultimately, then, the 'wild longing for clarity' of which Camus speaks is really a longing for Meaning. In other words, it is—if we take the term in a broad enough sense—a religious hunger. When Camus goes on to consider the 'philosophical suicide' of the existential philosophers who recognize the apparent absurdity of our existence, but then (as Camus sees it) 'leap' beyond reason to find a Meaning in it, it is to God that they leap (whether the personal, biblical God of Shestov and

---

[37] See also his preface to the 1955 English edition of *The Myth*, where he says that the 'fundamental subject' of the book is that 'it is legitimate and necessary to wonder whether life has a meaning; therefore it is legitimate to meet the problem of suicide face to face' (*MS*, p. v).

[38] As with my capitalization of Truth, I will from now on write Meaning with a capital M when I refer to the sort of ultimate metaphysical meaning with which Camus is concerned, as opposed to more local or particular meanings.

THE ABSURD   33

Kierkegaard or the vaguer but still recognizably quasi-theistic 'transcendence' of Jaspers). However, the Absurdist's sense of the world as lacking Meaning is not simply equivalent to atheism. It seems to involve two main aspects. The first is the sense that there is nothing normative about reality; that it does not prescribe or ground any values that would give human lives meaning by indicating what was and was not worth doing. 'Belief in the meaning of life always implies a scale of values ... Belief in the absurd ... teaches the contrary ... Once for all, value judgements are discarded here in favor of factual judgments' (MS 60–1). The second crucial aspect is the denial of immortality; the insistence that death is the end. It is absurd that human life could be ended at any moment and that this end is final and absolute. And it is the mark of the absurd mind that it is not reconciled to death as an inescapable fact of nature; rather, 'death repels us ... death exalts injustice. It is the supreme abuse' (MS 89–90). The Epicureans, with their calm (at least on the surface) insistence that 'death is nothing to us', were not Absurdists in Camus's sense.[39] Indeed, it is the disbelief in immortality, rather than the disbelief in a transcendent God, that is most characteristic of the absurd mind. In accusing Dostoevsky of leaping from a perception of absurdity to a religious consolation, Camus is mainly concerned with the issue of immortality. It is not Dostoevsky's Christianity as such, but his acceptance of a future life, that marks his break with the absurd. (See MS 110–11.) Indeed, Camus claims that 'it is possible to be Christian and absurd. There are examples of Christians who do not believe in a future life' (MS 112). And in his Notebooks Camus even wrote: 'Secret of my universe; believing in God without human immortality.'[40] So, although Camus's notion of the absurd is defined in contrast to a religious view, it is not theism as such, considered merely as a metaphysical hypothesis about a First Cause, that concerns him. A God who neither prescribed values for us to live by, nor offered immortality, would do nothing to alleviate the absurdity of our existence.

Camus makes no claim to have discovered the absurd; on the contrary, he assumes throughout that the experience of it is a familiar one and notes moreover that it has been explored reflectively by many modern thinkers. It should be kept in mind that Camus's concern in the 'Philosophical Suicide' section of The Myth is, as he makes clear (MS 23, 28), not a scholarly examination of the philosophers he considers there, but a further exploration of the absurd sensibility and the options open or not open to it, through an impressionistic invocation of thinkers who have tried to articulate that sensibility. His attitude to those he calls 'the

---

[39] It is, therefore, curious that Camus chose as an epigraph for the Myth Pindar's lines 'Oh my soul, do not aspire to immortal life, but exhaust the limits of the possible' (MS 2). A happy or resigned acceptance of one's mortality is not Absurdist. There is an interesting contrast with the epigraph Camus used a year later for the fourth of his 'Letters to a German Friend', from Obermann: 'Man is mortal. That may be, but let us die resisting; and if our lot is complete annihilation, let us not behave in such a way that it seems justice!' (RRD 27).

[40] NB II, 12.

34   THE PHILOSOPHY OF CAMUS

existential philosophers' is interestingly complex and ambivalent. He includes
under this heading Kierkegaard himself, Lev Shestov (or Chestov, in the common
earlier transliteration from the Russian), Jaspers and Heidegger, and it is clear from
his later discussions of Dostoevsky and Kafka that he considers these very philosophical novelists to fall under the same category. What he admires about them
is their perception that the world as we experience it does not make sense; that
our reason can find no Meaning in it. 'These men vie with one another in proclaiming that nothing is clear, all is chaos, that all man has is his lucidity and his
definite knowledge of the walls surrounding him' (MS 27). But he also admires the
deep personal concern and disturbance with which they experience this break-
down of reason's ambition for a comprehensive explanation of things—a concern
that differentiates them from relaxed sceptics or empiricists with whom they might
agree on the purely epistemological plane. The existential philosophers are deeply
troubled by their inability to find Meaning in the world, and Camus shares their
attitude.

Camus describes Kierkegaard as 'perhaps the most engaging' of the existential philosophers, apparently because 'Kierkegaard, for a part of his existence at
least, does more than discover the absurd, he lives it' (MS 25). Kierkegaard was
very insistent on the importance of living in the categories in which one thinks,
rather than merely thinking in them; but can he be said to have embraced the
absurd—intellectually, existentially, or both—in Camus's sense?[41] Camus continues: 'Don Juan of the understanding, he multiplies pseudonyms and contradictions, writes his Discourses of Edification at the same time as that manual of
cynical spiritualism, The Diary of the Seducer. He refuses consolations, ethics,
reliable principles' (MS 26). This might seem to suggest that Kierkegaard's existence was 'absurd' in the sense that he simultaneously inhabited contradictory
attitudes to life; but that judgement would seem to depend on ascribing to him
all the views of his pseudonyms. Certainly, one might say that Kierkegaard could
not have written the pseudonymous literature unless he had felt within himself
the possibility of those different attitudes to life, but, as Camus the novelist was
aware, to enter imaginatively into a perspective is not the same as to share it
oneself.

One might say that Kierkegaard did—as we have noted already—endorse the
Camusian absurd in a limited epistemological sense (reason cannot find any overall Meaning in our experienced world) while rejecting it on a metaphysical level
(the idea that there is no Meaning). But this is where Camus accuses him—and the
other existential philosophers—of losing his nerve. He accuses them all of looking

---

[41] Kierkegaard and his pseudonyms sometimes talk about 'the absurd', but in a different sense; in
Fear and Trembling, Abraham's trust in God to preserve or restore Isaac is said to be 'absurd' in the
sense of going beyond and against all rational calculation. But this, of course, is not what Camus means
by the word.

THE ABSURD   35

for an 'escape' from absurdity, rather than finding the strength to dwell with it.[42] This is what he means by 'philosophical suicide' (as an alternative to literal suicide as a response to the absurd)—the abandonment of reason, the 'leap' to some form of consolation. Putting this criticism succinctly in regard to Shestov, he says: 'To Chestov reason is useless but there is something beyond reason. To an absurd mind, reason is useless, but there is nothing beyond reason' (MS 35). The existential philosophers allow their deeply felt *need* for Meaning (which, as we have seen, Camus commends) to let them posit its *reality* without intellectual justification. This is true of Kierkegaard too; he does not, in the end, Camus charges, leave us with an undecidable polyphony of differing perspectives, but leaps beyond them to a consciously and defiantly irrational version of Christianity. 'Despite apparently opposed writings, beyond the pseudonyms, the tricks, and the smiles, can be felt throughout that work, as it were, the presentiment (at the same time as the apprehension) of a truth which eventually bursts forth in the last works: Kierkegaard likewise takes the leap' (MS 37). But, as with Shestov, the God to whom he leaps is beyond our rational or perhaps even our moral categories, which means that our rational desire for clarity and certainty is never satisfied. Although Kierkegaard and the existential philosophers try to escape from the absurd, all they really manage is a kind of conjuring trick (MS 35) by which they end up deifying, rather than really escaping, the absurd. For Kierkegaard, 'antinomy and paradox become criteria of the religious. Thus, the very thing that led to despair of the meaning and depth of this life now gives it its truth and its clarity' (MS 37). In a way this is the worst of both worlds; Kierkegaard turns from the apparent absurdity of our existence to a God whose existence is not rationally justified and who is Himself absurd in the sense of being bound by no standards of reason or morality. In response Camus states what might be called a modest rationalism: 'if I recognize the limits of the reason, I do not therefore negate it, recognizing its relative powers. I merely want to remain in this middle path where the intelligence can remain clear. If that is pride, I see no sufficient reason for giving it up' (MS 40).

Is this critique fair to Kierkegaard? It seems to me that Camus is reading Kierkegaard too much in the light of Shestov—as more of an irrationalist and antinomian than he was. It is interesting, though, to note that Camus soon became aware that Kierkegaard was a more complex thinker than he had presented him as being. Although I am not primarily concerned with biographical/historical detail, it is relevant that *Either/Or* was not available as a whole in French translation until 1940 (although 'The Seducer's Diary' was published separately as early as 1929).[43] A *Notebook* entry from late 1942 shows Camus responding to his reading of *Either/Or*, volume ii (containing Judge William's letters in defence of the

---

[42] It is interesting that he tries to substantiate this claim against all the existential philosophers (and novelists) he mentions except for Heidegger. But the comments he does make on Heidegger are rather vague and do not seem to reflect any first-hand knowledge of his work.

[43] Stan, 'Albert Camus', 74–5.

36   THE PHILOSOPHY OF CAMUS

ethical). If he was reading it for the first time (which seems to be the case), then it was shortly before *The Myth* was published—too late, perhaps, for Camus to want to make any revisions in the light of his reading. But the note is interesting. Having complained in *The Myth* of Kierkegaard taking 'the leap' and by doing so making 'the sacrifice of the intellect' (*MS* 37), Camus now recognizes that, in Judge William's work, we have an 'Apology for the *general*'—for universal standards. '*Kierkegaard is not mystical.* He criticizes mysticism because it stands apart from the world—because it does not belong to the general. If there is a leap in Kierkegaard, it is an intellectual leap. It is the pure leap; on the ethical plane. But the religious plane transfigures everything.'[44]

This remark already points the way to the ethics of universal human concern that Camus fully articulated in *The Rebel*. And it suggests a way out of the aesthetic, or the absurd, that is not anti-rational. If it is still a 'leap' this is because it requires decision, commitment, an act of will, not just detached ratiocination. But this leap is itself an 'intellectual' one. Still, Camus is of course right that for Kierkegaard in the end the ethical is not enough; really to escape from the absurd, we need to make a further move, to the 'religious plane', and it is this that Camus is complaining of in *The Myth*. Is he right, though, that this second transition— the notorious 'leap of faith' (though Kierkegaard never uses that exact phrase in either his signed or his pseudonymous writings) really is a 'sacrifice of the intellect'? It is important to note that Kierkegaard does not treat belief in God itself as paradoxical or 'absurd'. One cannot indeed prove the existence of God through dispassionate 'sideways-on' metaphysical reasoning, but for Kierkegaard we have an innate sense of and attunement to God, understood primarily and in Platonic terms as the Good, an absolute and eternal standard of value.[45] This is implicitly present to us in our moral experience, and that it is not something that can be demonstratively proved to a sceptical mind (not much can) does not mean that it requires a 'sacrifice of the intellect'. Kierkegaard (through Climacus) identifies this generic 'Religiousness A' as 'Socratic' and associates it with a demythologized version of Platonic Recollection; the Truth is within us, though buried and repressed. It may need a struggle with ourselves for us to recognize it, but no great leap in the dark.[46]

This 'Socratic' religiousness does not represent Kierkegaard's own final position, though, and he certainly wanted to stress the paradoxical—and not merely paradoxical but, to the natural (sinful) human sensibility, offensive— nature of Christian belief.[47] But Christianity as paradox is 'Religiousness B'—the

---

[44] *NB II*, 39–40.

[45] This identification of the Platonic Good with God is in line with a long tradition of Christian Platonism. See especially the long discourse 'On the Occasion of a Confession' (often known as 'Purity of Heart') in *UDVS* 5–154, where he uses 'God', 'the Good', 'The Eternal', more or less as synonyms.

[46] See *PF*, chs 1, 2; *CUP* i. 205–10, 555–61.

[47] See, especially, *PC*, pt II *passim*, 69–144.

THE ABSURD   37

paradoxical and the absurd arise only once one is already in the religious sphere.[48] Insofar as Kierkegaard thinks that the preceding stages—the ethical, Religiousness A— are inherently unstable because of their inability to handle the problem of guilt and sin, then Camus is right that Kierkegaard does think that the only ultimate way out of the aesthetic sphere is paradoxical. (Although it still has its own rationale, in the solution it offers to what Kierkegaard argues is the otherwise insoluble and crippling problem of moral failure.) But it should not be overlooked that Kierkegaard does also explore the possibility of both ethical and religious alternatives to aestheticism (and thus I think to Camusian Absurdism), which are not paradoxical or anti-rational. Camus himself eventually took an ethical path away from the absurd. And Kierkegaard's account of a possible 'Socratic'—Greek rather than biblical and paradoxical—religiousness may serve at least as a comparison case for Camus's own eventual efforts to develop an outlook that would go beyond the humanistic ethics of *The Rebel*.

It should be noted that Camus does include under the same heading of 'philosophical suicide', not only the religious philosophies of Shestov and Kierkegaard, but also the religiously neutral Phenomenology of Husserl.[49] And this might seem to call in question my claim that Camus's Absurdism is essentially defined in opposition to a religious outlook. I shall try to show that in fact it does not; but also that considering Camus's attitude to Husserl is quite helpful for further explicating his notion of the absurd. Husserl had sought a descriptive philosophy that would 'suspend' or 'bracket' the assumptions that we usually make about the objects of our experience, and instead simply describe them as they are given to consciousness. Camus is initially enthusiastic about this project, seeing it as happily congruent with absurd thought, and as confirming its principle that there are truths but no Truth. For Husserl, 'thinking is not unifying or making the appearance familiar under the guise of a great principle. Thinking is learning all over again to see ... phenomenology declines to explain the world, it wants merely to be a description of actual experience' (*MS* 43). (One can see how this might be an attractive philosophy for a novelist.) Everything, considered as an object of experience, is placed on the same level: 'From the evening breeze to this hand on my shoulder, everything has its truth' (*MS* 43), but none of these truths is privileged. They just are, 'beyond all judgements' (*MS* 43). What is interesting about this is the positive tone; Camus (or the Absurdist for whom he is speaking) does not seem frustrated by the lack of unifying explanation in this phenomenological world, but finds in this pure descriptive phenomenology a 'profound enrichment of experience and

---

[48] *CUP* i. 555–6. Although Kierkegaard distinguishes Religiousness A from Christianity (Religiousness B), he sees the latter as building on (though also transforming) the former rather than simply contradicting it.

[49] I use an upper-case 'P' for Phenomenology when referring specifically to the philosophical movement initiated by Husserl; a lower-case 'p' when referring to a first-personal descriptive approach to philosophy more generally.

38   THE PHILOSOPHY OF CAMUS

the rebirth of the world in its prolixity' (*MS* 44). We are already getting a hint here of how Absurdism will be reconfigured in the later parts of *The Myth* as a positive philosophy.

But, Camus complains, Husserl is not content to stick with this 'modest' enumeration of phenomena. He looks to our experience to give us not simply a succession of fleeting particulars, but insight into the essential natures of actual and possible beings.[50] (Hence his method of 'eidetic variation', by which one alters in imagination the objects of one's experiences, in order to see in what respects or how far they can change without losing their identities.[51]) This leads Camus to reproach Husserl for moving from a purely descriptive, experiential philosophy to a sort of semi-Platonism: 'Husserl speaks ... of "extra-temporal essences" brought to light by the intention, and he sounds like Plato' (*MS* 44). Camus is aware that this is not full-blown Platonism—Husserl's essences are not transcendent or ideal paradigms—but this is not enough to reconcile Camus to them. 'Platonic realism becomes intuitive, but it is still realism' (*MS* 45). Seeking, as he was, to provide clear foundations for the mathematical and natural sciences, Husserl aimed to disclose an objective rational structure in experience; but this is what the Absurdist finds unbelievable. In the end, Camus finds in Husserl, not 'a taste for the concrete' but 'an intellectualism sufficiently unbridled to generalize the concrete itself' (*MS* 47).

Considered as a scholarly analysis of Husserl's philosophy, Camus's discussion is problematic in various ways.[52] But, as I pointed out above, Camus was not really intending such an analysis. He was, rather, trying to explicate the sense of the absurd through considering what an Absurdist might find acceptable and what unacceptable in certain contemporary intellectual currents. And, whatever the deficiencies in detail of his treatment of Husserl, his broad sense of what in Husserl is relevant to the issues he is concerned with seems plausible. The initial promise of Phenomenology as a purely descriptive discipline that nevertheless offered an 'enrichment' of everyday experience was felt by philosophers more academically rigorous than Camus. A well-known anecdote recounted by Simone de Beauvoir tells of how Raymond Aron was explaining Phenomenology to her and Sartre over drinks:

> Aron said, pointing to his glass, 'You see ... if you are a phenomenologist, you can talk about this cocktail and make philosophy out of it!' Sartre turned pale with emotion at this. Here was just the thing he had been longing to achieve for years— to describe objects just as he saw them and touched them, and extract philosophy from the process.[53]

---

[50] A programme set out in, e.g., Husserl, *Ideas: First Book*, pt one, ch. 1.
[51] For a lucid account of this method, see Sokolowski, *Introduction to Phenomenology*, ch. 12.
[52] The shortcomings of Camus's account are pointed out—and indeed somewhat exaggerated—in Hefferman, 'Camus and Husserl', 186–94.
[53] De Beauvoir, *The Prime of Life*, 135.

THE ABSURD   39

Husserl might have complained that both Sartre and Camus were guilty of a mis-understanding if they had hoped for such results from a philosophy that he had intended as a 'rigorous science' that would provide clear and certain foundations for knowledge.[54] But, however vague Camus may have been about some of the details of Husserl's philosophy, his contrast between a possible phenomenology devoted to evoking the texture of lived experience, and Husserl's actual founda-tionalist search for intellectual certainty, remains legitimate and suggestive.[55] It is worth noting, indeed, that most of Husserl's successors abandoned the Carte-sian and foundationalist aspects of his philosophy, thus moving closer to Camus's preferred version of phenomenology.[56] This did not, however, necessarily involve their abandoning essentialism (properly understood), and, as we shall see in the next chapter, a crucial part of Camus's eventual move away from Absurdism was his rejection of his former nominalism for what I shall argue was a form of Phe-nomenological essentialism about human nature (although he does not present it explicitly as such).

Even if one accepts Camus's claim that Husserl's version of phenomenology rep-resents an evasion of the absurd, it might still seem to be a different, and purely secular, evasion from that of Kierkegaard and other religious philosophers. But, for Camus, this is not really so. Both are guilty of 'starting from a philosophy of the world's lack of meaning' and ending up 'by finding a meaning and depth in it' (MS 42). Hence, he insists, 'from the abstract god of Husserl to the dazzling god of Kierkegaard the distance is not so great. Reason and the irrational lead to the same preaching' (MS 47). What explains this perhaps surprising claim? I think what is going on just below the surface of Camus's apparently epistemological criticism of Husserl's essentialism is really a concern to reject the idea that there might be a *normative* structure in reality, a proper order that we can recognize as such, and thus feel at home in. This is the 'broad sense' of 'religious' that I mentioned above; and this is, I think, what Camus complains of when he charges Husserl with restor-ing 'depth to experience' (MS 44) and thus providing a 'metaphysic of consolation' (MS 46). I think Camus's intuition that, beneath the austerely rationalistic surface of Husserl's philosophy, lies a concern with Meaning, and even a religious sense, is defensible.[57] But perhaps a better example than Husserl for what Camus is really

[54] Sartre, of course, did go on to acquire a much fuller scholarly understanding of Husserl than Camus did, although he also remained capable of reading his own interests and concerns into Husserl, as in his brilliant short essay, 'Intentionality'.

[55] It is interesting that Merleau-Ponty (consciously or otherwise) echoes Camus's claim that properly phenomenological thinking 'is learning all over again to see' in his remark that 'true philosophy entails learning to see the world anew' (Merleau-Ponty, *Phenomenology of Perception*, preface, p. lxxxv).

[56] It should, however, be said that the contrast between Husserl and his 'existential Phenomenologist' successors, though real, can be exaggerated. Husserl himself developed a strong interest in themes such as embodiment and the 'life-world' of everyday experience that were further articulated after him by thinkers such as Merleau-Ponty.

[57] According to Leszek Kolakowski, the 'search for certitude' that drove Husserl 'has little to do with the progress of science and technology. Its background is religious rather than intellectual; it is, as

40   THE PHILOSOPHY OF CAMUS

opposing (or one that makes the reason for his opposition more explicit) might be Confucianism—or, more specifically, the 'Neo-Confucianism' of the Song-Ming era. For here we find an essentialist philosophy that is very explicitly concerned to present reality as a rational order that is normative and descriptive/explanatory at once—a vision of the world in which we humans have our proper place, which itself involves rightly valuing things according to their real worth. Bryan Van Norden notes that, 'according to neo-Confucian metaphysics, *qi* and the Pattern [*li*] are the two aspects of everything that exists ...While *qi* is the physical "stuff" that constitutes individuals, it is Pattern that determines both the descriptive and the normative structure of the universe.' He then quotes Zhu Xi (1130–1200): 'It is certain that everything in the world has a reason why it is as it is, and a standard to which it should conform. This is the Pattern.'[58] By contrast, in the Absurdist vision of the world, things have neither reasons why they are as they are (as distinct, perhaps, from partial causal explanations) nor any normative standards to which they should conform.[59]

III Is Absurdism Consistent?

The absurd, as Camus defines it, then, involves a deep human longing for reality as a whole to embody values that would give direction and purpose to human life. We feel that the world *ought* to be a Meaningful order in which we can feel we have a proper place. But the absurd also involves the conviction that the world is not in fact such an order. This combination has a certain instability built into it. One experiences life as absurd if one experiences within oneself a need for the world to be Meaningful, and also experiences the 'unreasonable silence' of a world that does not appear to meet that need. But, if one comes to believe that there is no ultimate Meaning to life, might one not do better to give up on the demand, or desire, that it have such a Meaning? Or: if that 'wild longing' does not go away—or if one feels that one would be in some sense impoverished if it did—then why not reconsider the conviction that the world *does* offer no response to that longing?

To start with the second question: Camus's Absurdist, without claiming to know with metaphysical certainty that the world is Meaningless, does clearly suppose that is the most reasonable thing to believe. The argument here seems broadly empiricist—there is no evidence to support the idea of such a Meaning. He thinks

Husserl perfectly knew, a search for meaning. It is a desire to live in a world out of which contingency is banned, where sense (and this means purpose) is given to everything'. Kolakowski, *Husserl and the Search for Certitude*, 84.

[58] In Tiswald and Van Norden (eds), *Readings in Later Chinese Philosophy*, 171.

[59] I do not mention Confucianism here to suggest that Camus himself had it in mind; my point is that we can understand his views better by contrasting them with those he is committed to rejecting, and that these include a wide range of different outlooks—so not just Christian theism, or the Western rationalist tradition.

that the 'existential philosophers' leap beyond reason when they posit a Meaning that is not justified by our experience; and he refuses to make such a leap, even if reason is not enough to satisfy him emotionally. But is there in fact no reason to think that the world has a Meaning? Even if we accept the ultimacy of the appeal to experience, there are lots of people who do *experience* the world as Meaningful in a strong sense—as expressive of God or Dao or Brahman; or simply of itself, but as a locus of wonder and beauty. In trying to explain the feeling of the absurd, Camus writes about 'perceiving that the world is "dense" ... with what intensity nature or a landscape can negate us ... The primitive hostility of the world rises up to face us across millennia' (*MS* 14). No doubt Camus is here evoking a real experience of the natural world as alien to us, or even 'hostile' (though, of course, that is itself an anthropomorphism). But he was also evoking a real experience in an earlier essay, 'Nuptials at Tipasa', when he wrote:

> Sea, landscape, silence, scents of this earth. I drank my fill of a scent-laden life and bit into the already golden fruit of the world, overwhelmed by the feeling of its strong sweet juice flowing along my lips. No, it was neither I nor the world that counted, but solely the harmony and silence that gave birth to the love between us.[60]

Here we have harmony rather than estrangement, love, rather than hostility. It might be said that this ecstatic vision of our harmony with nature does not show nature to be Meaningful in a sense that answers our desire for 'clarity', for an explanation that makes sense of it all. But, as I have suggested above, Camus's real concern is not primarily epistemological—it is to feel that we are at home in the world; that there is a sense that we can live and experience, whether or not we can intellectually articulate it, that the world both embodies certain values and demands of us that we live by them. There is a right way and a wrong way to respond to the world, and to respond rightly to it is to live well. In his ecstatic communion with nature at Tipasa, Camus felt 'I had played my part well. I had performed my task as a man and the fact that I had known joy all one livelong day seemed to me, not an exceptional success, but the intense fulfilment of a condition which, in certain circumstances, make it our duty to be happy.'[61] To feel joy in our love for the world is the right way to live; even our task and duty. There is indeed something pantheistic about this attitude to nature; Camus begins and closes the essay from which I have been quoting by invoking 'the gods' (though he does suggest in between that we can dispense with that language— 'those who

---

[60] Camus, 'Nuptials at Tipasa', in *SEN* 74 (also *LCE* 71). Tipasa is a ruined Roman city on the Algerian coast that Camus visited often in his youth.

[61] *SEN* 74 (*LCE* 70–1).

42   THE PHILOSOPHY OF CAMUS

need myths are indeed poor'[62]). And looking back on his youth close to the end of his life, Camus refers to 'the world which I worshiped as my God'.[63]

Faced by the choice between this positive vision of the world and the negative one expressed in the *Myth*, why choose the negative? We could ask this biographically, as a question about Camus personally, but that is not my primary concern. And we could of course ask, as I noted above, to what extent Camus himself believed the Absurdist philosophy he advanced in *The Myth*. I will return to this question. But my main concern is philosophical; are there good reasons for favouring the Absurdist view of the world, even if it goes against the experience we have of it as Meaningful and our wild longing for it to be so?[64] Does Camus suggest such reasons in *The Myth*? Certainly, the most influential argument for supposing that the world is without Meaning is that given by philosophical naturalism—the claim that the natural sciences have given an account of the world that can satisfy as far as is reasonable the desires we have for purely intellectual clarity and completeness of explanation, but that contradicts Zhu Xi's conviction that the order of nature is normative as well as descriptive. On this view, science shows that the universe offers no support to human values, hopes, or aspirations. But Camus, as we have seen, is much too sceptical about what natural science can achieve to take this line. It may give pragmatically useful explanations of various phenomena, and even unify them under laws to some extent, but it cannot offer an adequate explanation of all of reality—especially not human reality. Simple human experience is irreducible to any scientific account and is not inferior to it as a source of knowledge: 'The soft lines of these hills and the hand of evening on this troubled heart teach me much more' (*MS* 20). In a later essay he notes that 'there is no absolute materialism, since simply to form this word there must be something in the world apart from matter'.[65] The consciousness that makes claims about materialism cannot itself be adequately explained by materialism—of course, a controversial judgement but, I think, an entirely correct one.[66] In any case, it is clear enough that Camus has

---

[62] *SEN* 71 (*LCE* 67); for the preceding and following references to the gods, see *SEN* 69, 74 (*LCE* 65, 71).

[63] Preface (1958) to the reprint of *Betwixt and Between* (*L'Envers et l'endroit* (originally published 1937)), in *SEN* 18 (*LCE* 6). It is significant that, although now critical of the stylistic clumsiness that he finds in these early essays, Camus still holds to the truth of what he tried to say there: 'I know no more about life itself than what is awkwardly said in *Betwixt and Between*' (*SEN* 24; *LCE* 12). ('Nuptials at Tipasa' appeared in his second volume of 'Lyrical Essays', *Nuptials*, in 1938.)

[64] Someone who really does not feel that longing and has never had that experience is unlikely to be persuaded to believe in an ultimate Meaning by dispassionate argument. The question is about whether the converse holds; whether there are good reasons for someone who is disposed to believe in an ultimate Meaning nonetheless to reject that inclination as illusory.

[65] Camus, 'The Enigma', in *SEN* 145 (*LCE* 158-9). In *The Rebel* he again rejects 'absolute materialism', which would 'deny thought' (what we would now call 'eliminative materialism') and also has some caustic comments about the less radical view that thought, though real, is 'absolutely determined by exterior reality' (*R*. 198).

[66] It is worth noting that the most strictly consistent forms of materialism have ended up rejecting, or at least calling into question, the notions of (semantic) meaning, rationality, truth, and knowledge (let alone consciousness); which means that, in the end, they cannot even account for the very science

no interest in appealing to scientism in rejecting the idea that the world has a Meaning.

However, there is an argument that Camus does seem to make for the alienated view of our relation to the world that appeals precisely to the irreducible and distinctive nature of human consciousness:

> If I were a tree among trees, a cat among animals, this life would have a meaning, or rather this problem would not arise, for I should belong to this world. I should *be* this world to which I am now opposed by my whole consciousness ... This ridiculous reason is what sets me in opposition to all creation ... what constitutes the basis of that conflict, of that break between the world and my mind, but the awareness of it? (*MS* 51–2)

Here Camus is very close to Sartre, for whom consciousness has no substantial being in itself, but exists simply as an awareness of its objects—of what it is not.[67] But human rational consciousness, as distinct from the consciousness of, say, a cat, is *self*-conscious. (As Sartre puts it, even when it is not engaged in explicit acts of introspection, it always has a 'pre-reflective' awareness of itself accompanying its awareness of other beings.[68]) It is always aware of itself as distinct from the objects it knows; and hence, Camus suggests here, the break or opposition between mind and world. This argument has the advantage, if it is correct, that it would show the absurd to have an ontological basis in the fundamental distinctiveness of human consciousness itself. However, although I think Camus and Sartre are right that to be self-conscious is to be aware of oneself as distinct from one's objects, alienation does not follow simply from differentiation. Differentiation is a prerequisite for any kind of relationship with what is other than oneself—including relations of love and harmony, as well as those of hostility or alienation. That our relations—whether to nature or to other people—are essentially hostile is an idea that seems

to which they appeal to validate their materialism. (See, e.g., Paul Churchland, 'Eliminative Materialism and the Propositional Attitudes' and Patricia Churchland, 'Epistemology in the Age of Neuroscience.') Even more modest versions of philosophical naturalism (notoriously) face deep difficulties in giving any adequate account of human consciousness; to the extent that they manage to do so, they tend to undermine their own initial materialist commitments, or reduce them to something merely verbal. (See, e.g., Strawson, 'Real Materialism', which argues for a form of panpsychism, according to which all of reality has a mental, or at least proto-mental, aspect. 'Real' materialism thus ends up looking more like a kind of objective idealism.)

[67] See Sartre, *Being and Nothingness*, esp. the introduction, pt one, ch, 1, and pt two, ch. 1. Whether Sartre directly influenced these thoughts of Camus is unclear. *Being and Nothingness* was not published till after *The Myth of Sisyphus*, and it was not until a year after that that Sartre and Camus became personally acquainted. But Camus did know, and had reviewed, Sartre's pre-war literary works, and a good deal of Sartre's philosophy appears in his novel *Nausea*. (Camus indeed complains, in his otherwise positive review, that the philosophy is not always well integrated into the literary narrative. See *SEN* 168–9 (*LCE* 200).) Whether Camus had read any of Sartre's pre-war academic philosophical monographs, I do not know, but Camus's line of thought here does seem rather similar to that of Sartre's short essay 'Intentionality' (1939).

[68] See Sartre, *Being and Nothingness*, introduction, sect. III (pp. l–lvi).

44   THE PHILOSOPHY OF CAMUS

to go very deep with Sartre; but I cannot see that he shows any ontological necessity why this should be the case, and this depressing conviction is not generally characteristic of Camus.

One might try to develop the argument from self-consciousness in a slightly different way. Thomas Nagel, in his classic essay 'The Absurd', claims that the crucial thing about self-consciousness is that it enables us to go beyond the implicit, pre-reflective sense of ourselves that is always present in our experience, to a more explicit self-awareness. When we make this move, we step back from the activities, passions, and interests that structure our lives and make sense of them to us, and look in on ourselves as though from outside. And, when we do that, the 'seriousness' with which we cannot help taking our lives appears 'gratuitous'.[69] Nagel presets this explanation of the absurd as an alternative to Camus's,[70] but Camus does, as I noted above, have quite a similar account of how the feeling of the absurd can arise, through our capacity to step back from and question the ordinary routines that make our world intelligible to us (see MS 12–13). Stepping back from *many* of our routines—or our desires, enthusiasms, and so on—may well lead us to experience them as pointless. But why should it *always* do that? If I ask myself: 'Is there any point in this?' when I am delighting in the beauty of nature (as Camus at Tipasa), or making love with my beloved, or trying to save somebody's life— or maybe even when plodding away at my work in the office—why shouldn't the answer just be, 'Yes!' Of course, getting too self-conscious in any of those moments may not be a good idea in any case. One notoriously tends to fall out of 'the flow' if one is too aware of being in it. But the point is not simply a psychological one—do not think too much if you want to avoid the absurd! The point is, rather, that the mere fact we can ask the questions we do not usually stop to ask about the value of our actions does not mean that those questions cannot be answered positively. The reason for thinking that they cannot be must come from the conviction that the things we concern ourselves with are *not* really of value, not worth bothering about as we think they are.[71] (Tipasa is not really beautiful; my beloved is not really lovable; the life I am trying to save does not merit any respect or concern. In general: value is just a projection.) But the whole question was, do we have good reason to believe that? And, if there are moods in which it does seem that way, still my earlier question recurs: why should we think those moods have more revelatory value than those in which it appears the other way?

One possible response would be to point out that the main purpose of *The Myth* is not so much to argue that the world is absurd, as to describe and explicate

---

[69] Nagel, 'The Absurd', 14.

[70] Nagel, 'The Absurd', 17.

[71] This shows, incidentally, that Nagel is wrong to claim, explicitly contra Camus, that 'the absurdity of our situation arises not from a collision between our expectations and the world, but from a collision within ourselves' ('The Absurd', 17). The latter collision has the force Nagel thinks it does only because he is presupposing something like the former collision.

the experience of it as absurd, and consider whether that is a kind of experience that we can live with, and even find happiness in. So perhaps we should not be pressing Camus too hard on the question of why affirming the absurd is the rational option. As a form of experience, the absurd is real enough, and the—notably Kierkegaardian—issue that concerns him is with what it could mean to an existing individual to live with that experience. So the Absurdist is not denying that there are non-absurd experiences, and does not claim to be judging between absurd and non-absurd experiences from a neutral position; but is concerned with the way that he or she does in fact experience the world, and wants to remain true to that experience. This reminder is pertinent and important, but I do not think it shows the line of questioning that I have been pushing so far to be misplaced. First, the absurd is not *simply* a mood or a feeling; it involves claims about reality that, Camus is quite clear, can be assessed rationally (even if not decisively *proved* one way or another). Granted that he has provided a compelling phenomenological description of the experience of the absurd, it seems that more needs to be done to show us why we should trust this experience over other, more positive, ones. And, secondly, the absurd is constituted by a tension between the longing for Meaning and the disbelief in it, and it is legitimate to worry that this tension amounts to a basic incoherence in the attitude. If so, that would indeed prevent one from dwelling in the absurd if one approached that task with the lucidity that Camus prizes. We need, then, to investigate whether we have good reason for holding to both the longing and the disbelief.

Although, as we have noted, Camus objects to leaping beyond reason, he also seems to recognize that reason simply is not competent to pronounce on whether or not things have Meaning. Reason does not lead us to any kind of scientific positivism or materialism, and it does not even affirm atheism. Having noted that 'the absurd does not lead to God', Camus adds a footnote: 'I did not say "excludes God", which would still amount to asserting' (*MS* 40). His position, then, seems strictly agnostic or sceptical. He is indeed close to the Greek sceptics—except that he does not find *ataraxia*, peace of mind, in accepting that we cannot have metaphysical knowledge. But, if objective reasoning cannot exclude Meaning, why not (if one does have a longing for Meaning) make a (quasi-)Pascalian leap of faith and affirm it?[72] Is it a fear of being mistaken? Camus does say that 'the absurd mind, rather than resigning itself to falsehood, prefers to adopt fearlessly Kierkegaard's reply: "despair"' (*MS* 41). But, as William James points out, you can miss the truth through an excess of caution as well as through a lack of it. To believe nothing that is not certain is a sure way to cut yourself off from a great many truths. Why is that

---

[72] Again, it needs to be stressed that the issue arises only for someone who has that passionate longing. Someone who apparently does not is not likely to be persuaded by detached ratiocination that there *is* Meaning. But such a person is likely to find Camus's whole project in *The Myth* to be misplaced, as I will discuss below.

46 THE PHILOSOPHY OF CAMUS

an obviously rational option?[73] From a Jamesian perspective, the Absurdist rejection of Meaning is as much a choice as the acceptance of it.[74] And Camus himself seems to recognize this, using the Pascalian term 'wager' to describe his attitude: 'Is one going to die, escape by the leap, rebuild a mansion of ideas and forms to one's own scale? Is one, on the contrary, going to take up the heart-rending and marvelous wager of the absurd?' (MS 52). Here he seems to acknowledge that betting on the absurd is as much a choice, as much a gamble, as betting on faith, and some commentators have seen him as himself taking a 'leap' similar to that which he condemned Kierkegaard and others for taking.[75] But Pascal gave reasons for betting in the way he recommended; and Kierkegaard (as I have noted above) was by no means simply an irrationalist. So recognizing that reason cannot give us the answer to the question of ultimate Meaning may not mean that reason simply drops out of the picture, leaving us with a choice that is either arbitrary or a matter of personal inclination. I will return in the following section to the question of whether Camus gives reasons, and, if so, what sort of reasons, for making the 'wager' he does.

Of course, James thought that one could 'will to believe' only if the question was not one that could be settled rationally (he did not wish to justify believing *against* reason) *and* if the options in question were genuinely 'live' ones (which was in part a matter both of temperament and of historical and cultural context). So perhaps Camus opted for absurdity because the alternative, (broadly) religious outlook was simply not a live option for him. It may indeed be that certain kinds of religious outlook were just alien to Camus (or to the Absurdist outlook that he is articulating in The Myth.) The absurd man 'does not understand the notion of sin ... that he is losing immortal life ... seems to him an idle consideration ... He feels innocent' (MS 53). (One is reminded here of Meursault's outburst to the prison chaplain at the end of The Outsider.) But, even if Christianity was not a live option for Camus, this would not exclude other forms of religious consciousness, such as the pantheistic rapture of 'Nuptials at Tipasa' with its loving harmony with the world. In any case, it is constitutive of the absurd that the 'absurd mind' feels the 'wild longing' for Meaning. If that is taken away, if a Meaningless world is contemplated by a mind with no longing for Meaning, or for whom the very notion of Meaning is empty, then there is no absurd in Camus's sense. So, by definition, some belief in Meaning has to be a live option for someone who is an Absurdist in Camus's sense. And, if such a person does not believe in Meaning because he or

---

[73] See James, 'The Will to Believe'.

[74] Camus does say that the absurd man 'demands of himself ... to live solely with what he knows ... and to bring in nothing that is not certain' (MS 61). But, as James notes, it is not certain that this demand itself is right or even reasonable; and so, if one accepts it, there is an element of decision involved. If the resulting position is to avoid self-refutation, then that initial demand must be given a special status as a prior commitment, which cannot be taken as applying to itself.

[75] See Cruickshank, Albert Camus and the Literature of Revolt, 63–4.

THE ABSURD   47

she simply does not experience it (however much he or she would like to), then the other option I mentioned above becomes inescapable; why not then simply work at rooting out the delusive desire for Meaning?

Of course, one cannot make a powerful desire go away by snapping one's fingers, but one can work on weakening such desires so that over time they might wither away. It is interesting that Camus seems to think that the longing for Meaning with which he is concerned is a universal characteristic of the human mind, not a personal or cultural/historical contingency. But there are, after all, many people who seem not to feel such a need. And this is, of course, true of many intellectuals today—pragmatists, empiricists, postmodernists—who claim to have no nostalgia for absolute Truth or ultimate Meaning. Since they do not expect the world to make sense in any grand religious or quasi-religious way, they do not experience it as absurd when it fails to do so. In his own day, Camus was criticized from such a perspective by A. J. Ayer, who claimed that the idea of the world as a whole having Meaning was itself meaningless (in a simple semantic sense) and that it was therefore a mere confusion to get upset about the world lacking what it could (logically) never have had.[76] So, we might wonder whether someone who is convinced that he or she will never get anything more than 'unreasonable silence' from the world would do best to try to mitigate and eventually eliminate the 'wild longing' for Meaning. (Maybe by hanging out with relaxed pragmatic naturalists and reading the works of Richard Rorty.) For, once the desire for Meaning fades away, so does the disturbing perception of the world as Meaningless. The whole question of a global Meaning evaporates, leaving us placidly to return to our everyday local meanings and values.

By contrast, the strangeness of Camus's notion of the absurd is apparent; it is the attitude of a basically religious consciousness that cannot or will not believe in the Meaning that it cannot help yearning for. In the *Letters to a German Friend*, Camus tells his fictitious addressee (a nihilist intellectual who had thrown his lot in with the Nazis): 'for a long time we both thought the world had no ultimate meaning and that consequently we were cheated. I still think so in a way.'[77] One can only feel cheated of something that *should* have been the case. And how could a genuinely secular mind think that there should—or even could—have been any such 'ultimate meaning'? There is (as I suggested in the Introduction) something curiously Gnostic about Camus's position here (and it should be remembered that Camus was familiar with historical Gnosticism from his work for his *diplome* dissertation[78]). The soul feels alien, not at home in this world; its existence in the world is indeed absurd and alienated. But, for the Gnostic, there is another, higher

[76] See Ayer, 'Albert Camus'.
[77] In *RRD* 27.
[78] See *CMN*, ch. 2.

48   THE PHILOSOPHY OF CAMUS

world, to which the soul can escape and return. For the Absurdist there is nothing but this world, but we are still strangers and aliens in it.

But is this in fact Camus's view? Srigley has argued that Camus's own aim is really to get us to abandon the delusive desire to find any absolute Meaning. Srigley interprets the absurd as a sense of disconnection between the mind and its world, which is due to a 'sickness' of the mind itself, a malfunctioning of its normal ability to relate itself properly to the world. *The Myth*, on this view, is a work of philosophical therapy, which is intended to lead those suffering from this disease back to a sense of normal connection with reality, in which we can find plenty of everyday meanings, even if no grand Meaning.[79] Srigley thinks that at the start of *The Myth* we hear the voice of this sick mind, which yearns for ultimate Meaning, and that the book then traces its cure to the point where it abandons that yearning and returns to the ordinary pleasures and challenges of life. (So that the authorial voice and Camus himself start off divergent and converge as the book goes on.) It is clearly true that *The Myth* does follow a progression—from the contemplation of suicide as a response to a Meaningless world, to a 'happy' acceptance of life in such a world. The frustration at our inability to find metaphysical Truth gives way to relief: 'I understand then why the doctrines that explain everything to me also debilitate me at the same time' (*MS* 55). (As we saw already in the discussion of Husserl, the abandonment of the search for order and unity in experience can free us to appreciate the multifarious richness of that experience itself.) And the 'wild longing' for Meaning gives way to the conviction that 'life ... will be lived all the better if it has no meaning' (*MS* 53).

However, this turnaround in the course of *The Myth* does not simply represent a return from delusive metaphysical anxieties to a sound common-sense engagement with the everyday world. Although, as I noted above, Camus does not think the denial of absolute Truth undermines science and its limited truths, he *does* think that the denial of any absolute Meaning undermines conventional ethical claims. The later parts of *The Myth*, as I will discuss in the next section, go on to develop a disturbingly radical moral antinomianism. Moreover, the sense of absurdity never goes away (which it seems it should, if the desire for Meaning, which is one of the two poles that generates it, is dissolved) and Srigley's view cannot, I think, convincingly explain *The Myth*'s insistence that the absurd is something we need to live with, rather than be cured from.[80] But, although I do not think Srigley is right to think that Camus is working to dissipate the sense of the absurd, I do think the understanding of the absurd shifts as *The Myth* goes on. The world

[79] See Srigley, *Camus' Critique*, ch. 1. He does, however, admit that Camus was not entirely clear or consistent about this and that *The Myth* is complicated by frequent backsliding (as he sees it) towards nostalgia for Meaning on Camus's part. See Srigley, *Camus' Critique*, 46–7.

[80] We should note that Camus's complaint about Kierkegaard was that he wanted to be cured. See *MS* 38.

remains absurd, in the sense of lacking in Meaning, providing no scale of values; and it shows up as such by contrast to the human hunger for Meaning. And yet, Camus argues in the later sections of *The Myth*, we can come to accept that lack of Meaning as liberating. This is not, however, the relaxed empiricist view mentioned above, for which the whole issue of Meaning fades away. On the contrary, the Absurdist remains acutely conscious of the lack of Meaning, and finds that it liberates precisely because it washes us clean of those everyday meanings to which the relaxed empiricist is happy to return.

In its original senses, the absurd was constituted by a tension between the longing for Meaning and the disbelief in it, and we needed to ask whether this tension amounted to a basic incoherence. The tension seems in a sense resolved later in *The Myth* by abandoning the desire for Meaning; but only partially and at the cost of creating a different kind of tension. For the sense of the absurd in the later part of *The Myth* seems to involve keeping the hunger for Meaning alive in order to be vividly aware of the world as lacking it, while at the same time repudiating that desire so as to live with passionate lucidity in a world clearly and consciously experienced as Meaningless. Furthermore, the conscious and even happy acceptance of the Meaninglessness of existence is only half the story told in the later parts of *The Myth*; the other half is precisely that our attitude towards the absurd should be one of continual revolt, rather than a relaxed acceptance that there is no Meaning to be had. Revolt is 'an insistence upon an impossible transparency. It challenges the world anew every second' (*MS* 54). The demand for Meaning does not in fact go away but is still used as a standard to judge the inadequacy of our existence, even while that standard is itself recognized as 'impossible'. Srigley's response to this is to reinterpret 'revolt' as merely the attitude of questioning, contemplating, and even perhaps praying to 'the greater reality in which he ["the absurd man"] exists'.[81] This does not, to put it mildly, fit well with Camus's declaration: 'revolt is the certainty of a crushing fate, without the resignation that ought to accompany it' (*MS* 54). Clearly, a deep and unresolved ambivalence continues to run through *The Myth*: Sisyphus both scorns the world for its Meaninglessness and finds his happiness in it; the Absurdist both revolts against the absurdity of the world and feels liberated by it. I do not primarily note this ambivalence in order to criticize Camus; sometimes what matters in philosophy is to unearth and to dwell with ambivalences rather than rush to resolve them with intellectually elegant solutions that may fail to recognize the complexity of the situation. But we need at this point to look in more detail at what I started to sketch above: the practical and ethical consequences that Camus draws from the Absurdist outlook, his account of what a consciously Absurdist life looks like.

[81] Srigley, *Camus' Critique*, 29.

IV Absurdism and Value

Camus does insist that one cannot derive an ethics from the absurd. As we have seen, the absurd cancels the assumption that there is a 'scale of values' (*MS* 60). Indeed, it essentially involves the rejection of Moral Realism—the belief that values are built into the fabric of reality. Camus accordingly endorses the conclusion of Dostoevsky's character Ivan Karamazov: 'Everything is permitted' (*MS* 67). Many contemporary philosophers would object that this does not follow—even if we reject Moral Realism, we need not be left with a merely subjectivist or even nihilistic stance. Perhaps we can create or 'construct' values for ourselves, even if they do not simply pre-exist us, 'out there'? I will, however, postpone discussion of this question until my consideration in the next chapter of Camus's later works, in which he does try to develop an ethics. Interestingly, Camus does say in *The Myth* that 'there is but one moral code the absurd man can accept, the one that is not separated from God. But it so happens that he lives outside that God' (*MS* 66–7). Again, we see that the absurd is defined in contrast to religion; it is the alternative to religion, religion is the alternative to it. Secular humanistic morality is rejected at this point in Camus's development as an incoherent halfway house. And here we can see his answer to the 'relaxed empiricist'; moral values depend ultimately, though perhaps implicitly, on a sense of the world having Meaning. Scientific truths, for the Camus of *The Myth*, do not need to be underwritten by metaphysical Truth; but ethical values do depend on their being an ultimate metaphysical Meaning. Hence the loss of that sense of Meaning has drastic consequences—it is not something we can simply shrug off.

Camus does note that Ivan's maxim 'does not recommend crime' and that, 'if all experiences are indifferent, that of duty is as legitimate as any other. One can be virtuous through a whim' (*MS* 67). But this, as Kierkegaard and his ethical spokesman Judge William would remind us, is just wrong—it is a conceptual error. One can act in the way a virtuous person would act through a whim; but to *be* virtuous is to be committed to virtue; to recognize it as having an authority over one, whether one feels like it or not. But conversely, if all experiences are indifferent, that of crime is also as legitimate as any other, even if it is not particularly recommended as *more* legitimate. Still, if Camus cannot recommend any particular way of acting as inherently better than any other, he can and does recommend a certain attitude one should take to whatever one does. (Although he is 'officially' seeking only to describe the absurd life, he is clearly in the later parts of *The Myth* trying to portray it in a way that will commend it to the reader; to make it attractive.) The crucial virtue for him, then, becomes lucidity; whatever one does, one should do it in full awareness of its ultimate lack of Meaning, while choosing to do it anyway. He gives us certain images of the absurd life—Don Juan, the actor, the 'conqueror' or adventurer. But it is not what they do, but the spirit in which they act that makes them (as Camus imagines them) exemplars of the absurd. And that spirit can in principle be found just as well in a post office clerk or a civil servant (*MS* 68, 91). 'It is enough to know and to mask nothing' (*MS* 90–1). This consciousness must, of course, involve not only an awareness of the Meaninglessness of life and the finality of death, but a refusal to resign oneself to them, which is why it involves revolt. This, of course, becomes a crucial notion for Camus, but it is initially a metaphysical, rather than a political, stance; as I noted above, it is 'the certainty of a crushing fate, without the resignation that ought to accompany it' (*MS* 52).

The notion of revolt is what underlies the argument that Camus finally gives against suicide. But this argument, unfortunately, has a definite whiff of sophistry to it. Suicide negates the absurd by eliminating the consciousness that revolts against the Meaninglessness of things. But the question was whether it is possible to live with the absurd; so suicide is to be rejected as a kind of escapism (*MS* 53–4). Of course, *if* one is to live with the absurd, one cannot escape it through suicide. But the question was whether it *is* worth living with the absurd, and Camus now seems simply to beg that question. What is really going on, though, is not so much a logical deduction as a personal response to an existential challenge. 'It is essential to know whether one can live with [the absurd] or whether, on the other hand, logic commands one to die of it' (*MS* 50). But it is not really about logic. The question Camus is posing is whether we can affirm life even though it is without Meaning. Logic cannot show that we should affirm it. But, if we find the impulse or passion within us to do so, we can move on with Camus to the question of what form that affirmation should take. This is one sense in which the absurd life is a leap or a wager—though those terms perhaps make it sound too voluntaristic, when it may be more about an instinctive, pre-rational love of life. It needs to be distinguished, though, from the prior 'leap' (which it presupposes)—the acceptance of the absurd itself, against the competing options of either cultivating a faith in Meaning or working to whittle away one's longing for it. I will return shortly to the issue of whether Camus gives us reasons for this prior leap.

Before doing that, we should note that Camus does argue that, even if the absurd cannot prescribe a particular course of action or way of life, it does still suggest a *sort* of ethic (or perhaps anti-ethic)—one that he indeed calls an 'ethics of quantity' (*MS* 72). On this view, 'what counts is not the best living but the most living' (*MS* 61). Because no experience is in itself more valuable or important than any other, one should aim simply to accumulate as much experience as possible. This does not *necessarily*, though, point to the life of a Don Juan or an adventurer, rather than to a staider and less various kind of existence. 'It is a mistake to think that the quantity of experience depends on the circumstances of our life, when it depends solely on us ... To two men living the same number of years, the world always provides the same sum of experiences ... It is up to us to be conscious of them' (*MS* 62). Quantity seems here to get turned into quality, in a way;[82] what matters is

---

[82] As Camus indeed explicitly recognizes; see the footnote on *MS* 62.

52 THE PHILOSOPHY OF CAMUS

the lucidity with which I am conscious of whatever experiences come my way—or which I seek out. For, although the absurd life is not necessarily the active life of the 'conqueror', freedom is one of the main 'absurd' characteristics or virtues. Not necessarily free will in a metaphysical sense, but the recognition that there are no objective values to which I *ought* to conform, no *telos* that I ought to follow. I am free to set my own course:

> To the extent to which he [the 'absurd man'] imagined a purpose to his life, he adapted himself to the demands of a purpose to be achieved, and became the slave of his liberty ... to the extent to which I hope ... to the extent to which I arrange my life and prove thereby that I accept its having a meaning, I create for myself barriers between which I confine my life. (*MS* 58)

But the absurd man is bound, as well as free; and bound, most of all, by the fact of his vulnerability to death. Although it is up to me how much 'quantity' I get out of the experiences I receive from my engagement with the world, I need to go on getting that experience, and nothing I can do can guarantee that. No matter how much passion or consciousness I put into my living, it cannot compensate for that life being cut short. 'There will never be any substitute for twenty years of life and experience' (*MS* 63).

As I noted above, although Camus claimed that he was merely describing the Absurdist mindset and not making 'value judgements' about it (*MS* 61), it is pretty clear that, in the later parts of *The Myth*, he (or the authorial voice of *The Myth*, anyway) is working to commend it to us. And this is made explicit with the assertion I have referred to already, that 'life ... will be lived all the better if it has no meaning' (*MS* 53). But to make such a judgement is, at least implicitly, to presuppose certain values that serve as the criteria for what is or is not 'better'. And this is not surprising. Charles Taylor has argued, very convincingly to my mind, that it is impossible for a human being to live outside some framework of evaluation, some sense of what is qualitatively better or worse.[83] And those philosophies that claim to reject any such evaluative frameworks, or to reduce qualitative to quantitative evaluation, nonetheless cannot help presupposing certain qualitative values.[84] Camus's values are made explicit in the later sections of *The Myth*, where we find him describing the absurd life in terms of 'majesty' and 'pride', and appealing to 'everything that is indomitable and passionate in a human heart' (*MS* 55). Certain virtues are taken as admirable; honesty (with oneself; the refusal of self-deception) as well as 'generosity' and 'solitary courage' (*MS* 71). The absurd life is 'better' because it is freer; it expresses a commitment to a kind of radical autonomy and

---

[83] See Taylor, *Sources of the Self*, pt one.
[84] See Taylor, *Sources of the Self*, ch. 3, 'Ethics of Inarticulacy'.

to the inner strength that enables one to live without illusions and without dependence on anyone or anything. It cannot of course guarantee that it will be free from oppressive external circumstances; but, like Sisyphus himself, 'the absurd man' can still respond to them—and surmount them—with scorn (*MS* 121). But, if everything really is Meaningless in a sense that undermines conventional ethical values, it is not really clear why we should hold to these virtues of heroic independence; why they are not as arbitrary as any others. In any case, though, I think it is plausible to suggest that it is here that we see the real reason for the wager on the absurd; a commitment to an ideal of radical freedom in which one is beholden to nothing but oneself. The values of the 'absurd man' are not forced on us by a properly lucid, objective analysis that reveals the Meaninglessness of our existence; rather, existence is regarded as Meaningless because of a commitment to those values.

Camus himself explicitly rejects this claim that the metaphysics of Absurdism derive from its values rather than vice versa. Discussing Ivan Karamazov's 'all is permitted', he notes that

> it should not be taken in the vulgar sense ... it is not an outburst of relief or of joy, but rather a bitter acknowledgment of a fact. The certainty of a God giving a meaning to life far surpasses in attractiveness the ability to behave badly with impunity. The choice would not be hard to make. But there is no choice, and that is where the bitterness comes in. (*MS* 67)

No doubt the suggestion that it is a desire for 'the ability to behave badly with impunity' that drives the Absurdist's outlook would be a crude vulgarization of the Absurdist's concern with radical autonomy. But I find nothing implausible in the suspicion that it is the desire for such autonomy that is ultimately motivating the Absurdist's perception of the world as lacking intrinsic value; as making no normative demands on us. Indeed, I suspect that most, if not all, metaphysics, or world views, are, consciously or otherwise, formed as expressions of values. And I do find it hard not to read Camus here as sounding a little defensive. Having previously spoken of the absurd as a 'wager', he is now denying that there is a choice involved; and, for all his metaphysical scepticism, he is now presenting Ivan's 'all is permitted', and the atheism from which it is derived, as an undeniable 'fact'. Perhaps Ivan (and Camus?) feels that other options are ruled out or have no force; but is that feeling itself justified? It should be said, though, that Ivan has deeper reasons for his atheism than appear in this context, and we will be considering those—and Camus's consideration of them in *The Rebel*—in the next chapter.

I think it is clear enough by now that the absurd life, as presented by Camus, is indeed one form of what Kierkegaard means by an 'aesthetic' life. It is, of course, to recall the distinctions I made in the Introduction, a highly reflective form of aestheticism. A lucid self-consciousness is a crucial defining characteristic of the absurd life. What makes it aesthetic is the awareness of living outside any set

54 THE PHILOSOPHY OF CAMUS

of moral or religious values, and, indeed, the commitment to so living. In some respects, Kierkegaard's main aesthetic character, 'A', especially as he expresses himself in the essay 'Crop Rotation' in *Either/Or*, seems a close forerunner of Camus's Absurdist. As I mentioned in the Introduction, the primary concerns of 'A' are to maximize his freedom and his sense of being in control. And, like Camus's Absurdist, he seeks to achieve this primarily by the attitude he adopts. Like the Absurdist, he rejects teleology, the purposive pursuit of long-range projects, as confining; and, also like the Absurdist, rejects hope. 'Not until hope has been thrown overboard does one begin to live artistically'[85] by being thus freed to focus on savouring the present moment. (Camus, very similarly, describes Revolt as 'devoid of hope' (*MS* 54) but insists that this hopelessness is liberating, as it prevents us from looking anxiously towards the future.) Moreover, 'A' rejects the 'vulgar, inartistic' method of keeping life interesting by simply changing what one is doing all the time;[86] for him, as for the Absurdist, what counts is *how* one experiences whatever one does. It might seem, then, that an aesthete of his kind (like Camus's post-office clerk) could be indistinguishable from either an unreflective conformist or an ethicist. But, just as Camus does draw our attention to certain ways of life as more clearly embodying the absurd attitude (Don Juan, the actor, the 'conqueror'), so 'A' too does seem to favour certain ways of life over others, in his warnings against serious commitments, such as marriage, friendship, a career. Of course, one could take on such roles in a spirit of ironic detachment from them, but, as Judge William observes, playing a role that one can choose to abandon at any time is very different from a real commitment to a way of life.[87] This is why Camus takes the actor as a particularly telling image for the absurd life (which is not of course the same as to claim that all actors are Absurdists); and Kierkegaard does also seem to see an affinity between aestheticism and the theatre. If one includes opera as theatre, then four of the six essays in *Either/Or*, part one, are concerned with the theatre, while the protagonist of the final piece, 'The Seducer's Diary', is someone who lives his whole life as a play in which he 'directs' and manipulates others into playing the parts he needs them to.[88]

Given these affinities, I think *The Myth of Sisyphus* can properly be read as a defence, against Kierkegaard, of one version of the aesthetic life in Kierkegaard's sense. Whether Camus consciously thought of it as such is unclear; as I noted above, the only part of *Either/Or* he had read when he wrote *The Myth* was 'The

---

[85] *E/O* i. 292.

[86] See *E/O* i. 291.

[87] *E/O* ii. 165–6.

[88] It is interesting that both Camus and Kierkegaard take Don Juan as an exemplar of aestheticism/the absurd; although Kierkegaard sees him as expressing a pure unreflective sensuality, while Camus's version is, of course, characterized by a lucidity without illusions. In a way, his Don Juan is closer to the highly reflective Seducer of the Diary—except that Camus's Don Juan is a more commonplace and less rarified figure: 'He is an ordinary seducer. Except that he is conscious ...' (*MS* 72).

THE ABSURD   55

Seducer's Diary', though that would certainly have given him some sense of what Kierkegaard meant by the aesthetic in its more radical, amoral form. In any case, he certainly has Kierkegaard (as the 'most engaging' of the 'existential philosophers') in mind as he tries to articulate an alternative response from theirs to the perception of the absurdity of existence that he shares with them. And the fact that the response he offers seems itself to be a version of the Kierkegaardian aesthetic does show that he shares something of Kierkegaard's sense of the possible options.[89]

Is Camus's Absurdism nihilistic? It may not recommend crime, but it still seems to permit it. As he says in the review of Absurdism with which he begins *The Rebel*, 'awareness of the absurd ... makes murder seem a matter of indifference, to say the least, and hence possible' (*R*. 5). He goes on, however, to claim that there is an argument from Absurdism to a rejection of murder. If suicide is, as he argued in *The Myth*, an escapism that is contrary to the absurd, then murder is too: 'From the moment that life is recognized as good, it becomes good for all men. Murder cannot be made coherent when suicide is not considered coherent' (*R*. 6). He concludes that, since opposed conclusions can both consistently be deduced from the absurd, Absurdism itself must be rejected as contradictory (*R*. 8). But if, as I have argued above, the argument against suicide fails, then it cannot function as a premise for a further argument against murder. However, as I also suggested above, I do not think the argument against suicide is best construed (despite Camus's own presentation) as an exercise in logic, but as an appeal to each person who feels the sense of the absurd to see whether he or she has enough sheer love of life to want to go on living despite the lack of Meaning. But someone who answers 'yes!' to that question is doing so for him- or herself, in a radically first-personal way; no general conclusion about the value of human life as such is involved. I will look at the real grounds for Camus's rejection of murder in *The Rebel* in the next chapter. But sticking for now to the Absurdist phase, I think we have reason to worry, not only that the Absurdism of *The Myth* gives us no basis for condemning murder, but that it might in fact even seem to 'recommend' it.

In a discussion of Dostoevsky's character Kirilov, Camus notes his reasoning: 'If God does not exist, I am God' but admits that it is 'rather obscure' (*MS* 106). Elucidating it, he claims: 'If God exists, all depends on him ... If he does not exist, everything depends on us. For Kirilov, as for Nietzsche, to kill God is to become god oneself' (*MS* 108). Kirilov himself draws the conclusion that he must kill himself, in order to demonstrate his radical independence; his life is entirely in his own hands, he is responsible to no one for it, and he will exercise sovereign authority over it. Camus, of course, disapproves of this conclusion; one should demonstrate

---

[89] Although, as we have seen, for Camus, the alternatives, for those who are aware of the absurd as a phenomenon, are between the conscious embrace of Absurdism and the 'leap' away from it into some kind of religious existence. The ethical, as a stage distinct from the aesthetic and the religious, does not really feature at this point.

56   THE PHILOSOPHY OF CAMUS

one's godlike independence, not by choosing death, but by living in sovereign freedom, as a 'tsar' of the absurd (*MS* 109). He bestows this title on two other Dostoevsky characters, Stavrogin and Ivan Karamazov—both of whom, if not actually murderers, become complicit in the deaths of others. Interestingly, though, there is another very relevant Dostoevsky character whom Camus does not mention: Raskolnikov, the protagonist of *Crime and Punishment*, who *does* murder—on one level for money, but, more deeply, in order to prove to himself that he is a sort of superman, who stands above moral laws and can exercise sovereignty over other people's lives. Camus does not explicitly endorse this reasoning, but it is present as an insistent subtext in the section on Dostoevsky in *The Myth*. Raskolnikov, after all, finds a way—unlike Kirilov—to demonstrate his godlike independence while still living to experience it. (At least, he *tries* to find that way—Dostoevsky's novel shows him ultimately buckling under the strain of trying to live up—or down—to his inhuman ideal.)

That Camus was disturbingly haunted by this idea of an innocent criminal— who kills out of metaphysical indifference, or even to demonstrate his godlike status – is clear from his fiction. In his first, unpublished novel, *A Happy Death*, the protagonist, Patrice Mersault, kills and robs a rich but crippled acquaintance, Zagreus.[90] Like Raskolnikov, he kills for the money he needs to be independent, but also, it seems, to show himself to be capable of the deed. He experiences no remorse.[91] The book is in some respects a trial run for *The Outsider*, whose hero, Meursault, kills without premeditation or purpose, but is, again, presented as innocent. In *Caligula*, Camus shows the Emperor's atrocities as motivated by an acute and honest perception of the absurdity of existence. And, in *The Misunderstanding*, the mother and daughter make a practice of murdering and robbing their lodgers, and Martha, the daughter, insisting on the emptiness of existence, refuses any notions of guilt, remorse, or pity. Of course, one cannot identify Camus with his fictional protagonists. In *Caligula*, Camus makes a point of presenting the Emperor as a tragic hero, rather than a monster; but whatever sympathy it has for him, the play clearly ends up siding with his assassin, Cherea.[92] But, in exploring the notion of the absurd, Camus was clearly fascinated by the idea that murder might be in some sense a proper response to an absurd world. He even gives this idea a particular twist. Anthony Rizzuto suggests that the young Camus

---

[90] This is somewhat complicated, since Zagreus seems to set up his own killing. There is also a heavy (too heavy) overlay of symbolism; 'Zagreus' probably did not appear very often in a 1930s Algiers telephone directory, but it was one name of the god Dionysus.

[91] 'Mersault realized that not once since Vienna had he thought of Zagreus as the man he had killed with his own hands. He recognized that power in himself to forget which only children have, and geniuses, and the innocent. Innocent, overwhelmed by joy, he understood at last that he was made for happiness' (*HD* 62).

[92] Although it seems that in the first version of the play, completed in 1941, Camus really did present Caligula as the hero. The play was substantially rewritten before its first performance in 1945.

THE ABSURD   57

was haunted specifically by the question of whether 'a man, in order to achieve divine solitude, [would] kill his mother?'[93] Matricide, the ultimate repudiation of the most basic social and natural bonds, would be the most extreme possible affirmation of 'the man-god's disaffiliation from family and society'.[94] Rizzuto argues that Caligula symbolically kills his mother when he murders his older mistress, Ceasonia, and that, in *The Outsider*, Meursault too symbolically kills his mother.[95] (In *The Misunderstanding* the tables are turned, and the mother (unwittingly but literally) kills her son.) In the 'Metaphysical Rebellion' section of *The Rebel*, Camus considers and criticizes those who, from Sade to the Surrealists, had concluded that the absence of God, or a moral world order, made criminality at least legitimate, or even appropriate. But it is clear that this is a mindset by which he himself had been deeply tempted, and that he knew well, from the inside. This makes the critique all the more poignant, as well as powerful.

V Conclusion to Chapter 1

The Myth of Sisyphus is a hard work to try and get in focus. The central concept of the absurd is initially defined in terms of a tension between a hunger for Meaning and a disbelief in it that is psychologically possible but seems inherently unstable. As the book progresses, the wild longing for Meaning develops into an attitude towards the supposed-to-be-Meaningless world that is itself conflicted. On the one hand, there is a continuing desire for Meaning, which becomes the attitude of revolt—a neo-Gnostic defiance of the world for failing to have Meaning. On the other hand, there is an acceptance of the world's lack of Meaning as liberating, as freeing us to enjoy a godlike independence; but which requires us always to have clearly in mind that lack of Meaning. If these two can coexist, it is perhaps only because the attitude of revolt is itself taken to require a godlike strength and independence. The Absurdist rebel seems in some sense to want the world to be Meaningless in order to defy it for so being, and by so doing to demonstrate his or her own strength, pride, and freedom. Again, the attitude may be psychologically possible—and Camus's eloquent prose may even lend it a seductive appeal—but there still seems to be an instability built into this outlook. Can one, with the lucid, undeceived rationality that Camus praises, really combine a Nietzschean yea-saying to a Meaningless world with a Gnostic revolt against it? Whether Camus himself ever was an Absurdist in the sense articulated in *The Myth* is hard to say. He is at least trying to set out the position as convincingly as he can;

---

[93] Rizzuto, *Camus' Imperial Vision*, 11.
[94] Rizzuto, *Camus' Imperial Vision*, 11.
[95] See Rizzuto, *Camus' Imperial Vision*, 10–28.

but, in so doing he, deliberately or not, brings out the tensions and—perhaps—contradictions that run through it. However, when he comes explicitly to reject the Absurdist outlook, it is not because of its internal incoherence, but because its radical immoralism had become intolerable to him. It is to this development in his thought that we must now turn.

2

Rebellion

Camus' temptation to a kind of ethical nihilism, which we explored at the end of the previous chapter, was always balanced by strong ethical intuitions. I have suggested that he may never have fully endorsed the outlook that he articulated in *The Myth*, but what led him to move away from it explicitly was certainly his sense that it could not support—and might even actively hinder—the ethical commitments that he felt unable to repudiate. The tension between a drive to a radical godlike independence, and a sense of solidarity and justice, was already present in his pre-war Algerian life, but that tension was dramatically escalated by the Nazi Occupation of France, to which he responded by joining the Resistance. The 'ethics of quantity', according to which 'no depth, no emotion, no passion and no sacrifice ... could render equal a conscious life of forty years and a lucidity spread over sixty years' (*MS* 63), could hardly approve of risking one's life in the service of an ideal of justice that was in any case baseless. Hence his concern in 'Letters to a German Friend' (1944) to find some better guide for life, and to resist the nihilistic conclusions that seemed to derive from Absurdism. Addressing the fictitious Nazi intellectual (who represents a possibility he found in himself), Camus notes:

> You never believed in the meaning of this world, and therefore deduced the idea that everything was equivalent and that good and evil could be defined according to one's wishes ... I, believing I thought as you did, saw no valid argument to answer you, except a fierce love of justice which, after all, seemed as unreasonable to me as the most sudden passion.[1]

He is concerned to find reasons to support his passion, but does not, at this point, get much beyond stating, without really defending in any detail, a kind of humanism: 'I continue to believe that this world has no ultimate meaning. But I know that something in it has a meaning, and that is man, because he is the only creature to insist on having one.'[2] Here we have an explicit repudiation of the principle, more or less assumed in *The Myth*, that the absence of ultimate Meaning undermines particular meanings. And this repudiation opens conceptual space for an ethical sphere, distinct from either the aesthetic or the religious, thus questioning

[1] Camus, 'Letters to a German Friend', in *RRD* 27.
[2] Camus, 'Letters to a German Friend', in *RRD* 28.

The Philosophy of Camus. Anthony Rudd, Oxford University Press. © Anthony Rudd (2024).
DOI: 10.1093/9780198924869.003.0003

The Myth's assumption that the only real options are dwelling in the absurd or 'leaping' to some sort of (broadly speaking) religious outlook.

The 'Letters' thus mark an important turning-point in Camus's development. As for the actual argument that Camus briefly suggests in the quotation above, one might respond that one does not make something true simply by insisting on it. But perhaps Camus's point is, rather, that there is something self-validating in the very demand for meaning; a being that can make that demand for meaning (or, we might say, value) thereby shows that it *has* meaning—or value—in a way that other beings do not. Still, this is at most a hint; the direct philosophical argument in support of justice in the 'Letters' remains sketchy at best. But the 'Letters' do testify to Camus's sense of the dangers of the Absurdist attitude, and his recognition that philosophical ideas could have lethal political consequences. And with this recognition comes Camus's move from the Aesthetic (Absurdism) to the Ethical. In this chapter, I will consider Camus's ethical philosophy, the extent to which it does or does not parallel Kierkegaard's ethical stage, and whether Camus does succeed in showing how there can be 'meaning' or value in human existence, even if it is not present in 'the world' as a whole. Rather than tracing the development of Camus's thought, I will jump forward to the definitive statement of his ethical philosophy, *The Rebel*—his major philosophical achievement, and a work that is still, I think, unfairly underestimated.

I Rebellion as Revelation of Value

As noted in the previous chapter, *The Rebel* begins with a look back to *The Myth*— a review of Absurdism that reinterprets it as akin to Descartes's methodological doubt. 'It is ... impossible to see in this [Absurdist] sensibility, and in the nihilism it presupposes, anything but a point of departure ... the equivalent in the plane of existence of systematic doubt' (*R.* 10). Descartes tried to refute scepticism by pressing it as far as it could go, in order to see where it broke down. His aim was to find something he could not doubt, on the basis of which he could then start to reconstruct knowledge. Camus's 'equivalent in the plane of existence' tries to push nihilism—the belief that nothing has value—as far as *it* can go, in the hope of finding a point where *it* will break down. He hopes, that is, to find something he cannot treat with indifference, something that inescapably lays a claim on him. Both procedures are necessarily first personal. Cartesian doubt ends with the doubter realizing the impossibility of doubting his or her own existence *qua* thinking being. It is crucial, of course, that what Descartes finds he cannot doubt is not the existence of René Descartes, this psycho-physical being with these particular characteristics and history; but, first personally, *my own* existence. And each person following Descartes's reasoning must do so first-personally for him- or herself: '*I* think, therefore *I* am.'[3] Still, Descartes's procedure aims at universality; anyone following it should reach the conclusion that one's own mental existence is indubitable.

Camus not only reinterprets his Absurdist philosophy in the light of Descartes's methodological doubt, but also makes a point of comparing his way out of it with Descartes's way out of scepticism. 'In our daily trials, rebellion plays the same role as does the *cogito* in the realm of thought; it is the first piece of evidence' (R. 22). Camus's equivalent of Descartes's procedure is in one sense less radically first personal; it need not appeal to the reader's individual experience, but can bring in (as we will see) data from history. But, in another way, it is also more radically first personal. There is nothing to guarantee that everyone will find themselves having to agree. Each of us can only ask: do *I* find myself compelled to recognize a real value here, something *I* have to care about, whose claim on *me* I have to acknowledge? There is no logical/conceptual guarantee that someone might not say: no, nothing does resist the nihilist devaluation of all values. And yet one must be careful to distinguish this decidedly Kierkegaardian sense in which the argument is 'subjective' from what is standardly thought of as ethical subjectivism. In discovering something I cannot help caring about, I experience it as making a genuine claim on me; its value is not something I project onto it. The consistent nihilist may not see this (arguably because he or she is refusing to see it), but here the nihilist is mistaken. That I cannot force someone out of nihilism by pure logic does not mean that it is a valid option. But, crucially, although Camus's appeal to experience is inescapably first personal, it does not leave us in an existential equivalent of the theoretical solipsism that Descartes then struggled to escape. On the contrary, this existential equivalent of the cogito takes us out of the *practical* solipsism in which *The Myth* had left us. Camus continues: 'But this evidence lures the individual from his solitude. It founds its first value on the whole human race. I rebel—therefore we exist' (R. 22).

Let us look more closely at Camus's argument. It arises, as I suggested above, from his personal experience that he could not treat the Nazi occupation as a matter of indifference; the evil of Nazism and the good of resisting it were experienced by him as givens, which demanded action—even personally very dangerous action—from him.[4] He experienced that good and evil could *not* 'be defined according to one's wishes'. In *The Rebel* he starts his argument with the example of a rebellious slave:

A slave who has taken orders all his life suddenly decides that he cannot obey some new command. What does he mean by saying 'no'? He means ... 'there is a

[3] Descartes, *Discourse on Method*, 18.
[4] This does not imply that no decision was needed; he still had to choose to give assent to those appearances rather than withdrawing from them into a sceptical suspension of judgement, or an Absurdist rejection of the normative.

62 THE PHILOSOPHY OF CAMUS

limit beyond which you shall not go'. In other words, his no defines the existence
of a borderline ... Thus the movement of rebellion is founded simultaneously on
the categorical rejection of an intrusion that is considered intolerable, and on the
confused conviction of an absolute right. (*R.* 13)

Rebellion, as Camus understands it, is not simply a reactive attitude, a blind rage,
but is founded on a conviction, however implicit or inarticulate, that the one being
abused should not be treated like that; that there is something about him or her
that makes such treatment *wrong*.[5] The one being abused need not be oneself:
rebellion 'can also be caused by the mere spectacle of oppression of which someone
else is the victim' (*R.* 16). In any case, beyond all considerations of expediency
or advantage, some behaviour is experienced as unacceptable—and unacceptable
because it violates something of value in its victim, something that should not be
violated. And this is something universal; something that exists in all of us. What
the slave rebels against is 'a command [that] has infringed on something in him
which does not belong to him alone, but which is common ground where all men
... have a common community' (*R.* 16). What is presupposed in rebellion is the
value of humanity as such, and therefore the reality of a normatively significant
notion of human nature. 'Analysis of rebellion leads at least to the suspicion that,
contrary to the postulates of contemporary thought, a human nature does exist, as
the Greeks believed' (*R.* 16).

The appeal back from Sartre—at whom this jab is obviously directed—to Plato
and Aristotle is striking.[6] According to Sartre,

existence precedes essence ... man first of all exists, encounters himself, surges up
in the world—and defines himself afterwards. If man as the existentialist sees him
is not definable, it is because to begin with he is nothing. He will not be anything
until later, and then he will be what he makes of himself ... Man is nothing else
than that which he makes of himself.[7]

On this view, we have neither fixed individual characters, nor a shared, universal,
human nature. And, crucially for Sartre, this means that there is no set of normative
standards to which I ought to conform. Both the standards by which I live, and the
person that I am, are my own creations. In opposing this view, Camus argues not

---

[5] His claim is not that all historical instances of revolt against oppression have been 'rebellions' in
this particular sense. Nor is he claiming that it is always easy to distinguish principled rebellion from
blind reactive anger. He *is* committed to the claim that, at least in many instances of revolt, there has
been an at least implicit sense of value of the sort he describes.

[6] Of course, Plato and Aristotle accepted and even tried to justify slavery. But Camus is implicitly confronting their willingness to rationalize their privileged position in ancient Greek society with
the universalistic implications of their own essentialism about human nature. For an *explicit* argument that Aristotle's defence of slavery—and of the inferior status of women—is incompatible with the
fundamentals of his own philosophy, see MacIntyre, *Ethics in the Conflicts of Modernity*, 85–7.

[7] Sartre, *Existentialism and Humanism*, 28.

just that there is a relatively fixed human nature (a biological reductionist would agree with that) but that it is one that is intrinsically normative. Someone's humanity sets moral limits on how I may treat that person. And that remains true, even when the person in question is a perpetrator of oppression and injustice. 'The slave who opposes his master is not concerned, let us note, with repudiating his master as a human being. He repudiates him as a master' (R. 23). What is brought to light in rebellion is a universal value.[8]

I do not think Camus is claiming that the analysis of slave rebellion is the only way in which the universal value of humanity may come to light, and thus the only way to reveal the basis of ethics. There may be many such experiences—many of them less dramatic or extreme—in which one recognizes that it is not right that someone, whether myself or another, be treated in a certain way. This situation of the rebellious slave brings these structures to light in a particularly vivid way, and in a way that is obviously of particular relevance to the historical/political argument that Camus wants to make. Although he does not say so explicitly, Camus, in his appeal to certain experiences as bringing to light a universal essence, is acting as a Phenomenologist, and it would have been helpful for clarifying his methodology if he had revisited his critique of Husserl from *The Myth* at this point. For what is experientially manifested in an episode of rebellion is not simply a discrete phenomenon, but a normative universal. The rebel recognizes in the abused person (whether him- or herself or another) a humanity that makes claims on all of us who share that humanity, and sets limits to how we should treat one another. One might call his approach a sort of Phenomenological Kantianism, in that the value of humanity, which is the basis of Kantian ethics, is revealed through experience—not, however, through an empiricist inductive argument, but Phenomenologically, through the recognition of the universal as given in the particular.[9]

We can compare Camus's account of rebellion—rather favourably, I think—with what is perhaps the most influential attempt to give a Phenomenological grounding for ethics—Levinas's phenomenology of 'the face'.[10] Like Camus starting with Absurdism and its nihilistic implications, Levinas starts with the threat of a radical moral scepticism: 'Everyone will readily agree that it is of the highest importance to know whether we are not duped by morality.'[11] Levinas finds his answer to this threat, like Camus, through the analysis of a situation of violence and inequality; in his case, the plea, or demand, written on the face of the victim

---

[8] Again, this is not a claim that rebellions have, historically, always been guided by such values. Indeed, much of *The Rebel* is devoted to recounting and trying to explain how the original ethical spirit of rebellion has repeatedly been corrupted in revolutionary practice.

[9] Jeanine Grenberg has argued that Kant himself is a (proto-)Phenomenological Kantian in this sense. For her important distinction between 'empirical' and 'phenomenological' experience as a basis for ethics, see her *Kant's Defense of Common Moral Experience*, 16–17, 40–6.

[10] See Levinas, *Totality and Infinity*, sect. III.

[11] Levinas, *Totality and Infinity*, 21.

64 THE PHILOSOPHY OF CAMUS

not to be killed.[12] Just as Camus is aware that slaves may become so downtrod-
den as to lose a sense of their own humanity—or become so vindictive as to lose a
sense of the master's humanity if they do revolt—so Levinas is painfully aware that
the 'impossibility of killing'[13] is not a literal or practical impossibility; all the time,
killers fail to see what in the faces of their victims *should* make murder impossible.
But those who do really *attend* to the face of the other[14] do find that impossibility
in it. Levinas's phenomenology, like Camus's, is not a purely intellectual refuta-
tion of moral scepticism, but a first-personal appeal that, nonetheless, brings to
light something universal—indeed, 'infinite'. Camus's account seems to me superior to Levinas's, not only in the clarity and simplicity of Camus's language—not a
trivial point, if one places value on the need to address and communicate with the
other—but also in his refusal of Levinas's tendency to hyperbole and radical asym-
metry. There is no real sense of mutuality in Levinas's ethics; the other overwhelms
the subject with an infinite demand—which the subject in turn can place back on
the other.[15] For Camus, by contrast, the recognition of our shared humanity is the
basis for an ethics, and a politics, of mutuality and reciprocal respect. It also takes
him back metaphysically to 'the Greeks', to a kind of essentialism that seems to
me more promising than the convolutions that Levinas gets into when he tries to
develop his phenomenology of the encounter with the other into a philosophy that
will take us somewhere 'otherwise than being or beyond essence'.[16]

Camus does not, in *The Rebel*, do much to develop the metaphysical essentialism underlying his ethics; I will return to this issue in the following chapter. But he
does say enough to make it clear that he is committed to a form of moral realism.
His account of human nature is an inescapably normative one; the rebel acts out
of a sense of the value of the humanity that we share. This sense is in the first place
immediate and even instinctive: you cannot do that to a human being! But this is
the experiential recognition of a value that is there, whether or not it is recognized
(either by the master or by the slaves themselves). John Foley has claimed that
'Camus makes no appeal whatever to transcendent values in *The Rebel*. Instead,
he argues that, on the basis of a common humanity (something that is universal but
not transcendent) it should be possible to create values, such values as come into
being in the act of rebellion itself'.[17] Foley does not define 'transcendent' here; we
can agree that Camus's intention in *The Rebel* is to articulate a humanistic ethics

---

[12] Levinas, *Totality and Infinity*, 198–9. One could say that Levinas's scenario is the flip side of
Camus's—where Camus starts from the experience of the victim, Levinas starts from that of the 'master'
(here the would-be killer) who realizes that he cannot kill.

[13] Levinas, *Totality and Infinity*, 199.

[14] Attention is a fundamental notion in the thought of Simone Weil, by whom Camus was significantly influenced. I will say more about this in Chapter 3.

[15] See Paul Ricoeur's criticisms of Levinas: Ricoeur, *Oneself as Another*, 188–90, 335–41.

[16] The title of Levinas's second major work. Ricoeur complains that Levinas in this book takes
hyperbole 'to the point of paroxysm' (*Oneself as Another*, 338).

[17] Foley, *Albert Camus*, 85.

that does not appeal to a transcendent God. But Foley's talk of *creating* values seems quite wrong; that is precisely what Camus rejects when he turns away from Sartre. His phenomenology of rebellion commits him to moral realism; human beings have a value that sets certain limits to what can legitimately be done to them, and this is true whether it is acknowledged or not. Value is not created by rebellion; rebellion is based on the recognition of value. If value were created by rebellion, then oppression would be legitimate up to the point at which the slaves do rebel.[18]

It is true that Camus's language is not always entirely clear or consistent. In a 1945 essay, he did write 'it is essential for us to know whether man, without the help either of the eternal or of rationalistic thought, can unaided create his own values ... France and Europe must now create a new civilization or else perish.'[19] His thinking was still in transition at this point, but I think even here one can take his talk of creating values as a loose way of saying the same thing as when he talks of creating a new civilization. What I think he came to see more clearly was that a civilization could be created only on the basis of values that were not themselves merely our creations. By 1948, with the essay 'Helen's Exile', his mature thought is in place. Passionately advocating for ancient Greek against modern European ideals, he notes that, 'for the Greeks, values were pre-existent to every action and marked out its exact limits. Modern philosophy places its values at the end of action. They are not, but they become ...When they disappear limits do as well ...'.[20] (This analysis is repeated, almost verbatim, in *The Rebel* (R. 16)). Only when action is guided by values that therefore existed before the action can it keep to limits and avoid rushing off to the murderous extremes that Camus is concerned to diagnose.[21]

I have suggested above that one can see Camus's exploration of Absurdism as akin to Kierkegaard's pseudonymous explorations of the various stages of life, trying to articulate them from the inside, to show how it would be to live them. Kierkegaard deliberately refuses to take a polemical approach, denouncing the shortcomings of different views of life from an external position. But his accounts of them are intended to show, not only, for example, the possibilities and the real attractions of the aesthetic life, but also where and how it does break down. For Camus, the Absurdist project of living with godlike indifference and independence

---

[18] A certain kind of Nietzschean might accept this consequence: as long as the slaves accept their oppression, they show that they deserve it. But I think Camus had, by the time of *The Rebel*, long since rejected any temptation he might have felt for this sort of heroic philosophy.

[19] Camus, 'Pessimism and Courage', in *RRD* 58.

[20] *SEN* 138 (*LCE* 151).

[21] Even in *The Rebel* there are some remarks that can seem to point to a more constructivist view, as when he talks about 'the confused values that are called into play by incipient rebellion' and continues 'the basis of these values is rebellion itself' (*R*. 21–2). This is not very perspicuous, but I think here, as in the 1945 quotation, he is referring to specific political proposals that might emerge from rebellion, rather than the basic values that underlie and justify rebellion.

66   THE PHILOSOPHY OF CAMUS

breaks down with the recognition of human suffering and the injustice that adds needlessly to that suffering. The 'fierce love of justice' that forced him to stand against the Nazis could not be accommodated within the Absurdist outlook; hence that outlook had to be repudiated. For Kierkegaard, the aesthetic shows its inadequacy through the boredom and depression that result when one tries, in full consciousness, to live a reflectively aesthetic life.[22] For Kierkegaard's underlying assumption is that the aesthete—like all of us—has a need for coherence and meaning in his or her life; indeed a need for the Good.[23] (This is the teleological aspect of Kierkegaard's philosophy, which connects him to the ethics of 'the Greeks'.[24]) 'A' tries to repudiate it, but is left dissatisfied and depressed precisely because he cannot really turn away from that un-met need. One might say that Kierkegaard's main concern is with what the aesthetic life does to one who tries to live it; how it fails, in its own terms, to provide the satisfying (happy, interesting) life it seemed to promise. Camus, by contrast, is more concerned with what Absurdism may lead someone to do to another. It is not that the Absurdist life fails in its own terms; it is derailed by a concern for justice that has no part in it, but that Camus, at least, finds he cannot repudiate.

But the contrast, though real, may be less stark than it appears. Although we do not learn of 'A' himself treating anyone with particular injustice or even unkindness, the protagonist of the 'Seducer's Diary' is indeed a cold-blooded manipulator of other people and their feelings; a liar and deceiver. The Diary is placed at the end of volume one of *Either/Or* (which explores the possibilities of the aesthetic life) to suggest that a consistent aestheticism is liable to lead, not only to an unsatisfactory life for the aesthete, but to mistreatment of those the aesthete encounters. The fictitious editor of *Either/Or*, Victor Eremita, who takes the diary to be a story written by 'A', notes how 'A' himself seems to be disturbed by the character of the Seducer that he has (supposedly) created.[25] The genuinely sympathetic part of his nature is worried by the realization of what his own manipulative tendencies could lead to. The Diary inescapably forces on him (and us) the question of whether he is to judge it in ethical, or merely in aesthetic, terms. If he does the former, he would be abandoning his aesthetic world view;[26] but choosing the latter would force him to take a decisive stand *against* the ethical—something he has hitherto wanted to avoid, and that would itself be incompatible with his concern to avoid

---

[22] This theme runs through *Either/Or*; it is repeatedly expressed by 'A', the aesthete, himself, but is also diagnosed and analysed at length in the letters of Judge William.

[23] On this, see, especially, Kierkegaard, 'Purity of Heart', in *UDVS* and also in *SUD*.

[24] See Rudd, *Self, Value and Narrative*, ch. 2, for a discussion of teleology in Kierkegaard.

[25] *E/O* i. 8–9; and see 'A''s introduction to the diary (*E/O* i. 303–13). In a way it does not really matter whether we take the diary to be 'A''s fiction or accept his claim that he found and surreptitiously copied it. In either case, it is important to distinguish between 'A' himself and Johannes the Seducer.

[26] As a total attitude to life, that is; Judge William insists that the aesthetic element in life should be subordinated to the ethical but not thereby destroyed; it is indeed, he argues, enhanced by this subordination.

decisive commitments.[27] So volume one of *Either/Or* ends with a challenge to 'A'—and to any reader who might be tempted to identify with 'A''s attitude—which is akin to Camus's challenge. Faced with a situation that calls for moral judgement and perhaps, if possible, action, can you abstain from such judgement and action, and evaluate the situation in purely aesthetic terms?

II Metaphysical Rebellion

In Kierkegaardian terms, then, *The Rebel* marks Camus's move from the aesthetic to the ethical—a transition that, though not identical to the one Kierkegaard describes, still has significant parallels with it. Camus continues, though, to reject the religious. While Kierkegaard's Judge William sees the ethical and the religious fitting smoothly together—and while Kierkegaard himself takes a serious religious perspective to show up the inadequacies of the purely ethical—Camus's ethical philosophy seems to be sharply opposed to the religious; at least to Christianity or, more generally, monotheism as he understood it. His initial account of rebellion as the discovery of the value of humanity leads, not directly to an investigation of political revolt, but to an extended discussion of 'Metaphysical Rebellion'. He defines it as 'the movement by which man protests against his condition and against the whole of creation' (R. 23). As in the case of slave rebellion, it is a protest guided by value, and directed against perceived injustice: 'we find a value judgement in the name of which the rebel refuses to approve the condition in which he finds himself' (R. 23.) The Metaphysical Rebel 'attacks a shattered world in order to demand unity from it'. His is a 'protest against the human condition both for its incompleteness thanks to death, and its wastefulness, thanks to evil' (R. 23–4). There is, therefore, still a very close link between the attitude of the Metaphysical Rebel and that of the Absurdist. For both of them, the spectacle of a fragmented, incomprehensible world haunted by death and suffering gives rise to a sense that *it ought not to be like this.* There was a tension in *The Myth*'s depiction of 'the absurd man'; on the one hand, he eventually accepts the Meaninglessness of existence and the inevitability and finality of death—and indeed finds happiness in consciously living without Meaning. But, on the other, he continues to rebel against his condition, to respond to it with scorn. In the later work, of course, rebellion is emphasized; but now it is clearly motivated and directed by the sense of value, the hunger for justice, which the absurd man abandoned.

---

[27] As Judge William puts it: 'the person who lives aesthetically does not choose and the person who chooses the aesthetic after the ethical has become manifest to him is not living aesthetically, for he is sinning and is subject to ethical qualifications, even if his life must be termed unethical ...' (*E/O* ii. 168). (I have altered the Hongs's spelling 'esthetic' to 'aesthetic' throughout.) The latter character would in effect be committed to what, in other works, Kierkegaard calls the 'demonic'—the conscious rejection of the good. (See, e.g., *CA* 118–54.)

68   THE PHILOSOPHY OF CAMUS

But the demand for a basic order and intelligibility in life, the horror at death and evil, is, as Camus recognizes, still a basically religious protest:

The rebel obstinately confronts a world condemned to death and the impenetrable obscurity of the human condition with his demand for life and absolute clarity. He is seeking, without knowing it, a moral philosophy or a religion ... if the rebel blasphemes, it is in the hope of finding a new god. (R. 101)

For a consistent naturalist, the world is what it is and has the degree of intelligibility it has; death is a natural biological process, and 'evil' is simply a term (perhaps an anachronistic one) for human tendencies to destructiveness, which are in principle explicable in terms of our biological and social history. But, for Camus, once we have realized the value of humanity, and not just of humanity as a universal, but of each individual human being, we cannot simply accept with equanimity, as a natural fact, that we are abandoned to chance and death as we are. The Metaphysical Rebel rejects God, because he sees God as the one who is responsible for this unjust creation: 'the father of death and ... the supreme outrage' (R. 24). As in *The Myth*, we continue to see Camus's curiously Gnostic sensibility: the sense that the world is not as it should be and that we find ourselves frustrated and alien within it. And, as in Gnosticism, we now (in *The Rebel*) see the rejection of the evil God of this world justified by appeal to something higher. For the Gnostics, this was the true spiritual God; for Camus, it is nothing transcendent, but 'the principle of justice which he [the rebel] finds in himself' (R. 24). This principle is based, as we have seen, on the value of human nature. But how can it make sense that humans have value in a world that is created on the principles of injustice? The Gnostics had complicated stories about how human souls fell from a higher realm into this evil material world; but Camus has no such story to tell.

Camus is also notably un-Gnostic in his love of physical nature. And, while he shares the indignation of the Metaphysical Rebel, his Hellenism—first clearly articulated in 'Helen's Exile'—pulls him in a very different direction, to a serene but passionate joy in the beauty and order of the world. He claims, indeed, that Metaphysical Rebellion is directed primarily at the God of Judaism and Christianity. (He does not refer to Islam in this context, but it would clearly be involved in the indictment also.) Hence it did not really occur among the ancient Greeks. 'The only thing that gives meaning to human protest is the idea of a personal god who has created, and is therefore responsible for, everything. And so we can say, without being paradoxical, that in the Western world the history of rebellion is inseparable from this history of Christianity' (R. 28). For the Greeks, 'to rebel against nature amounted to rebelling against oneself. It was butting one's head against a wall' (R. 27). Greek thought was not irreligious; 'it carried nothing to extremes, neither religion nor reason, because it denied nothing, neither reason nor religion'.[28] But the Greeks did not see a simple juxtaposition or even opposition of God and the world, or of good and evil: 'Metaphysical rebellion presupposes a simplified view of creation—which was inconceivable to the Greeks. In their minds, there were not gods on one side and men on the other, but a series of stages leading from one to the other' (R. 28). So, although Camus, as we have seen, occasionally referred to his whole 'Rebellion' cycle as 'The Myth of Prometheus', he admits that it is not really Prometheus but Cain who is the true mythical prototype for the rebel (R. 32).

I suggested in the Introduction that it might be helpful to think of the Metaphysical Rebel, like the Absurdist, as akin to a Kierkegaardian pseudonym. In articulating the Metaphysical Rebel's view, Camus is exploring an outlook and a sensibility to which he is strongly attracted, and which he thinks is important to understand as clearly as possible. But one should not assume that this view is—at any rate wholly—Camus's own.[29] The early parts of The Rebel are confusing because Camus is giving expression to two distinct and not fully compatible world views, sometimes reporting on them, sometimes speaking from within them, but not always clearly distinguishing which he is doing when. On the one hand, he articulates a Hellenic ideal of limit, moderation, and love of beauty—not an effete and historically false image of 'sweetness and light' but a vision of meaningful order, which sees 'excess' as 'the only definitive crime' (R. 28) and according to which we are part of the nature that it would be meaningless to think of turning against. But, on the other hand, he speaks in the voice of a rebellious or heretical Christian, denouncing the creation—even such a basic feature of the natural, biological world as death—in the name of values that cannot simply come from the nature they condemn. The Metaphysical Rebel is 'not definitely an atheist ... but he is inevitably a blasphemer' (R. 24). But, even when he does become an atheist, denying rather than simply defying God, he remains in rebellion. He does not return to a Greek harmony with the world but remains outraged by it. The 'Greek' mind, by contrast, in rejecting the God of Abraham rejects the presupposition of metaphysical revolt, and is reconciled with the world—a world from which divinity or the sacred is not absent. (Abrahamic monotheism is not the only sort of religious sensibility.) So, we need to ask which voice represents the real Camus. Or should we regard both as though they were pseudonyms, neither fully identifiable with Camus himself?

The later parts of The Rebel, and the later writings by Camus that I will review in the next chapter, do (as I shall try to show) express Camus's adherence to the Greek outlook, as he understands it. However, he certainly sees something crucially right about the Metaphysical Rebel's protest as well. But can they be

---

[28] Camus, 'Helen's Exile', in SEN 136 (LCE 148).
[29] It should be remembered that Kierkegaard by no means rejected everything that his pseudonyms said; he was indeed in very substantial agreement with several of them.

70   THE PHILOSOPHY OF CAMUS

reconciled? Srigley sees Camus as trying to work through Metaphysical Rebellion, in order to emerge from it and return to 'Greek' values, on the other side of it.[30] On this account, Camus thinks the rot set in with Christianity's repudiation of Hellenism; Metaphysical Rebellion gives a justified critique of Christianity, but is unable to establish alternative values, and falls into nihilism. In order to escape from this dead end, we need to repudiate the whole Christian–Modern development and return to the Greeks. There is a good deal that is right about this as an interpretation, but I think it is still an oversimplification. My alternative reading will take the rest of this book to develop; but I can say here that, although I think Camus's developed outlook is predominantly a 'Greek' one, a creative tension between Greek, quasi-Gnostic, and even Christian tendencies remains in Camus to the end of his life.

Both the 'Greek' and the Metaphysical Rebel in Camus agree at any rate in rejecting the God of the Hebrew scriptures, finding in Him little more, it seems, than an arbitrary tyrant, ultimately responsible for creating a world of injustice.[31] (Which was, of course, exactly how the Gnostics saw Him.) In this Camus may have been influenced by Simone Weil, also a passionate Hellenist, who was given to making sharp contrasts between Athens and Jerusalem, much to the discredit of the latter. Weil, however, became a passionate if unorthodox Christian. Camus, in The Rebel, sees Christianity as an attempt to mitigate the stark outlines of Hebraic monotheism by introducing Christ as the mediator between God and humanity, and by his taking suffering and death on himself. However, at least from the perspective of the Metaphysical Rebel, this, in a way, makes matters worse. Christ's sufferings serve to validate and justify ours. 'In that Christ had suffered, and suffered voluntarily, suffering was no longer unjust and all pain was necessary' (R. 34). Christianity, even more than theism in general, thus becomes the target of the Metaphysical Rebel's indignation, denounced as a legitimization of human suffering.

This judgement can easily be put into a political form, the Rebel now seeing Christianity as supportive specifically of social and political injustice. It is accused of teaching either that the existing power structures have been directly willed by God; or that they are an effect of, and punishment for, sin, which we should patiently endure since our ultimate good is not in this life anyway.[32] With this

---

[30] See Srigley, Camus' Critique, chs 2, 3. He does not, however, think Camus saw things clearly enough at the time of The Rebel to avoid falling into serious contradictions there.

[31] This is a rather unsubtle reading of the Hebrew scriptures, of course. One might wish that Camus had learnt more about the possibility of a more nuanced reading from Martin Buber, whom he admired. (The admiration was mutual: see Friedman, Encounter on the Narrow Ridge, 342.) However, Camus's main aim here is not to engage in careful exegesis of Hebrew Scripture, but to trace the ways in which the Metaphysical Rebels reacted to how they read the Scriptures; and the God they rejected was the one they constructed from their unsubtle readings.

[32] These claims about the politically conservative tendency of religion in general and Christianity in particular are backed up in The Rebel by historical observations concerning the support given by Christian Churches to oppressive political structures in, for example, ancien régime France and

REBELLION 71

move, Metaphysical Rebellion now passes over into Historical (socio-political) Rebellion. Camus does not think that the former must *necessarily* lead to the latter. The protests of the splenetic dandies and Romantics that he examines (*R.* 47–54) may remain purely individualistic and asocial. But, once God has been either defied or denied, it is natural (though not inevitable) that the Rebel comes to see the urgent task as the revolutionizing of the world, its refashioning so as to eliminate, as far as possible, the injustice with which it is permeated. Once the theology that had legitimated the old order is rejected, then that order itself is revealed as ripe for revolutionary overthrow. As Marx says, 'the criticism of heaven turns into the criticism of the earth ... the *criticism of theology* into the *criticism of politics*.'[33]

Metaphysical Rebellion thus leads naturally, though not inevitably, to Historical (political) Rebellion; but does Historical Rebellion require Metaphysical Rebellion as a premise or presupposition? Must 'the criticism of earth' depend on 'the criticism of heaven'? Camus does assert that the sacred and rebellion are necessarily opposed. 'Only two possible worlds can exist for the human mind: the sacred and the world of rebellion. The disappearance of the one is equivalent to the appearance of the other' (*R.* 21). If one takes this 'metaphysically', then the claim is almost analytic; Metaphysical Rebellion is, by definition, the rejection of the sacred.[34] But does the acceptance of the sacred preclude *political* rebellion? That it does may seem plausible enough at first glance; if the order of the world is good, to rebel against it is sin or (as the Greeks held) folly. But this is moving too quickly. One can rebel against political injustice without repudiating the basic normative order of the world. And this is something Camus himself pointed out. Describing, towards the end of his life, the attitude that he formed in his youth and that, so he claims, shaped his whole subsequent outlook, he writes: 'Poverty prevented me from thinking that all is well under the sun and in history; the sun taught me that history is not everything. Change life, yes, but not the world which I worshipped as my God.'[35] Here we see both a sense of the world as a sacred order *and* a commitment to revolt, 'aimed at lifting up everybody's life into the light'.[36] But this is precisely a qualified revolt; one that recognizes limits. I will return to the question of the relationship between Metaphysical and Historical Rebellion. But first we need to pause and look more closely at the precise nature of the challenge that Camus thinks suffering raises for religion in general and theism in particular.

Tzarist Russia. (Of course, this line of thought could be questioned by bringing in a wider range of historical examples than Camus considered, such as the Puritan revolution in England, or the Abolitionist movement in America.)

[33] Marx, 'Towards a Critique of Hegel's Philosophy of Right: Introduction', 28–9.

[34] It may seem, though, that they are not exclusive opposites, as Camus claims; one can reject the sacred on the basis of a 'cooler', sceptical attitude, without the dramatic moral indignation of the Metaphysical Rebel. Or is such scepticism still a kind of rebellion in Camus's sense?

[35] Camus, preface (1958) to the new edition of *L'Envers et l'endroit*, in *SEN* 18 (*LCE* 6).

[36] *SEN* 18 (*LCE* 5).

72 THE PHILOSOPHY OF CAMUS

The standard philosophical 'problem of evil' has to do with whether the existence of God is consistent with the suffering and evil that exist in the world. Traditionally it has taken the form either of a logical challenge—the claim that the admitted facts of evil are logically incompatible with the existence of God as traditionally conceived (that is, as all-knowing, all-powerful, and entirely benevolent)—or as an evidential challenge: that those facts make it unlikely that such a God exists. Since it is hard to deny that an infinite being might have reasons for permitting suffering, whether or not finite minds can fully grasp those reasons, the logical challenge seems implausible, and few philosophers today maintain it. And, since it does not seem that finite minds would necessarily be good at calculating whether the amount of suffering makes it implausible that an infinite mind might have good reasons for allowing it, it seems that the evidential challenge is at best inconclusive. But, behind these often very technical arguments lies a concern that one might call the existential problem of evil: can one accept or worship a God who—for whatever reasons—is supposed to allow such extensive and often horrendous suffering? This is the challenge posed by Dostoevsky's Ivan Karamazov, who is willing to admit that this world with all its suffering might have been created by God for good reasons; but who also refuses to accept such suffering, even if there are reasons for it that his finite mind cannot grasp.[37] Hence his attitude is one of—precisely—rebellion. He does not make cool intellectual assessments of the likelihood of God's existence, given the fact of evil; he refuses to accept the world that God—for whatever reasons—is supposed to have made, feeling that, if he did, he would be complicit in the crimes endlessly committed in it.[38] It is this existential version of the problem of evil that exercises Camus in *The Rebel* and, of course, in his novel *The Plague.*

In *The Plague*, the Jesuit Father Paneloux preaches two sermons. In the first he confidently announces that the plague in Oran is a divine punishment for the sins of the city and calls his congregation to repentance (*P.* 72–7). The death toll continues to rise, and Paneloux is traumatized by witnessing the protracted death agony of a young child. In his second sermon, adopting a much humbler tone and using the pronoun 'we' instead of 'you', he abandons all attempts to explain why the plague is happening and argues that faith is to love God without being able to understand His ways, to continue to love Him through the pain and apparent injustice of the world He created (*P.* 172–6).[39] (Paneloux also joins the 'health teams' that Dr Rieux has established to help slow the spread of the plague; he eventually dies of an illness that might or might not be a form of the plague.) Camus fiercely rejects any type of rationalizing theodicy, as in the first sermon,

[37] Dostoevsky, *The Brothers Karamazov*, 235–6.
[38] See Dostoevsky, *The Brothers Karamazov*, bk 5, ch. 4, 'Rebellion'.
[39] In both sermons Paneloux appears to assume that whatever occurs has been directly willed by God, whether or not for reasons that we might be able to comprehend; he does not make any distinction between what God wills and what God permits.

REBELLION   73

that would purport to give a justificatory explanation for suffering. He does recognize the possibility of a faith that does not rationalize in that way, and can respect it in others, especially if it is combined with a practical commitment to alleviate suffering.[40] But, without judging others for doing so (if they do so honestly and without self-deception), he refuses to make any leap of faith for himself. The 'problem of evil' for Camus is not so much a rational conundrum, the solution to which would tell us whether or not faith is a reasonable possibility; it is a personal existential challenge. (Again, this is a very Kierkegaardian attitude to take, even though Kierkegaard himself responded very differently from Camus to that challenge.) I noted that in *The Myth* Camus did not really explain why the Absurdist would continue to reject the belief in a Meaning to existence for which he or she feels a deep need. I suggested that the implicit reason for that refusal in *The Myth* was the Absurdist's overriding desire for radical freedom and independence. When the Absurdist becomes the Rebel, a more compelling answer becomes available. The Rebel wants there to be a Meaning to existence, but, for moral reasons, either refuses to accept a Meaning that would involve accepting unjust suffering, or refuses to accept that a world that is characterized by so much suffering can be regarded as a Meaningful order at all (the distinction, basically, between the blasphemer and the atheist).

What is distinctive of Camus's treatment, though, is that he is acutely aware that there is a problem of evil for the atheist too. 'From the moment that man submits God to moral judgment, he kills Him in his own heart. And then what is the basis of morality? God is denied in the name of justice, but can the idea of justice be understood without the idea of God?' (*R*. 62). As we saw in *The Myth*, the Absurdist became an amoralist through the conviction that ethics could be viable only on a religious basis. This conclusion is precisely what Camus now wishes to resist in *The Rebel*, but he still takes the challenge very seriously. It might be thought that the argument he considers is not really very challenging, as it seems to presuppose a rather simple, and not very plausible, divine command theory of ethics—God decides what is right and wrong, so, if there is no God, then 'all is permitted'. But God can be seen as foundational for morality without supposing that moral obligations are based on (ultimately arbitrary) divine commands. A long tradition of Christian Platonism has identified the Platonic Good—the ultimate, eternal normative standard—with God, and has argued that the relative goodness of created beings—and thus the moral imperative to behave appropriately towards them—derives from their participation in the (necessarily) absolute goodness of

---

[40] See, e.g., the moving tribute to his friend and fellow *resistant* René Leynaud, in Camus, 'The Flesh', in *RRD* 46–54.

74   THE PHILOSOPHY OF CAMUS

God's nature.[41] Kierkegaard, I believe, stands in this tradition.[42] In any case, I think Camus's argument can be generalized beyond theism. In *The Myth* it is the loss of belief in Meaning generally, not just in theism, that undermines the belief in particular ethical meanings.[43] And it seems that the Ivan-like Rebel would be committed to rejecting, not only the idea of a transcendent God who establishes or underwrites the moral order of the world; but also, and more generally, the idea that there *is* a coherent, morally significant order to the world. For to accept such an idea would—according to this Rebel—be to accept the actual injustice that occurs within this supposed order.

It seems then—despite Camus's own claim that rebellion is at least primarily a response to Abrahamic theism—that one can rebel against a Stoic immanent logos, or a Neo-Confucian world of all-pervading Principle as much as one can against the God of Abraham. The intensely personal nature of the latter of course makes revolt a more dramatically personal act, but it is not clear that it changes what is essentially at stake. Hence the tension in Camus's thinking that I referred to above, for it seems that the Metaphysical Rebel would also be inclined to revolt against the order of balance and limit that characterizes the Greeks' beautiful and sacred cosmos. As, indeed, the Gnostics did. Camus's project therefore requires him to articulate a form of moral realism that will be metaphysically robust enough to form a basis for ethics, without succumbing, as he thinks theism does, to what is legitimate in the Metaphysical Rebel's protest.[44] *The Rebel* raises the issue powerfully, but it cannot be said that it resolves it. Whether Camus does provide enough material (fragmentarily in *The Rebel*, and elsewhere) to suggest a plausible resolution will be a central theme of the third chapter. Essentially, then, the challenge he sets up is this: the passion for justice that motivates the Rebel is based on the perception of human beings as having intrinsic value. This passion leads the Rebel

---

[41] For a thorough and rigorous modern defence of such a view, see Adams, *Finite and Infinite Goods.* In part three of that book Adams argues for a 'modified' divine command theory, but this is subordinated to his Platonism; God's commands are not arbitrary but expressive of the (necessary) goodness of the divine nature. See also, for a broadly similar line of thought, Evans, *God and Moral Obligations.*

[42] C. S. Evans has argued that Kierkegaard is a Christian Platonist and that, although he has a divine command theory, this is only in something like Adams's 'modified' sense. See Evans, *Kierkegaard's Ethic of Love.* I am not convinced that Kierkegaard really holds anything that can be properly called a divine command theory, even in the modified sense, but I agree with Evans about the centrality of his Platonism.

[43] As I noted, Camus's comments on Husserl indicate that he (or the Absurdist of *The Myth*) saw a belief in an immanent order of normative essences, as well as theism, as an unjustified form of philosophical escapism.

[44] One kind of view that would not, I think, be robust enough would be the minimalistic version of moral realism defended by some contemporary philosophers. (See, e.g., Shafer-Landau, *Moral Realism.*) These philosophers maintain that there are irreducible moral truths, but do not try to give any further metaphysical account of them. Essentially, they just add irreducible normativity on to an otherwise standard naturalistic account of a world of brute facts. I have argued elsewhere that this cannot be adequate; a serious moral realism needs a metaphysics that can *make sense* of there being value in the world, and this requires us to postulate a genuine normative world order. See Rudd, *Self, Value and Narrative,* 146–54.

REBELLION 75

to reject indignantly the idea of a moral world order. But he or she is then left with a vision of reality as, morally speaking, chaotic—a world in which predation and aggression are as 'natural' as anything else. But in that case, how can humans have the value that the Rebel started off by assuming? How can there be a morally relevant human essence in a naturalistic world of merely brute facts? But, if there is not, then the passion for justice that the Rebel started from is itself an absurdity.

Many contemporary philosophers would still see Camus's concern as based on an oversimplification of the alternatives. They suppose that, even if we reject moral realism—the idea that values are somehow 'built in' to reality, or, at least, to some parts of reality (human persons)—we can still think that there is an objective—at least, non-arbitrary—basis for morality. A wide variety of options has been proposed—for example, Rawls's and Korsgaard's Constructivism, Scanlon's Contractualism, Habermas's Discourse Ethics, and Dworkin's strict separation of the normative from the ontological, to mention only some.[45] So someone defending Camus's sense of the options would have to do a lot of work to show that these attempts to find a middle way between moral realism and subjectivism fail. But I think they do; I think none of them can really stand up to sceptical scrutiny. This is not the place to attempt to show that.[46] It is, however, worth noting that, for all their ingenuity, they are all decidedly philosophers' inventions. None of them, it seems to me, captures the phenomenology of moral outrage and protest that Camus vividly evokes. When I feel outrage at seeing someone abusing someone else, this is not because I can, for instance, reflect that rational people under hypothetical conditions of free and open discussion would agree to create a set of rules for social cooperation that would exclude such behaviour. On the contrary: I would hope they would agree to exclude it because they could see that it was wrong prior to and independent of any such agreement.[47]

Is this sort of argument unfair? The philosophers are, after all, seeking to give rational justifications to underpin our immediate or instinctive moral reactions; they know perfectly well that people in real moral situations do not engage in anything much like their reasoning. But the Camusian point is that what is given in

[45] See Rawls, 'Kantian Constructivism in Moral Theory'; Korsgaard, *The Sources of Normativity*; Scanlon, *What We Owe to Each Other*; Habermas, *Moral Consciousness and Communicative Action*; Dworkin, *Justice for Hedgehogs*.

[46] Though see the critique of Korsgaard in Rudd, *Self, Value and Narrative*, 107–17.

[47] It is worth noting that Kant, who has influenced more than any other thinker the project of developing an objective but non-realist ethics, was himself a moral realist. Contrary to what is often supposed, he did not think ethics could simply be based on the demand for rational consistency in action (the ability consistently to universalize my maxims). Having set out the first (purely formal) formulation of the Categorical Imperative, he notes that it could be applicable only if 'there were something the *existence of which in itself* has an absolute worth' (Kant, *Groundwork of the Metaphysics of Morals*, 36). This, for Kant, is humanity; hence the more substantive formulation: 'So act that you use humanity, whether in yourself or in the person of any other, always at the same time as an end, never merely as a means' (*Groundwork*, 38). As he says, 'if nothing of absolute worth would be found anywhere ... then no supreme practical principle for reason could be found anywhere' (*Groundwork*, 37).

76   THE PHILOSOPHY OF CAMUS

moral experience is a—veridical—sense that people are of value, that they share in a normative essential nature,[48] and that this sets limits to how one should treat them. The philosophers mentioned above, by rejecting moral realism, reject that claim. They may give arguments for why we should in fact act in the same way as Camus's outraged rebel does, but they do not justify the rebel acting as he or she acts *for the reasons that he or she actually has*. Some philosophers may be content for there to be this disconnect between actual moral experience and an account of how we should behave rationally. I think that Camus is right, though; if there is an objective basis for ethics, it needs to be present in ethical experience itself. And I think he is also right that moral realism—the simple conviction that persons do actually have intrinsic value—is present in that experience. However complex its subsequent elaborations might get, moral realism is, at its heart, an experiential given, not a philosophical theory.[49]

I think, then, that Camus is right to see a serious problem for those who want to combine a commitment to a non-arbitrary ethics with a metaphysics that denies that values are really present in the world (or that at least human beings have inherent, intrinsic value). He dwells on the contradictions of the nineteenth-century Russian radicals who combined crude materialism with Utopian socialism (see *R*. 154–6), but the problem remains even when the two sides of the opposition take less extreme and exaggerated forms. Those who adopt the metaphysics of disenchanted naturalism—a vision of the world as lacking any intrinsic or inherent value—may do so because they think this is what science shows us. (We have noted Camus's own scepticism about such scientism in the previous chapter.) The combination of such a view with a sceptical or subjectivist account of ethics may be internally consistent. But those who reject any view of the world as possessing intrinsic value for the *moral* reasons sketched above do face the painful problem that Camus so clearly diagnosed—that Metaphysical Rebellion seems to undermine its own basis. If there is no metaphysical basis for value, then it seems that 'all is permitted'—that even murder becomes an indifferent act, and so the indignation that drove the rebellion undercuts itself (*R*. 57–8).

Again, this might seem exaggerated. Even if we do accept that morality has no deep metaphysical or rational basis, but is merely a part biological and part contingently historical and social adaptation to ensure social cooperation, can we not still endorse it as such? This would be a sort of pragmatic Humean approach to ethics,

---

[48] Of course, I too am using philosophical jargon here to make my point. But the conviction that I am describing is what someone in real life might invoke in protesting against cruel or abusive behaviour by saying: 'he/she is human!' Or: 'he/she has feelings!' or: 'how would you like it if someone did that to you?' (The latter is an appeal not to an abstract principle of consistency, but to a substantive sense of a shared nature—Kant's point, as mentioned in the previous note.)

[49] Camus's basic position is, I think, close to the moral, or more broadly evaluative, realism elaborated in much greater detail by Phenomenologists such as Max Scheler and Dietrich von Hilderbrandt (see Scheler, *Formalism in Ethics*, and Hilderbrandt, *Ethics*). Camus does discuss Scheler in *The Rebel*, but only his monograph on Resentment (*R*. 17–19).

which would base it in part on emotional sympathy (which is, after all, just as natural to our species as more aggressive or selfish feelings are) and in part on practical considerations about the need for security and reliable social interactions.[50] The trouble is that all these considerations are contingent. We are sometimes sympathetic, but sometimes we are not. On a purely empirical approach, it is hard to see how we get to the further idea that we *ought* to feel sympathetic even when we do not; or that we ought to act as if we were feeling sympathetic even in the absence of such feelings. And, insofar as I come to regard my feelings of sympathy simply as an evolutionary adaptation bred into members of a social species by natural selection (and/or inculcated by social pressures) rather than a kind of metaphysical insight into the real value of persons, then I cannot see how that outlook (if taken seriously) could fail to debunk and undermine those feelings. That I feel sympathy for someone who is suffering may be natural (though a quick look around the world will show that it is far from inevitable), but (on a purely naturalistic view) that I have this causally explicable reaction does not by itself give me any *reason* to act in one way rather than another.

As for practical considerations of social utility: I may indeed recognize that, as a practical matter, it is good for society to have moral rules, but I may also calculate, just as practically, that it may be advantageous to me to break them from time to time. Moreover, if morality is simply a way to hold society together, then why should the disadvantaged in society care about that? And, on the other hand, why should the advantaged feel any moral inhibitions about oppressing the disadvantaged? Morality for the advantaged would mean holding society together in a way that advantages *us*. And the thought that this is wrong, that society *should* be run in a more just fashion, clearly implies a higher set of moral standards that do not coincide with the practical social and legal standards that a particular society now has. But, *ex hypothesi*, the purely practical sense of morality under consideration can make no such appeal (although it could allow for an argument that society would be more stable if it does not foster radical discontent). One could, of course, fall back from this hard-nosed Hobbesian account of morality as a practical social necessity to a gentler Humean appeal to natural humane sympathies; but that would run into the problems already noted above.

The practical/empirical approach still seems to have no answer to the Russian nihilist Pisarev, as discussed by Camus: 'Pisarev asks himself ... whether he is justified in killing his own mother' (as we have seen, a touchstone case for Camus) 'and answers, "And why not, if I want to do so, and if I find it useful!"' (R. 154). This justification of crime through an appeal to inclination and utility cannot be adequately answered by a philosophy that can itself appeal only to inclination and utility. Of course, it is tempting to say that Pisarev is just crazy and needs

---

[50] See, e.g., Blackburn, 'How to Be an Ethical Anti-Realist'; Rorty, *Contingency, Irony and Solidarity*, esp. chs 3, 9; Street, 'Coming to Terms with Contingency'.

78   THE PHILOSOPHY OF CAMUS

no answer, though we would have reason to restrain or punish him if he were to go ahead and attempt matricide. But I would like to think that he would be *wrong* if he were to do so; not just a social danger or an inconvenience, and not just someone whose acts produced feelings of disapproval in most people. I want to say, on the contrary (and Camus would too), that his acts produce disapproval because they are wrong; not that they get defined as 'wrong' because they (mostly) produce disapproval. Obviously these remarks are merely a sketch for a full argument against the claim that there can be a kind of ethical subjectivism that does not collapse into outright nihilism. But I hope they can at least help to indicate that the problem that Camus identified—that Metaphysical Rebellion undermines its own foundation—is a real and serious challenge, and that it is far from obvious that what I have called the 'Humean' response to it is adequate to meet that challenge. And I hope the discussion above also makes it clear exegetically that, in *The Rebel* as in *The Myth*, Camus is far removed from the outlook of relaxed pragmatic naturalists or empiricists (such as Rorty) and is, in his sense of the issues, even if not in his conclusions, much closer to Kierkegaard. Of course, Camus is committed to maintaining a form of moral realism that does not depend on any theistic basis, and that will be able to stand up (as he thinks theism cannot) to the Metaphysical Rebel's protest. Or, to put it another way, he wants to endorse a form of Metaphysical Rebellion that will be robust enough to justify the rejection of theism without undercutting itself. Whether or not he succeeds in this will be a central issue for the rest of this book.

III Refusing to Be a God

So, in Camus's diagnosis, moral outrage at the suffering of the world leads the Metaphysical Rebel to reject the belief in a moral order to reality; but this then undermines his or her original moral protest. This may lead to a kind of cynicism in which murder becomes a matter of indifference in itself (even if there are good practical reasons for discouraging it[51]). But it might also lead the Rebel back to the Dostoevskian project of becoming a god. Continuing his summary of Ivan Karamazov's reasoning, Camus writes:

> The master of the world, after his legitimacy has been contested, must be overthrown. Man must occupy his place. 'As God and Immortality do not exist, the new man is permitted to become God.' But what does becoming God mean? It means, in fact, recognizing that everything is permitted and refusing to recognize any other law but one's own. (*R*. 58–9)

---

[51] Although this will depend. In many societies, being willing at least to condone or be complicit in murder is indeed the best way to get on in a practical way. Complicity is in some cases even necessary for survival.

REBELLION 79

The idea of becoming God is liable to seem outlandish, especially to sensible Anglophone empiricists. Of course, talk of self-divinization is imagistic and hyperbolic, although it is worth noting that people do find it natural to use the language of 'playing God' in the context of debates about, for example, genetic enhancement.[52] What it means primarily for Camus (and Dostoevsky) is an insistence on radical autonomy. The Dostoevskian anti-heroes who want to become gods are obviously modelling themselves, not on the intrinsically good God of theistic Platonism, but on the voluntaristic God of the Nominalists, understood as a pure sovereign will, which defines good and bad by a choice for which no further reasons can be given.[53] What is supposed to make them godlike is their insistence that there are no normative constraints on them; that they are bound by no law but their own. As they see it—and whether or not they feel the need to prove it, like Raskolnikov, by murder—I have supreme authority over myself; hence, imagistically, I am my own god.

One way of approaching this idea of self-divinization is through the closely related idea of self-creation. Most philosophers (apart from hard determinists) would agree that we have the ability not only to choose specific actions, but, beyond that, to plot the course of our lives (at least to some extent). And many would further agree that we have the capacity to choose (to some extent) what kinds of persons we become; we can work on developing character traits, including virtues (and indeed vices), cultivating interests, trying to grow some desires and reduce others. The (as far as we know, specifically human) ability to have higher-order desires (desires about desires) means that we can choose to identify with some desires and repudiate others. Emphasizing that ability, Harry Frankfurt claims that 'the person in making a decision by which he identifies with a desire, *constitutes himself* ... These acts of ordering and rejection ... create a self out of the raw materials of inner life.'[54] In a rather different context and idiom, Richard Rorty has also used the language of self-creation, declaring that 'we ironists hope, by ... continual redescription, to make the best selves for ourselves that we can.'[55] One can, while recognizing the importance of higher-order desires (or better, volitions[56]) and the ability they give us to form our characters, still find this talk of self-creation excessive,[57] and in subsequent work Frankfurt has heavily qualified his claims.[58] But other philosophers have been uncompromising.

[52] For a good discussion of 'playing God' in such contexts, see McPherson, *The Virtues of Limits*, ch. 1.

[53] See, e.g., Gillespie, *Nihilism before Nietzsche*, ch. 1, and Pfau, *Minding the Modern*, ch. 7.

[54] Frankfurt, 'Identification and Wholeheartedness', 170.

[55] Rorty, *Contingency, Irony and Solidarity*, 80. He also comments that (ideally) 'the point of social organization is to let everybody have a chance at self-creation' (p. 84).

[56] See Frankfurt, 'Freedom of the Will and the Concept of a Person', 16

[57] I have suggested 'self-shaping' as a more appropriate expression; see Rudd, *Self, Value and Narrative*, 16.

[58] See Frankfurt, *The Reasons of Love*, for a clear summary of his developed thought.

80   THE PHILOSOPHY OF CAMUS

Christine Korsgaard, for instance, insists 'there is no *you* prior to your choices and actions, because your identity is in a quite literal way *constituted* by your choices and actions.'[59]

Korsgaard's view seems quite strikingly close to Sartrean existentialism, which was, of course, the most influential and radical expression of the idea that we create ourselves in Camus's immediate intellectual environment. And it was precisely this that Camus repudiated when he appealed back from 'the postulates of contemporary thought' to Greek essentialism about human nature. As I noted above, it is crucial for Sartre that the absence of an essential human nature means not only that I am free to create or define myself; it also means the absence of any normative or teleological constraints on how I might do so:

> Human reality cannot receive its ends ... either from outside or from a so-called inner 'nature'. It chooses them and, by this very choice, confers upon them a transcendent existence as the external limit of its projects. From this point of view ... human reality in and through its very upsurge decides to define its own being by its ends. It is therefore the positing of my ultimate ends which characterizes my being and which is identical with the sudden thrust of the freedom which is mine. And this thrust is an existence; it has nothing to do with an essence ... the for-itself is wholly selfless and cannot have a 'profound self'.[60]

This view contrasts notably with Kierkegaard's. Kierkegaard does accept—up to a point—the idea of self-creation, or at least, self-shaping; as we saw in the Introduction, he sees selfhood as a task, not as something that is simply given. But he sees that task in a fundamentally normative and teleological context; we are responsible for becoming or failing to become selves, but we can become fully the selves that we *should* be only through a proper relation to God. Without any such normative context (theistic or otherwise) Sartre's radical idea of self-creation merges with the Dostoevskian theme of self-divinisation.[61] On this view, I have absolute autonomy; there is no normative authority standing over me, which might determine whether I do badly or well in defining myself.

Human self-divinization can take a collective as well as an individual form. I noted above that Metaphysical Rebellion can turn into Historical (political) Rebellion, but there are two ways it can do this. The first is simply that Metaphysical Rebellion entails the rejection of the notion that established socio-political systems are willed by God or built into the order of the Universe, and thus opens up the

---

[59] Korsgaard, *Self-Constitution*, 19.

[60] Sartre, *Being and Nothingness*, 443–4.

[61] Sartre does explicitly argue that we have an ineradicable desire to be God, although he sees this, not quite in Camus's sense (the desire to be one's own ultimate legislator) but as the (impossible) desire to combine the freedom of the for-itself with the substantiality of the in-itself. See Sartre, *Being and Nothingness*, 565–8, 621–3.

possibility of their being legitimately challenged.[62] And the indignation at human suffering that underlies Metaphysical Rebellion may then naturally translate into a determination to act so as to minimize the suffering caused by socio-political injustice.[63] This does not by itself involve anything like self-divinization. But Metaphysical Rebellion can turn, and sometimes has turned, into the project of putting, not some strong-willed individual, but humanity itself, in the place of God. Historical Rebellion, when motivated by this sort of metaphysical ambition, aims, not simply at the piecemeal correction of injustices, but at a Utopian transformation of the structures of human existence. Humanity, collectively, can become its own (re-)creator, without reference to any independent normative constraints. (Dostoevsky was also deeply concerned with how self-divinization could take this revolutionary political form. As one of his characters says: 'For socialism is not only the labour question ... but first of all the question of atheism ... the question of the tower of Babel built precisely without God, not to go from earth to heaven, but to bring heaven down to earth.'[64])

As we saw in the previous chapter, Camus—or the Absurdist persona that he created—was strongly tempted by the idea that, if one rejects God, one must then try to become a god oneself. By the time of *The Rebel*, though, he has firmly rejected that idea, insisting on the principle, 'in order to be a man, to refuse to be a god' (*R*. 306). His whole project now is to show how there can be a modest humanism, one that resists the temptation, having rejected God, to deify either oneself individually, or humanity collectively. But he has an acute sense of how strong that temptation can be, and much of *The Rebel* is concerned to trace the ways in which it was succumbed to, from nineteenth-century thought and literature to twentieth-century political practice. Although his implicit critique of Sartre is significant (he never mentions him by name in *The Rebel*), Camus saw Marx and Nietzsche as the most important exponents of a form of Metaphysical Rebellion in which atheism served as the premise or presupposition for a philosophy of radical self-creation. (We take God's place by becoming our own creators.) The difference, of course, is that Marx thought of the collective self-creation of humanity through political action, while Nietzsche's vision was of individual self-creation—though this was a vision that had its own political implications.[65] Nietzsche was a deep influence on

---

[62] Although, as I have noted above, one does not need to reject the idea of a normative, or even sacred, order in the world to challenge particular socio-political structures. Metaphysical Rebellion may be one way to delegitimize such structures, but there are less drastic options available.

[63] Of course, the worry is that Metaphysical Rebellion may also undercut such a determination by leading to a kind of moral nihilism.

[64] Dostoevsky, *The Brothers Karamazov*, 26 (bk 1, ch. 5).

[65] Camus was writing at a time when it was still quite common to condemn Nietzsche for providing the intellectual basis for Fascism. Camus is concerned to defend him against this charge, but he does recognize the real importance of a vulgarized Nietzscheanism in the formation of Fascist ideology, and does not think that Nietzsche can escape all blame for this. See *R*. 75–7, 79. For a good discussion of Nietzsche's politics, see Gillespie, *Nietzsche's Final Teaching*.

82   THE PHILOSOPHY OF CAMUS

Camus, and his vision of self-creation was one by which Camus himself was personally tempted. But in *The Rebel* he rejects both Marxism and Nietzscheanism as forms of the same self-deifying *hubris*. And he also notes how both in fact not only exalt self-creation but oscillate between radical voluntarism and a fatalistic giving-over of the self to wider, impersonal forces.

It is a familiar point that the Promethean humanist in Marx coexists uncomfortably with the economic determinist. I will return to Camus's critique of Marxism shortly, but, as for Nietzsche, Camus notes his rejection of the idea of any purpose or value, any moral order, in nature. At times, this seems to lead him simply to exalt in the creative freedom that results from the absence of any objective moral constraints (the recognition 'that everything is permitted'). But Camus is well aware that Nietzsche's outlook is more complex than that. He sees that a world without aim or values would be a world in which there is no good reason for doing anything in particular rather than anything else. (This is why Kierkegaard's aesthete sees boredom as the real threat—the sense that all action is, quite literally, pointless.[66]) Hence Nietzsche rejects 'absolute anarchy' since 'chaos is also a form of servitude. Freedom exists only in a world where what is possible is defined at the same time as what is not possible. Without law there is no freedom' (R. 71) This is a thought that Camus certainly accepts himself—and it is also a very Kierkegaardian thought. As we have seen, Kierkegaard regarded the self as (ideally) a synthesis of transcendence and immanence, held together by its overall orientation towards God, or at least to an orienting objective Good.[67] When that orientation is lost, then the self is liable to fall into either the form of despair that denies finitude and necessity (its proper limits) or the form that denies infinitude and possibility.[68] The former finds philosophical expression in doctrines (like Sartre's) of radical self-creation, the latter in forms of materialism and determinism. But, as Marx and Nietzsche show, it is also possible to shuttle back and forth between these two forms of imbalance without finding the proper equilibrium between them. And Camus's critique of Marx and Nietzsche shows his own implicit commitment to a view of selfhood that is strikingly congruent with Kierkegaard's—except, of course, for the specifically theistic element.[69]

One strain in Nietzsche's thinking sees the 'law' that must limit one's freedom so that it does not degenerate into mere whimsicality as something that strong creative individuals must impose on themselves. The trouble with this, as Kierkegaard had already pointed out, is that a law you impose on yourself is also one you can relax, remove, or replace at will. 'In despair the self wants to enjoy the total satisfaction of making itself into itself ... it wants to have the honor of this poetic, masterly

---

[66] See 'A''s essay 'Crop Rotation', in *E/O* i, 281–300.
[67] *SUD* 13–14.
[68] See *SUD* 29–42.
[69] I will discuss Camus's positive view of selfhood and human nature more fully in the following chapter.

construction ... And yet ... in the very moment when it seems the self is closest to having the building completed, it can arbitrarily dissolve the whole thing into nothing.'[70] Nietzsche is, in a sense, aware of this, which is why his praise of the radically creative free spirit gives way to his insistence on *amor fati*—the undiscriminating acceptance of the processes of nature, of which human subjects are merely fleeting manifestations. As Camus puts it: 'On the point of achieving the most complete liberation, Nietzsche therefore choses the most complete subordination' (R. 71). Failing to find anything equivalent to the Kierkegaardian 'synthesis' of possibility and necessity, Nietzsche thus slides instead from one extreme to the other.[71] 'Total acceptance of total necessity is his paradoxical definition of freedom ... The movement of rebellion, by which man demanded his own existence, disappears in the individual's absolute submission to the inevitable' (R. 72–3).[72] The aim, it should be noted, remains a kind of self-deification; but now one becomes a god, not through passionate self-assertion, but through becoming one with the divinity of nature—by identifying with the sublimely amoral pantheistic energies of a nature that indeed has no laws other than its own: 'There is in fact a god—namely the world. To participate in its divinity, all that is necessary is to consent' (R. 73–4). Such consent involves abandoning any pretentions to pass moral judgements on what happens in the natural world—which is to say, for Nietzsche, *everything*, including the human world.[73] For Nietzsche, then, Metaphysical Rebellion ends in absolute affirmation—an unlimited consent to the world of suffering and death. Whether or not Camus was directly and consciously influenced by Kierkegaard in this (Kierkegaard is not explicitly mentioned in his critique of Nietzsche), I think Camus saw Nietzsche as representative or exemplary (albeit on a higher level of self-awareness) of the European mind in general after the 'Death of God'— lurching between extremes of hubristic self-creation and an abject surrender to impersonal forces of nature or history.

The idea that, after rejecting God—or, more broadly, the idea of a moral world order to which we ought to conform and which sets limits to what we can rightly do—we are then free to alter both nature and society (ourselves) as we like according to our own wills has been an immensely powerful driving force in Modernity.

[70] *SUD* 69–70. This critique could well apply to Sartre, as well as to (aspects of) Nietzsche.

[71] One could describe this as the oscillation between Nietzsche's existentialism (or, in a rather different mode, his proto-postmodernism) and his naturalism, which continues to exercise commentators. See, for instance, the contrasting interpretations of Nietzsche in Nehamas, *Nietzsche: Life as Literature*, and Leiter, *Nietzsche on Morality*.

[72] In this interpretation of Nietzsche, I think Camus shows the continuing influence of Shestov. See Shestov, *Athens and Jerusalem*, 204–25.

[73] Julian Young gives a detailed argument for regarding Nietzsche as, essentially, a pantheist (Young, *Nietzsche's Philosophy of Religion*). He notes that Nietzsche, qua pantheist, is faced by the problem of evil even more starkly than the Christian theist, since he has no possibility of a free-will defence; and that he 'solves' the problem by accepting the world, with all its suffering and cruelty, as 'perfect ... there is no possible way in which the world could be better than it is' (Young, *Nietzsche's Philosophy of Religion*, 200).

84   THE PHILOSOPHY OF CAMUS

For the Absurdist of *The Myth*, this passion for maximal freedom and control takes an individualistic and apolitical form.[74] But, in *The Rebel*, Camus is concerned to trace what happens when these self-deifying ideals are transposed onto the collective and political level. Not that the concern to take control of the circumstances in which we live is necessarily bad. On the contrary: it has led to much that has been beneficial in the way of technological and medical advances, and in changing oppressive social structures that had been thought of as natural, sacred, and unalterable. But it has often also turned into a dangerous hubris. It underlies an attitude to nature that sees it simply as raw material to be controlled and exploited to serve human needs. Camus protests eloquently against this:

> Nature ... sets up its calm skies and its reasons against the folly of men. Until the atom too bursts into flame and history ends in the triumph of reason and the death-agony of the species. But the Greeks never said that the limit could not be crossed. They said that it existed and that the man who ignored it was mercilessly struck down.[75]

Nowadays we can see nemesis operating through the effects of climate change, as well as in the risk of nuclear war, to which Camus was referring here. But his themes of hubris and nemesis, being timeless, could hardly be more timely.

Hubris operates in our attitude towards societies as well as to nature. Much of *The Rebel* is concerned to trace the ways in which the initial generous impulse of rebellion was perverted into a collective will to power that allows itself to recognize no limits in its efforts to re-create society according to a Utopian schema. The collective human subject (whether humanity as a whole or a part of it, such as the proletariat, the nation)—often embodied in the person of The Great Leader— becomes godlike and finds satisfaction in worshipping itself as its sets about its work of (re-)creation. This tendency to turn politics into a secular religion accelerated in Europe from the French Revolution, where it first became clearly apparent, up to Camus's own time. The Industrial Revolution, the growth of capitalism, and the imperial expansion of the European powers in the nineteenth century, were certainly marked by this hubristic sense of an unlimited power to remake the world, with the continual exercise of the power becoming its own justification. Such self-deifying hubris was seen at its most plainly nihilistic in Fascism and, especially, Nazism; Camus notes that the Nazi *Fuhrerprinzip* is a 'degraded form of mysticism' that 'restores idolatry and a debased deity to the world of nihilism ... The Germany of Hitler gave [Mussolini's] false reasoning its real expression, which was that of a religion' (*R.* 182). But the most blatant instance of political rebellion

---

[74] This is true even of 'the Conqueror'—one of the exemplary Absurdist figures in *The Myth* (*MS* 84–90), who sees the social and political realm simply as a field for individual self-expression.
[75] Camus, 'Helen's Exile', in *SEN* 138–9.

turning into a pseudo-religion based on worship of the collective god–man was, of course, Communism. 'Russian Communism ... has appropriated the metaphysical ambition that this book describes, the erection, after the death of God, of a city of man finally deified' (R. 186). In all these movements we can see the same tendency we saw in Nietzsche, to oscillate between a radical voluntarism and a surrender to impersonal forces beyond the self. On the one hand, we get an insistence on the unlimited power of the human will to remake its (social or natural) world; on the other, a fatalistic historicism according to which history is moving inevitably in a certain direction, and we need simply to identify ourselves with its movements. But, although theoretically opposed, these stances often go together easily enough in practice.[76] And, if one believes that one is the agent of the historical process—if one has identified one's will with History—then one is liable to feel oneself intensely empowered, one's will-power greatly strengthened. The followers of those theologies that stress God's all-determining providence have often been not fatalistic, but passionately activist. If one identifies one's will with God's (and therefore with what is right), one is then motivated to impose that will even where circumstances might have seemed unpropitious. The same applies if one replaces God with History.

Camus's critique of Communism was highly controversial in his own time—at least in France —especially as he did not spare Marxist theory from responsibility for the moral catastrophe of Soviet practice.[77] Camus is genuinely appreciative of some of Marx's insights into the workings of capitalism, but he notes the extent to which Marx mixes close empirical investigations with a pseudo-Messianic belief in History, derived from Hegel. 'Thus it is not astonishing that he could blend in his doctrine the most valid critical method with a Utopian Messianism of highly dubious value ... his critical method ... has found itself further and further separated from facts, to the exact extent that it wanted to remain faithful to the prophecy' (R. 188). Like Popper, Camus notes that Marx's predictions were repeatedly falsified; but that, rather than revise the doctrines, his followers clung to them as dogmas. 'When the predications failed to come true, the prophecies remained the only hope' (R. 189). Camus certainly recognizes that Marx would have been as horrified by Stalin as Nietzsche would have been by Hitler; but Marx, by his deification of the historical process and his positing of a Utopian end that can then serve to justify any means, created a doctrine that can recognize no moral limits. 'Utopia replaces God by the future. Then it proceeds to identify the future with ethics; the only values are those that serve this particular future. For that reason, Utopias have almost always been coercive and authoritarian' (R. 208). Again, 'when

[76] Lenin is the obvious example of a voluntarist in practice with an officially determinist philosophy.
[77] Even his willingness to criticize Stalinism was shocking enough for some of his critics—including, unfortunately, Sartre.

good and evil are reintegrated into time and confused with events, nothing is any longer good or bad but only either premature or out of date' (*R.* 209).

I shall not go into the detail of Camus's criticisms of Marxism here; they seem to me correct on all essential points. For my purposes what I do want to emphasize is the way that Camus sees Marxism in religious terms, as the outcome of a process that began when Christianity turned away from the Greek concept of nature itself as a Meaningful order. Eventually Christianity gave way to Enlightenment Rationalism, where a personal God was replaced by abstract principles. But that in turn gave way to historicism, when any sense of transcendence was lost. 'Marx destroys, even more radically than Hegel, the transcendence of reason and hurls it into the stream of history' (*R.* 200). Marxism—and modern historicism in general—thus represent the nihilistic culmination of a history that began with Christianity: 'It was Christianity that began to replace the contemplation of the world by the tragedy of the soul. But Christianity at least referred to a spiritual nature and consequently retained a certain fixity. Now that God is dead, all that remains is history and power.'[78] Using Kierkegaard's schema, one might say that, for Camus, the religious (Christianity) leads away from an ethical stance grounded in nature and then collapses into the aesthetic (nihilism). But this would be a little too simple; as noted above, this Greek sense of nature as cosmos is itself in some sense a religious outlook. This—as well as Camus's complex and conflicted view of Christianity—is an issue to which we will need to return.

David Sprintzen has, very strangely, claimed that Camus 'totally misses (as Sartre suggested) the center of Marx's vision: humanity's collective self-creation through time.'[79] This is odd, because Camus in fact saw very clearly how central this theme was to Marx—and this was a crucial part of the reason why Camus rejected him. It is interesting to compare Camus here to his Italian contemporary, Augusto Del Noce. Del Noce was a Catholic philosopher who was tempted during the last years of Fascism by the view of some left-wing Catholics that Marx's atheism was simply a personal opinion, separable from his social and political views, so that Catholics would be free to affirm the latter while rejecting the former. However, Del Noce's close study of Marx led him to conclude that 'all of Marx's thought is a consistent development of the radical *metaphysical* principle that *freedom requires self-creation*, and thus the rejection of all possible forms of dependence, especially dependence on God'.[80] Hence, *pace* the 'Catholic Left', Marx's atheism is not a personal preference detachable from his political and economic thought, but is at the basis of his whole system.[81] Camus was not of course bothered by Marx's rejection of Christian theism *per se* (although he was disturbed by the *reasons* for

[78] Camus, 'Helen's Exile', in *SEN* 138.
[79] Sprintzen, *Camus: A Critical Examination*, 277.
[80] Lancellotti, 'Translator's Introduction', in Del Noce, *The Crisis of Modernity*, p. xii.
[81] See, in particular, Del Noce's essays, 'Marx's "Non-Philosophy"' and Communism as a Political Reality' and 'Marxism and the Qualitative Leap'.

which Marx rejected theism), but he also saw the idea of radical self-creation as incompatible with the acknowledgement of any proper limits on human willing. To think of oneself as one's own creator is to make oneself a kind of god. Del Noce rejects this for religious reasons, Camus for the sake of a humbler humanism.

Although self-creation is a crucial part of Marx's philosophy, Marx, like Nietzsche, oscillates between declaring humanity's potential for self-liberation, and subordinating human agency to impersonal forces—in his case, of history. The distinction between Marx the revolutionary humanist and Marx the economic determinist has sometimes been articulated chronologically, as a distinction between the early and the later Marx, but it is really a tension that runs throughout his thought. Insofar as it is resolved, it is by seeing humanity—or, more specifically, the proletariat—as the (collective) agent of a total transformation of the human situation, and of humanity itself, while also seeing its actions as (in the last analysis) merely the embodiment of unconscious historical processes (the development of productive forces, and so on). Although he calls himself a materialist, Marx subordinates human subjectivity to history rather than to nature, and Camus indeed notes Marx's distain for the natural world, claiming that he sees it 'as an object, not for contemplation, but for transformation ... for the Marxist, nature must be subdued' (R. 190). In this, he argues, Marxism follows Christianity (it is hostile to Christianity because in a sense it is a rival to it on its own ground), while being deeply opposed to the classical Greek view of things. 'In contrast to the ancient world, the unity of the Christian and the Marxist world is astonishing. The two doctrines have in common a vision of the world which completely separates them from the Greek attitude' (R. 189).

The claim that Christianity as such has this proto-Marxist attitude to either nature or history is, I think, questionable, although Hegelian–Marxist historicism certainly has its roots in certain aspects of Christianity. But Camus proposes an interesting contrast and comparison: 'For Marx, nature is to be subjugated in order to obey history, for Nietzsche nature is to be obeyed in order to subjugate history' (R. 79). Both start from a radical idea of human self-creation and end up in 'obedience' to something beyond humanity. Camus seems more sympathetic to Nietzsche's option, and he himself sometimes declared an allegiance to 'Nature' in opposition to 'History' (see R. 299–300). But, for Camus, nature is at least akin to the Greek *cosmos*, whose order we can joyfully contemplate (more on this in the next chapter), and this is not really what it meant for Nietzsche. As we have seen, Camus rejects the ecstatic naturalism of Nietzsche's Eternal Return and *amor fati*, in which the individual is lost in the amoral pantheistic sublimity of the world; and he also rejects the cooler kind of scientific, reductive naturalism that is so widespread in today's intellectual world—and to which Nietzsche was also sometimes drawn.[82] (And, of course, Camus also rejected the Nazis'

---

[82] See Leiter, *Nietzsche on Morality*, for an interpretation of Nietzsche as a 'naturalist' in this sense.

reductionist pseudo-science of race, the most degraded form of the naturalistic impulse to subordinate individuality to biology.) However, given the time and place in which he was writing, it is not surprising that Camus paid more attention to the threat to individualism and humane values posed by historicism rather than by naturalism. Since history is both something made by humans and also—according to historicist philosophy—a realm operating according to its own laws, it can tempt us, more readily than nature can, to think we can find in it the elusive prospect of a genuine synthesis of the voluntary and the impersonal, or of possibility and necessity, without resorting, as Kierkegaard thinks we must, to God or the Good.

It was, of course, Hegel who was the main philosophical source of historicism, and Camus sees him as having played a pivotal role in the tragic history of modern rebellion. He recognizes that Hegel's rejection of the abstract rationalism of the Enlightenment was motivated by his sense that the merciless forcing of abstract principles onto a messy and recalcitrant reality was what led to the French Revolution's degeneration into Terror (R. 133). And Camus agrees with Hegel's analysis here. His account of the French Revolution emphasizes the extent to which it was a religious struggle between the principle of the divine right of kings—Christianity underwriting absolutism—and the new, secularized, 'religion of virtue' (see R. 112–32). But, as Camus sees it, the subsequent rejection of the Jacobins' fanaticized abstract virtue did not lead the revolutionary movement back to a more modest and self-critical sense of justice, but rather led it to a cynical rejection of virtue itself in the name of a (supposedly) hard-headed philosophy of history. And it was by Hegel that this philosophy was first clearly formulated. Hence, 'the repudiation of the Terror, undertaken by Hegel, only leads to an extension of the Terror' (R. 136). Camus is happy to recognize the complexity and ambiguity of Hegel's thought, and that its historical influence derived in part through simplifications or misunderstandings of it (see R. 135, 136–7, 142). But what the radical Left Hegelians took from Hegel was really present in him. Camus highlights Hegel's rejection of transcendence—whether of moral principle (R. 142–3) or of God. Hegel was not an atheist, but he replaced the transcendent God with a Spirit (*Geist*) that was purely immanent to this world. Moreover, this immanent God is not eternal, but in process of development: 'this immanence ... has nothing in common with the pantheism of the ancients. The spirit creates itself and will finally prevail' (R. 142). (Self-creation on the cosmic scale.) This immanent God who creates Himself through our historical development was not hard for the Left Hegelians to secularize: 'immanence in the process of development is, if one can say so, provisional atheism' (R. 145). An ever-receding future, the end of history, takes the place of transcendence, and we are thus left with no guidance except that we should keep the process of history moving on. 'If nothing can be clearly understood before truth has been brought to light at the end of time, then every action is arbitrary and force will finally rule supreme' (R. 146).

REBELLION   89

A critical attitude to Hegel is certainly one thing Camus and Kierkegaard have in common. (Camus does indeed refer approvingly to Kierkegaard in a footnote in his discussion of Hegel, citing him on the impossibility of deriving divinity from history (R. 145).) They seem very close in their attitudes to Hegel, though their emphases differ. Neither simply rejects or dismisses Hegel, and both learn from him; but they both see some of the main tendencies of his thought as extremely dangerous. Kierkegaard regularly denounces or mocks Hegel's idea of system; we have already seen his insistence that reality can be apprehended as a 'system'— a rationally ordered whole—only by an infinite mind, and that finite existence is incompatible with such systematic understanding. Camus certainly shares this rejection of Hegel's systematic ambitions; in *The Rebel* he complains that 'Hegel rationalized to the point of being irrational ... he gave reason an unreasonable shock by endowing it with a lack of moderation' (R. 133). The main focus of Camus's criticism, as we have seen, is on the ethical dangers posed by Hegel's historicism, and Kierkegaard emphatically agrees with him on this.

> [From] the world-historical point of view ... it often seems that there is a cer-
> tain magnitude of crime and cunning linked to millions and the nation, where
> the ethical becomes as shy as a sparrow in a dance of cranes. But looking again
> and again at this incessant quantifying is harmful to the observer, who easily
> loses the chaste purity of the ethical, which in its holiness infinitely scorns all
> quantifying ...[83]

The ethical, he sternly insists, is one thing; the historically significant and effective is quite another. For both Kierkegaard and Camus, the real, suffering, ethically struggling human being cannot be sacrificed to some grand vision of historical progress; and is also not entitled to use such a vision as a justification for crimes. As Camus put it: 'Suffering is never provisional for the man who does not believe in the future. But one hundred years of suffering are fleeting in the eyes of the man who prophecies, for the hundred and first year, the definitive city' (R. 207).

Camus (like Kierkegaard also) has been accused of misunderstanding Hegel, or of criticizing a version of him constructed by his commentators, rather than the real Hegel. Sartre (falsely) asserted during their famous quarrel that Camus had only a vague and second-hand knowledge of Hegel's works.[84] Even more sympathetic commentators, such as Maicej Kaluza, have charged that 'Camus directs his criticism ... by judging Hegel primarily in the light of the twentieth century Hegel commentaries'[85]—especially the work of Alexandre Kojeve. I think such claims are, at best, exaggerated. No doubt, Camus's understanding of Hegel was influenced by commentators such as Kojeve. But it does not follow that he did

[83] *CUP* i. 142.
[84] Sartre, 'Reply to Albert Camus', 145.
[85] Kaluza, 'Camus and his Hegel(s)', 200.

90 THE PHILOSOPHY OF CAMUS

not seriously engage with 'the real' Hegel. Kaluza claims that his interpretation of Hegel's thought as leading to the materialism of the Left Hegelians was one-sided and accuses him of 'choosing to present this progression as grounded in Hegel's own work, thus depriving Hegel of ambiguity and of the possibility of being interpreted differently'.[86] But Camus explicitly describes Hegel's system as 'the most ambiguous in all philosophic literature' (R. 135). He was well aware that what the Left Hegelians—including that very influential contemporary Left Hegelian, Kojeve—took from Hegel was only one aspect of his thinking; but what they took— the historicism, the rejection of non-historical moral principles, the master–slave dialectic—was all in Hegel himself. Certainly, Camus was not setting himself up as an academic Hegel scholar; he was primarily concerned with the general tendencies of Hegel's thought, and with what was dangerous in its influence. But I do not think he can be fairly accused of failing to engage properly with Hegel, or with attacking a straw man.

One thinker who is not mentioned in *The Rebel*, but who would fit well into its argument, is Heidegger,[87] and it is instructive to see how the principles that guide Camus's critiques of Nietzsche and Marx can be applied to him too. There are some interesting similarities between Camus's and Heidegger's projects—both, in their critiques of Modernity's self-understanding, seek to reach back behind Modernity's Christian origins, in order to recover certain insights that they see as present in ancient Greek thinking. For both of them (certainly for the *later* Heidegger) this involves recognizing the importance of the natural world as a context for human life, one that sets limits that we need humbly to acknowledge, and that even forms a kind of sacred space in which we live out our lives.[88] However, Heidegger also embraced a radical historicism, which seems to leave little room for ethical thinking. In *Being and Time*, he largely follows Kierkegaard in seeing *Dasein* (human existence) as a synthesis of finitude/necessity and infinitude/possibility. But, while for Kierkegaard our 'infinitude' consists in our constitutive relation to an actually infinite being (God), for Heidegger it simply consists in our ability to transcend our finitude so as to be aware of it as such. There is nothing beyond the finite; what is uniquely human is our capacity to recognize explicitly the ultimate groundlessness of our finite being. Thus Heidegger rejects Kierkegaard's further claim that the self is a synthesis of temporality and eternity. *Dasein* just *is* temporality. Necessity and possibility are themselves interpreted in essentially temporal terms, as equivalent to the past and the future, with the present as the moment of decision that takes the trajectory of the past and directs it into the future.

[86] Kaluza, 'Camus and his Hegel(s)', 200.

[87] As I noted in the previous chapter, Camus does mention Heidegger in *The Myth*, but what he says there is vague and clearly second hand. Whether he came to know Heidegger's work better later on, I do not know, though I am not aware of any evidence of it.

[88] It is intriguing to note that the poet Camus most admired, René Char—who was also a close personal friend—was a friend and admirer of Heidegger.

REBELLION   91

Gregory Fried sums up Heidegger's radically temporal, anti-Platonic view:

There is no absolute transcendence for Heidegger, no way out of the cave in the sense of arriving at a timeless realm of ultimate truth; the truth is always given as a time-bound, particular openness to a world of meanings that has a necessary limit, a definite finitude. Historical meanings will shift, drift and ultimately pass away into the nothing that time brings to all finite things. All the more reason to embrace the cave, for it is all we will ever have.[89]

There are, therefore, no eternal—or even more modestly trans-temporal—values for Heidegger that might direct the self-projection of Dasein into its possibilities; if we can talk of values at all, they too are created in the course of that self-creating project.[90] (Equivalently, one can say that for Heidegger there is no human *telos*.) Accordingly, critics such as Heidegger's former student Hans Jonas have argued that Heidegger's radical temporalism makes his philosophy nihilistic: 'Such a loss of eternity is the disappearance of the world of ideas and ideals ... If values are not beheld in vision as being ... but are posited by the will as projects, then indeed existence ... becomes a project from nothingness into nothingness.'[91] It is true that in the later parts of *Being and Time* Heidegger moves away from the individual voluntarism that the earlier part of the book had seemed to be advocating; he adopts a communal perspective, and his temporalism becomes historicism. Authenticity turns out to consist in a conscious identification with one's community as it finds and follows its historical destiny. But there are still no trans-temporal moral standards to constrain the will of that community—or the great individual leading it—as it seeks its destined path in history. Heidegger's rejection of any philosophy of non-temporal value has, of course, been connected by his critics to his political choices. I do not think one can simply draw a straight line connecting the radical temporal ontology of *Being and Time* to Heidegger's support for the Nazis; the philosophy does not contain rules for its own application to particular historical circumstances, and Heidegger could, without inconsistency, have made different choices. But it can fairly be said that his philosophy offered few resources to support a principled opposition to the Nazis and left him dangerously open

---

[89] Fried, *Towards a Polemical Ethics*, 14. The references to 'the cave' are, of course, to Plato's Myth of the Cave in *Republic*, bk VII. It should be said that Fried is concerned about the ethical implications of this Heideggerian view and argues for the revival of at least a modest form of Platonism as a counterbalance to it.

[90] As Peter Trawny puts it: 'For Heidegger there is no moral law from which human reason could proceed, beyond the [inescapably historical] appropriative event of truth and the experience of it in thinking' (Trawny, *Freedom to Fail*, 25). Trawny goes on to note the relativizing consequences for ethics of Heidegger's 'refusal of Platonism and metaphysics'; it means that 'philosophizing in each case becomes finite. Kant was able to think the categorical imperative only precisely within the historical moment in which he thought it. The categorical imperative in Heraclitus? Impossible' (Trawny, *Freedom to Fail*, 43).

[91] Jonas, 'Gnosticism, Existentialism and Nihilism', 338.

92   THE PHILOSOPHY OF CAMUS

to the temptation offered by a leader and a movement that cast themselves as the embodiment of the national destiny.[92] Historicism and the philosophy of collective self-creation can lead as easily to the totalitarianism of the right as to that of the left.

I think Camus would have largely concurred with this critique; though he was too metaphysically sceptical to be confident about *eternal* values, he was, as we have seen, insistent at any rate that values are not our creations, but stand over us as criteria for the legitimacy or otherwise of our actions. Although Heidegger was no Utopian, and he did not think of history in terms of progress, much of what Camus says about Hegel's or Marx's replacement of morality with history could be applied, with some modifications, to Heidegger. Heidegger saw himself as inaugurating a new, post-metaphysical phase in Western thinking, which would overcome nihilism; Camus (if he had paid attention to Heidegger at the time of *The Rebel*) would, I think, have seen him as still thoroughly emmeshed in the historicizing nihilism of modern Western metaphysics. Perhaps he would have been more receptive to Heidegger's later work, which does involve a shift from voluntarism (even collective voluntarism, or that of the individual who embodies and expresses the collective will) to a kind of quietism. But this has problems too. According to Julian Young, Heidegger's later work eventuates in the realization that "'I am nothing', not a "substance" but a mere incident in Being's venture. One realises that the only agent is Being itself, that one is, qua ego, merely its conduit'.[93] On this interpretation, it would seem that Heidegger, like Nietzsche, like Marx, ends up swinging from a radical voluntarism to a view of humans and their willing as merely expressions of grander, impersonal processes—here, the historical destining of Being itself. Young's interpretation is fairly radical, and there are readings that see the later Heidegger preserving more of a sense of individual agency than his does. But there clearly is a shift to a kind of quietism in Heidegger's work, and certainly at least a tendency in it to the radical self-abnegation that Young articulates. And, in both phases, Heidegger remains committed to historicism and the rejection of trans-temporal values—a constellation of ideas that Camus regarded as, at best, politically irresponsible, and, at worst, disastrous.

IV Applications: Camus's Politics

We have a sense of what Camus rejects; but what is the positive content of his ethics? He has no ethical system and shows no interest in setting out any systematic list of either virtues or duties. Writing at a time of extreme political violence,

---

[92] Although, to be fair, Heidegger no more believed in the official Nazi ideology (based on its 'racial science') than Sartre believed in orthodox dialectical materialism during the period of his support for Stalinism.

[93] Young, 'Death and Transfiguration', 142.

REBELLION 93

when the most elementary ethical injunctions—against murder and torture—were being routinely flouted, he focuses on the need to respect human life and dignity at the most basic level. As I noted above, his ethics is a form of Phenomenological moral realism. If we simply attend to the realities of human life and human suffering, it should just be apparent to us that certain ways of treating people are wrong. But self-interest and ideology inhibit us from so attending; Camus's aim to is help remove some of the ideological blinders that prevent us from recognizing what ought to be obvious to us. The discussion of ethics in *The Rebel* occurs mainly in a political context, not because Camus thinks that ethics can be reduced to politics,[94] but, on the contrary, because he thinks that politics desperately needs to be restrained within an ethical framework.

Camus does not have a systematic political philosophy, and his critics, from Sartre and Jeanson onwards, have accused him of a sort of vague, moralistic idealism that fails to engage constructively with political realities.[95] As Simone de Beauvoir put it:

> Camus was an idealist, a moralist and an anti-Communist; at one moment forced to yield to History, he attempted to secede from it; sensitive to man's suffering, he imputed it to nature ... Camus was fighting for great principles ... Usually he refused to participate in the particular and detailed political action to which Sartre committed himself.[96]

This impression of Camus is largely based on his refusal to articulate any specific political (social, economic) programme, and also on his commitment to non-violence. But Camus's refusal to commit himself to a detailed political programme was itself a principled one, and rests on a general scepticism about grand programmatic schemes, whether political or intellectual. We have seen above his repudiation of both the Jacobins' dream of imposing pure abstract principles of right on the complex particularities of society, and the Bolsheviks' dream of acting as the executive agents of History in bringing about a radically new (though of course never more than vaguely sketched) social order. For Camus there are indeed 'great principles'—though they are also simple and even humble ones—of basic respect for persons and concern to alleviate human suffering. But there is no formula for how they are to be followed in particular circumstances, in *this* society at *this* point in history; they dictate no grand master plan that can then be imposed

[94] See Iris Murdoch's comment on Simone de Beauvoir: 'One sometimes has the feeling that she regards politics as the only kind of practical ethics' (Murdoch, 'De Beauvoir's *The Ethics of Ambiguity*', 123.) That was *not* intended as a compliment.

[95] For details of the famous quarrel between Camus and Sartre (and Sartre's acolyte Jeanson), which exploded in 1952, following the publication of *The Rebel* the previous year, see Sprintzen and Van der Hoven (eds), *Sartre and Camus*, which contains the primary texts from the controversy together with contextual and evaluative essays on it.

[96] De Beauvoir, *Force of Circumstance*, 260.

94 THE PHILOSOPHY OF CAMUS

by the visionaries who claim they can see it. (Here again his formula 'truths but no Truth' applies.) There are lots of particular actions one can and should take in particular circumstances—as Camus himself worked as a journalist to expose the French colonial government's neglect of Arab poverty in Algeria, joined the Resistance against the Nazi occupation, vocally opposed Stalinism while also continuing to denounce Franco, worked (unsuccessfully) for a civilian truce in the Algerian war, and campaigned against capital punishment. But there is no one right way that any society should be organized (whether it be called 'Socialism' or anything else). De Beauvoir's formula is, in fact, almost the opposite of the truth; it was Camus who was engaged with the particular and the pragmatic, while she and Sartre lost themselves in a world of grand abstractions—Revolution, Socialism, History; however brutal the particular actions they were willing to condone in the name of those abstractions. As Camus put it: 'It seems to me that I am arguing in favour of a true realism against a mythology that is both illogical and deadly.'[97]

Camus's principled refusal of any grand programme represents his pragmatic, particularistic side; his commitment to non-violence represents the absolutist aspect of his ethics. They might seem to stand in tension with one another. But really they belong together. He resists grand programmes precisely because they tend to violence. And, even when attempts are made to implement them without physical violence, there is still something violent in the very mindset that attempts to impose a grand scheme on all the messy historically contingent particularities of a real society. In any case, his commitment to non-violence is not in fact absolute. As we have seen, rebellion in his sense is based on the perception of the value of persons, which forbids violence and abuse. And yet rebellion cannot be effective if it wholly renounces any recourse to violence, even as a last resort. The rebel

cannot therefore absolutely claim not to kill or lie without renouncing his rebellion and accepting once and for all, evil and murder. But no more can he agree to kill and lie, since the inverse reasoning which would justify murder and violence would also destroy the reason for his insurrection. Thus the rebel can never find peace. He knows what is good and, despite himself, does evil … In any case, if he is not always able not to kill, either directly or indirectly, he can put his passion and conviction to work at diminishing the chances of murder around him. (R. 285–6)

Camus recognizes the validity both of the absolutist injunction against violence *and* the consequentialist recognition that we may be required to get our hands dirty in order to prevent the triumph of evil in the world; and also their incompatibility. Torn between these contradictory demands, 'the rebel can never find peace'. Camus insists on retaining the tension here; he refuses to collapse it by

---

[97] Camus, 'The Artist and his Time' (interview), in *MS* 208.

endorsing either a pure consequentialism, or an absolutist pacifism. But nor is he quite willing to work out a compromise solution by saying that killing in some circumstances (self-defence, protection of others) is straightforwardly justified— even though in his considered view it is sometimes unavoidable. The rebel has to live this paradox, recognizing genuine but genuinely incompatible imperatives. There are no formulas for how exactly one is to do this. Camus admired the pre-Bolshevik Russian revolutionaries who were prepared to kill Tzarist officials, but who then let themselves be captured and executed to atone for their killings (see *R.* 164–73; also Camus's play *The Just*). But he does not suggest that this is a general principle that any rebel who is willing to use violence must follow.

Camus is here struggling with the same issue that Christian theologians have faced, in trying to reconcile an ethics that explicitly commands that one should not resist evil, with the honest recognition that the refusal to do so would mean abandoning the victim to the oppressor and abuser. Some of them have, nonetheless, opted for complete pacifism, but most have not. (Interestingly Camus does say that, 'in the world today, only a philosophy of eternity could justify non-violence' (*R.* 287).) In a way, Camus's view is comparable to Luther's deliberately paradoxical claim that the Christian is both freed from the bonds of Law by the Gospel, but also remains a sinner, still living in a fallen world under the Law. Luther finds a kind of practical reconciliation of the two perspectives, arguing that for a Christian to use force in the service of civil order—even in the office of executioner—may be a work of love, aimed at ensuring the peace and security on which any sort of social life depends.[98] This goes beyond what Camus, with his passionate hostility to capital punishment, would be willing to tolerate.[99] But, as this example indicates, Camus's acceptance of paradox does not mean that he has no practical guidance to offer. On the contrary, he is clear that violence should be used only as a last resort, to the minimum extent that is absolutely necessary, and only against those who pose a direct threat. (Practically speaking, Camus is close to the Just War tradition here.)[100]

Camus firmly rejects the unlimited use of violence, aimed at, or justified as being necessary for, bringing about a vaguely sketched Utopia. But it is important to realize that his critique of Stalinism and other revolutionary movements is not, as Sartre liked to present it, a repudiation of practically effective political action for

---

[98] See Luther, 'On Secular Authority', 374–5.

[99] See Camus, 'Reflections on the Guillotine', in *RRD*, 175–234.

[100] All of this is missed by those critics who still cling to the oddly tenacious myth of Camus as an impractical idealist. Martin Crowley, for instance, claims that 'there is nothing in Camus' arguments that would allow us to distinguish between different instances of reactive violence, to decide whether some might be justified and others not; the only distinctions to be made are between the existential attitudes of the perpetrators, which is pretty flimsy ground for moral debate' (Crowley, 'Camus and Social Justice,' 103). Crowley does say that, although 'empty', Camus's idea of justice may still serve as a sort of reminder of the moral frontiers of politics (Crowley, 'Camus and Social Justice,' 103–4)—though it is rather hard to see how it could be both.

96 THE PHILOSOPHY OF CAMUS

the sake of moral scruples. Camus does have absolute values, but his critique of Stalinism is not purely absolutist—it is consequentialist as well. For consequentialism does not simply license any violent experiment that *might* turn out to have beneficial long-term results. The violence of the means has to be weighed against both the goodness of the intended end *and* the likelihood of those means actually leading to the end. Camus is critical of Utopian thinking in part because the end that it posits is by definition so incomparably great that it can seem to justify any means. But, while the absolutist in him does side with Ivan Karamazov's contention that even a state of perfect universal harmony would not justify the tears of an innocent child (*R.* 56), the hard-headed realist in him also notes that, the more paradisical the Utopia at the end of history is depicted as being (and therefore the more bad means it can be taken to justify), the more it tends to look like sheer fantasy. And fantasies do not justify murders. Moreover, the idea that ends and means can be neatly detached so that in principle any end (peace, justice) can be brought about by any means (war, despotism) is itself highly questionable.

Sartre, at the time of his polemic with Camus, liked to insist on his own 'realism', his willingness to set aside moralistic scruples and get his hands dirty for the sake of a greater good.[101] But if we take 'realism' to mean something more than just a willingness to be ruthless about the means to a desired end, Sartre had little claim to the title. As I noted above, even if one accepted in principle the use of violence to bring about a radically better state of affairs, one would still need good reason to think that *this* violence in *these* circumstances was in fact likely to have that effect. Maybe you cannot make an omelette without breaking eggs, but this does not mean you should approve someone who is simply smashing eggs by the cartonful against a wall, while proclaiming that an omelette of incomparable splendour will undoubtedly emerge from the resulting mess.[102] And why would anyone, *realistically*, think that Stalinism—one of the most brutally repressive political systems ever devised—was at all likely to usher in a glorious new future of justice and humanity? An orthodox Marxist would reply that the deterministic laws of History showed that the dictatorship of the proletariat was a necessary stage on

---

[101] Looking back, from the perspective of the 1970s, Sartre seems to have regretted having taken this 'realist' stance. Describing his earlier view, he said, 'you do it because it works and ... you evaluate it according to its efficacity [*sic*] rather than some vague notions having to do with morality, which would only slow things up.' He goes to admit, though, 'the whole idea didn't sit too well with me, it upset me no end, despite the fact that—ignoring my own better judgement—I carried it through and finally arrived at a pure realism ... when I had reached that point, what it meant was that I had blocked out all ideas of morality' (*Sartre by Himself*, 78; quoted in Foley, *Albert Camus*, 139). If his memory of being 'upset' by the realism that he forced himself to adopt is accurate, this may in part explain the viciously unfair nature of his polemic against Camus; in attacking Camus so bitterly, Sartre was really trying to silence the voice of his own 'better judgement'.

[102] See *CD* 27–8 (also in *RRD* 262 and in *SO* (under the title, 'The Artist and his Age') at 239) for Camus's own sarcastic take on the omelette–eggs metaphor, regularly trotted out by apologists for revolutionary violence.

the progress towards Communism; that the happy ending was guaranteed.[103] But Sartre was far too intellectually sophisticated to believe in such laws. As Camus indeed pointed out, he was trying to have things both ways—rejecting Marxism as a deterministic philosophy, while defending Soviet realities that could be defensible only if Marxism as a philosophy was correct.[104] For, without a deterministic philosophy of history, we would have to assess the chances of a given regime leading to a radically better state of affairs empirically. And why would anyone, looking at Stalin's Soviet Union with any empirical clarity, think that this gruesome dictatorship had any likelihood at all of leading to anything good?[105]

Camus rejects the idea that we are faced with a choice between (in Koestler's terms) the Yogi and the Commissar[106]—that is, 'between ineffective purity [of which Sartre of course accused him] and expediency' (R. 288). In fact, he insists,

the former chooses only the ineffectiveness of abstention and the second the ineffectiveness of destruction. Because both reject the conciliatory value that rebellion, on the contrary, reveals, they offer us only two kinds of impotence, both equally removed from reality, that of good and that of evil. (R. 288)

Stalinist methods may be 'effective' (at least in the short term) in building up a powerful militaristic state; they are utterly ineffective, unpractical, and unrealistic in bringing about a just society. Camus's willingness to take the side of 'the West' against the Soviet Union did not mean that he was in any way uncritical of the West or blind to its faults. But he preferred a society in which it was possible to criticize its abuses, with some real prospect of seeing at least some improvements, to one that systematically repressed all criticism. 'One may have to fight a lie even in the name of a quarter-truth. That is our situation at present. However, the quarter-truth contained in Western society is called liberty.'[107] He continued to identify himself as a man of the Left[108] while retaining an independence from all political parties or ideologies. He does express sympathy for various political movements, including the Mediterranean tradition of 'libertarian socialism' or syndicalism (R.

---

[103] Although, even on this view, it would still be necessary to justify the implausible assertion that the dictatorship of Stalin was the dictatorship of the proletariat.

[104] See LE 117 ff.

[105] Of course, Sartre was not looking at the Soviet Union empirically or realistically; as both Camus and another former friend of Sartre's, Raymond Aron, noted, he was viewing it (or trying to force himself to view it) mythologically—as the embodiment of such fantasized abstractions as The Revolution, The Proletariat, Socialism. See Aron, *The Opium of the Intellectuals*, pt one, 'Political Myths'.

[106] See Koestler, *The Yogi and the Commissar*.

[107] Camus, 'The Wager of our Generation', in *RRD* 248.

[108] See, e.g., 'The Artist and his Time', in *MS* 209, where Camus complains that the 'intellectuals of the left' have abandoned what 'the left' had historically stood for—the protest against 'injustice, obscurantism and oppression'.

98   THE PHILOSOPHY OF CAMUS

298–9), which he programmatically opposes to Marxism,[109] but also Scandinavian social democracy (see, e.g., R. 298n.).[110] One might note that the two are hardly compatible; and that syndicalism, as it flourished for a time in Spain and, to a lesser extent, in Italy and France, was both utopian in its aspirations and violent in its methods. (Indeed, it was driven as much as the Marxist tradition was by a fantasy of collective human self-deification.) Camus can, I think, be fairly accused of some naivety in his attitude to the syndicalist tradition, but what he admired about it (and what sometimes blinded him to its faults) was its bottom-up organization and decentralized vision (see R. 297–8). Scandinavian style social democracy, on the other hand, was admirably moderate in its aims and methods, but was also distinctly top-down in its approach, bureaucratic and centralized. In his rather vague references to these traditions, Camus was not, I think, really trying to sketch a programme or ideology, but rather was trying to draw attention to neglected alternatives in the simple stand-off between Communism and Capitalism. These alternatives were certainly neither perfect in themselves nor fully compatible with one another; but they might still offer some positive inspiration for those willing to engage with them in a critical spirit and apply lessons from them flexibly in different circumstances.[111]

The Rebel ends with a call for moderation; not in the sense of a tepid compromise, but a positive sense of the need to balance competing values and interests without wholly subordinating some to others, or suppressing any. (I will say more about the philosophical underpinnings of his political moderation in the next chapter.) Those who prefer the tidiness of a system may find this attitude contradictory—a refusal to make hard choices. (As in Sartre's sneer: 'You blame the European Proletariat because it has not publicly declared its disapproval of the Soviets, but you also blame the European governments because they are about to admit Spain to UNESCO. In this case, I can see only one solution for you: the Galapagos Islands.'[112]) And Camus does even say at one point that rebellion 'must never

---

[109] In this Camus sometimes plays rather fast and loose; Marx's principal 'libertarian socialist' opponent in the disputes in the First International that Camus refers to at R. 299 was Bakunin, whose nihilistic cult of revolutionary violence Camus had sharply criticized earlier in *The Rebel* (R. 156–60).

[110] See also his commentary on the British General Election of 1951, in which he expresses his admiration for the 'social reforms' of the outgoing Labour government, while admitting that 'I am not really a socialist, since my sympathies lie with libertarian forms of syndicalism' ('Albert Camus Talks about the General Election in Britain', in *SO* 115). In this talk he also notes, approvingly, that Labour is an 'example of socialism devoid of philosophy'—focused on practical issues, rather than grand theoretical abstractions, and thus, 'like Scandinavian socialism', able to 'remain more or less true to its [working-class] origins' (*SO* 116).

[111] In many ways—although he seemed uncomfortable about quite admitting it and made various rhetorical jabs at 'liberal individualism' and 'bourgeois freedom', Camus was really a classical liberal. He certainly maintained the central value of individual freedom (especially freedom of thought and speech) and saw the task of politics as a strictly limited one—not to solve the problems of life, but to give individuals the freedom and leisure they needed to pursue those problems for themselves (R. 302). His objection to classical liberalism was that its individualism led it to neglect social and economic problems, and thus left the freedoms it offered practically irrelevant to masses of people.

[112] Sartre, 'Reply to Albert Camus', 144.

abandon any of the terms of the contradiction that sustains it' (R. 285). But by 'contradiction' here he means tension—between principles of respect for humanity and of effective action; of justice and of freedom. They harden into actual contradictions only when pushed to rigid extremes: 'these contradictions only exist in the absolute They suppose a world and a method of thought without mediation' (R. 288).[113] Absolute freedom and absolute justice both become murderous; for the rebel, freedom and justice need to find their limits in one another. 'Rebellion itself only aspires to the relative ... Absolute freedom mocks at justice, Absolute justice denies freedom. To be fruitful, the two ideas must find their limits in one another' (R. 290, 291). It is much easier, in a way, to refuse limit, to rush to an extreme, than to live in a tension that is never definitively resolved. 'In 1950 [and not only in 1950!] excess is always a comfort and sometimes a career. Moderation ... is nothing but sheer tension' (R. 301).[114] And so far from it being opposed to rebellion, as some might think, 'rebellion in itself is moderation' (R. 301). As Camus argued at the beginning of the book, the original impulse of rebellion is precisely the recognition that something is being done to a human being that transgresses the limit that human nature should set to our interactions with one another. 'Rebellion, at the same time that it suggests a nature common to all men, brings to light the measure and the limit which are the very principle of this nature' (R. 297). Again, this is not mere hand-waving; it has precise practical consequences. Camus derives absolute freedom of speech from his principle of relativity (R. 290), and, while, as we have seen, he cannot rule out the use of revolutionary violence in all cases, he argues that 'a revolution is not worth dying for, [and presumably also not worth killing for] unless it assures the immediate suppression of the death penalty' (R. 292).

V Conclusion to Chapter 2: Some Kierkegaardian Questions

I hope to have shown that Camus has a serious ethical philosophy, and one that serves as the basis for a humane and flexible approach to politics. His ethical writings certainly show his concern to get beyond the nihilism that was at least explored in his earlier thought, and to articulate a positive, humanistic account of value. He offers a powerful phenomenology of rebellion as expressive of a perception of the value of persons, as well as a compelling diagnosis of what happens

---

[113] Kierkegaard attacked the Hegelians for using the language of 'mediation' to justify fudging distinctions and obscuring the need in practical circumstances to make decisive choices. But here Camus is arguing that 'mediation' is what allows us to resolve in practice contradictions that exist only in abstraction. I do not think that they are opposed here (their apparent differences can be mediated!), though their emphases are different.

[114] This might remind us of Kierkegaard's claim, in *Sickness unto Death*, that true selfhood is a synthesis—really a holding in creative tension—of forces that seem abstractly contradictory: finitude and infinitude, possibility and necessity, time and eternity.

100   THE PHILOSOPHY OF CAMUS

when rebellion ceases to be guided by that perception of value and turns into a project of unlimited self-creation. He calls for a kind of moderation, based on the limits that become visible in that awareness of value; a moderation that is not about lazy compromise, but is based on a concern to do proper justice to all that has value. All of this seems to me admirable, and to constitute a philosophical achievement that has still not been adequately recognized.

Let me return, though, as I conclude this chapter, to the comparisons with Kierkegaard. Obviously, the contexts of Camus's and Kierkegaard's discussions of ethics are quite different—Camus focuses on questions of political violence, while Kierkegaard does not. Kierkegaard *is* deeply concerned with social and, in a sense, political issues; but his brilliant analysis of 'the present age' in *Two Ages* is about the way in which a passionless society quietly dissolves all principles, ideals, and individuality in favour of a tepid conformity to ever-shifting fashions.[115] By comparison, he even seems to feel some sympathy for 'the age of revolution' (thinking of the French Revolution) as an era that at least exhibited some passion.[116] For all that, though, Kierkegaard certainly was not a revolutionary; and Kierkegaard's ethical stage, with its principal pseudonymous representative, Judge William, seems to be socially conservative in a way that contrasts with Camus's ethics of rebellion. (Many commentators have indeed found Judge William rather complacent in his solid commitment to the structures and institutions of the bourgeois society of his day.[117]) On the other hand, one might accuse Camus of valourizing—even glamourizing—rebellion over the unglamorous but necessary work of keeping an admittedly imperfect society functioning. There is no doubt something in both criticisms (and of course Kierkegaard was not intending us to take Judge William as expressing his own final opinion in any case). But—setting romantic stereotypes aside—Camus's rebel is essentially someone who recognizes the value of persons and who tries to act in ways that are consistent with that value. And that may involve, not only dramatic confrontations with radically unjust institutions, but also working to sustain as well as to improve institutions that—even though imperfectly—do uphold those values. Back in *The Myth of Sisyphus* Camus had noted that the absurd could be consciously lived by 'a sub-clerk in a post office' as well as by an adventurer or a Don Juan (*MS* 68). And likewise, according to the terms of his developed ethical philosophy, I think a Judge and respectable married man can still be a 'rebel'.

Although Camus and Kierkegaard's Judge William certainly look at the ethical life from different angles, I do not think there is anything essentially incompatible in their views of it. Their visions, while different in tone as well as in substance, are

[115] See *TA* 68–110.
[116] See *TA* 61–8.
[117] See, e.g., Turner, 'To Tell a Good Tale', 49–50; Furtak, *Wisdom in Love*, 82–7; Wietzke, 'Narrativity and Normativity', 105–6. For defences of Judge William, see Davenport, 'The Esthetic Validity of Marriage', and Ferreira, 'One's Own Pastor'.

complementary rather than contradictory. This is not to deny that there is tension between them, but tension is not contradiction. One might say that they represent forms of radicalism and conservatism that (in line with Camus's own philosophy of balance) act as necessary limits on one another; and they can do that because, despite their different emphases, they both recognize objective principles of justice and humanity, while also both recognizing the finitude of the human condition. The Judge does not blindly identify rightness with the standards of his society; nor does Camus call for a complete revolutionizing of all social structures. Both recognize that there is a time to tear down and a time to build up; that both protest and conservation have their valid place, although they may differ on when and where to identify those times and places. They certainly do differ, as I noted earlier in this chapter, in that the Judge sees the ethical and the religious as smoothly aligned, whereas Camus develops an ethical critique of the religious; but this, I think, represents a difference in their understanding of the religious, rather than of the ethical as such.

Still, from a Kierkegaardian perspective, the religious question is central. In contrast to Judge William, Kierkegaard himself sees the ethical as needing to be transcended by the religious; not, of course, abolished by it, but reinscribed within it. The ethical is not, for Kierkegaard, able to stand on its own as an adequate, self-subsistent form of life. And, as we have seen, Camus worries deeply about whether the ethical critique of religion ultimately undermines itself; that ethics leads us to reject religion, but that ethics needs religion to support itself. There are, I think, three questions that can, in a Kierkegaardian spirit, be raised for Camus at this point. First: has Camus really solved the problem he raised about the metaphysical foundation of ethics? Epistemologically or phenomenologically, he grounds ethics in the experiential recognition of the value of persons, not in a response to divine commands, or anything of that sort. But can a realist philosophy of personal value be compatible with a standard atheistic/naturalist picture of the world? As Camus himself asked in his *Notebooks*: 'if there is a human nature, where does it come from?'[118] When he asked himself that question (in 1946), I think it expressed a genuine perplexity. Camus clearly came to believe in a normatively significant human nature, which imposes (normative) limits on how a person should be treated; but does not this amount to saying that, in a sense, persons are sacred? And can one make sense of how that could be true on a generally de-sacralized view of the world? Camus notes that 'in ancient times the blood of murder at least produced a religious horror and in this way sanctified the value of life' (*R.* 279) and he contrasts this with the bureaucratic indifference of contemporary mass-murder. But is not that indifference merely a logical consequence of the Modern rejection of the sacred generally? If a human life is a merely biological phenomenon, is it not

[118] *NB II*, 144.

102   THE PHILOSOPHY OF CAMUS

just rational to reject the 'religious horror' at its violent termination as mere super-
stition? Camus does, in 'Helen's Exile' and *The Rebel*, hint at the idea of an order
of value running through nature as such, and at Nemesis as a sort of metaphysical principle. But can these hints be developed into a plausible metaphysical basis
for ethics? And, if not, can a merely humanistic ethics stand alone in an otherwise
value-less world?

A second question is whether Camus himself could really be content with recommending only a sensible humanism. We have noted throughout this study his
fascination (even if in many ways negative) with the religious, his perception that
the loss of a (broadly defined) religious belief in the Meaning of the world leads
us to a sense of absurdity. The religious impulse becomes psychotic when translated into politics,[119] but is he asking us to abandon it altogether and settle for a
placid humanism without absolutes? Many liberal humanists, in Camus's day as in
ours, would be happy with this solution,[120] but there is reason to think that Camus
remained haunted by a sense of God—or of the absence of God—that left him
discontented with standard liberal secularism. 'I don't believe in God, that is true.
But I am not an atheist, nonetheless. I would even agree with Benjamin Constant
that there is something vulgar ... yes ... worn out about being against religion.'[121]
Camus certainly attempts to articulate a humanistic ethics that can reject the temptation to respond to the 'death of God' by deifying either humanity in general or
certain would-be Supermen. But this is compatible both with the rejection of the
religious as such, *and* with the humility of a genuinely religious attitude, which
also refuses self-deification. Towards the end of *The Rebel*, he writes: 'The absolute is not attained, nor, above all, created, through history. Politics is not religion,
or if it is, then it is nothing but the Inquisition. How would society define an absolute?' But he continues: 'Perhaps everyone is looking for this absolute, on behalf
of all. But society and politics only have the responsibility of arranging everyone's
affairs so that each will have the leisure and the freedom to pursue this common
search' (*R*. 302). An essentially political ethics, dedicated to defending basic principles of freedom, justice, and welfare, does not by itself satisfy that in us—'perhaps'
in all of us, as a basic human drive—that seeks the 'absolute'. But if that drive—
we might as well call it the religious drive—is frustrated, then it is liable to find a
disguised outlet in political life, where the pursuit of absolutes is so deadly. If so,
there is something both shallow and unstable about a purely secular, humanistic
outlook, which (rightly) bans the absolute from politics, but which also refuses to

---

[119] Either in the form of politicized religion (theocracy) *or* in that of secular political movements that
seek to put themselves in the place of religion. It should be said that this leaves open the possibility of
legitimate political actions or movements inspired by religious faith, such as the Civil Rights movement
in America, or the Solidarity movement in Poland—both of which would indeed be excellent examples
of Camusian Revolt.

[120] One thinks of other contemporary critics of Marxism in particular, and revolutionary historicism
in general, such as Karl Popper and Isaiah Berlin.

[121] Camus, 'On Faulkner' (1956; excerpts from three interviews), in *LCE* 320.

find space for it elsewhere. The repressed will return, and the forms it takes will not be attractive.

There is a third problem too: given the gruesome history of human cruelty that Camus has recounted, it seems clear that, even if human beings can recognize ethical demands, they (we) are very bad indeed at living up to them. Kierkegaard argues (through some of his pseudonyms) that a purely ethical life—one without the resources of grace and forgiveness to turn to—would end either in self-deception, leading to hypocrisy and self-righteousness, or in despair. And, if we cannot live by ethical demands, do they not simply poison human life, filling it with dishonesty, guilt, or both? In a way this was the 'aesthetic' critique of morality presented by Camus in *The Outsider*. But, if Camus does not want wholly to repudiate that critique, while still wanting to distance himself from Meursault's amoralism, is there an option left? Can he articulate a humanly livable ethics that takes account of our tendencies to evil?

These Kierkegaardian questions and challenges are not simply posed to Camus from an external perspective. They are, as I have tried to indicate, questions that Camus himself was deeply exercised by. I believe that his third 'cycle' would have attempted to provide answers to them. How this would have gone, we cannot know in detail, but the direction in which his thought about these matters was headed will be the theme of the next chapter.

3

Nemesis

This chapter will consider Camus's responses to the worries that I raised at the end of the previous one about the adequacy of his ethical philosophy. I will try to show that Camus was very much exercised by these worries himself, and that he did indeed see them as pointing to the need for an outlook that went beyond the ethical philosophy of *The Rebel*—although not in a way that repudiated it, but rather in a way that deepened it and gave it a proper grounding. This more-than-ethical philosophy thus has structural similarities to Kierkegaard's religious stage, and, although it is a difficult question whether or to what extent we can ascribe a 'religious' philosophy to Camus, I do want to show that the similarities are more than just structural. I noted in the Introduction that Camus had planned a third 'cycle', organized around the theme of Nemesis, and was working on the cycle's novel, *The First Man*, when he died. This cycle would have given Camus's more-than-ethical philosophy its full articulation, but it was a work in progress that he never brought to completion. Accordingly, this chapter will differ from its predecessors in that there is no one Camusian text that I can take as the definitive statement of this phase of Camus's thinking. I will, therefore, need to draw on a number of his later essays, as well as on his *Notebooks*—and also look more closely at some of his literary work than I have done before. I will also be drawing on some of the later parts of *The Rebel*; just as the theme of rebellion was already introduced in *The Myth*, so the ideas of Nemesis, balance, and love all make their appearance in *The Rebel*, although not fully developed there. But, although my account of this last stage of Camus's thinking will necessarily be somewhat speculative, I do think that he left us enough—in however incomplete and fragmentary a form—to give us a pretty good sense of the direction of his later thoughts. And I think it is a worthwhile exercise to try and give a perspicuous overview of this material here— in part because it is less known than his earlier work and is often not included in the popular image of Camus.

It is worth noting that, although the Nemesis cycle was to have included an essay that Camus provisionally referred to as 'The Myth of Nemesis', it might not have taken the same discursive form as *The Myth of Sisyphus* and *The Rebel*. A note from 1951 runs: 'After *The Rebel*. Aggressive, obstinate rejection of the system. The aphorism henceforth.'[1] It is intriguing to speculate that Camus's third theoretical work might have taken the form of a collection of Nietzschean aphorisms.

---

[1] *NB* II, 269.

The Philosophy of Camus. Anthony Rudd, Oxford University Press. © Anthony Rudd (2024).
DOI: 10.1093/9780198924869.003.0004

He certainly had a talent for striking aphoristic formulations (which is why it is difficult to resist extensive quotation from him), and it is interesting to note his concern not to come across as a systematic thinker. Did he think it was a weakness of *The Rebel* that in it he had succumbed too much to the systematic form? Or did he think that such a form was unavoidable, given what he wanted to do in *The Rebel*, but that his subsequent thought would be distorted if it fell into that form? A later *Notebook* entry shows that he was contemplating a new collection of lyrical essays (to be called 'The Festival').[2] His earlier collections of 'lyrical essays' had not been included within the 'cycles', but might he have been wondering whether his thoughts on Nemesis might have been better expressed in this more personal, essayistic form, perhaps as an alternative to both the aphorism and the more formal, discursive treatise? Of course, we cannot know, but it is clearly possible that his theoretical articulation of the Nemesis theme would have taken a deliberately non-systematic form; *and* it is worth considering the possibility that his thoughts on this topic may have been such as to make such a form particularly appropriate. So, if the ideas I explore in this chapter seem inconclusive and suggestive rather than fully developed, this may be not just because they do not express Camus's final and definitive formulations, but because this phase of his thinking itself consciously repudiated finality and definitiveness.

I Beyond the Ethical

Camus's concern to articulate an outlook that would go beyond the ethical—and certainly beyond the quest for political justice that had animated *The Rebel*—is clearly expressed in his important 1953 essay 'Return to Tipasa'. As I noted in Chapter 1, his early (1938) essay 'Nuptials at Tipasa' is a lyrical celebration of his sensual immersion in the beauty of nature that he found in that ruined city on the Algerian coast. The later essay is a moving description of how he was able to rediscover, after all the political horrors of the intervening years, the freshness and joy of his response to the beauty he found again there. 'Amid this light and silence, years of night and fury melted slowly away.'[3] After noting his incapacity to abandon his concern for 'beauty and the sensual happiness it brings' in order to devote himself wholeheartedly to the struggle for justice, he continues by rejecting the idea that this would in fact be something that justice, properly understood, does demand of us: 'nothing is true which compels us to exclude. Isolated beauty ends in grimaces, solitary justice is oppression. Anyone who seeks to serve the one to the exclusion of the other serves nobody, not even himself, and in the end is doubly the servant

---

[2] *NB* III, 184.
[3] Camus, 'Return to Tipasa', in *SEN* 151 (*LCE* 167).

106   THE PHILOSOPHY OF CAMUS

of injustice.'[4] To put beauty above justice—a kind of aestheticism, represented in its most serious form by Nietzsche's prioritizing of aesthetic over moral value—is obviously to serve injustice (directly or indirectly). But to subordinate beauty to justice not only mutilates the fulness of our being; it also undermines justice itself. The struggle for justice needs to be constantly refreshed by a basic love of life and beauty if it is not to become bitter and self-defeating: 'the long demand for justice exhausts the love which nevertheless gave it birth.' But, without love, contemporary Europe 'can do nothing but confront one injustice with another ... in order to prevent justice from shrivelling up, from becoming a magnificent orange containing only a dry and bitter pulp, we had to keep a freshness and a source of joy intact within ourselves.'[5] Unless it is sustained by love, justice becomes cold, score-keeping, rule-bound and vindictive—and thus unjust.

This makes clear sense if we think of the love of people in this context; the argument would then be that justice cannot be a primary or self-standing virtue, but derives from and is sustained by love. In *The Rebel*, Camus had initially founded the demand for justice, not on love but on a universal respect for persons, based on the perception of the worth of the basic humanity that we all share. But by the end of the book he is indeed arguing that 'rebellion cannot exist without a strange form of love' (*R.* 304). This is an important move in itself. However, Camus is also concerned—and in 'Return to Tipasa' even more concerned—with the love of nature, the love of beauty. A compassion for fellow sentient sufferers is of course part of what he means by 'love' here. But by itself this may lead to no more than a grim stoicism, as we dutifully work to alleviate suffering—or indeed it may just lead to despair as we contemplate the extent of human misery. And despair may also come from contemplating our own moral failures. Contrasting his present state with his youthful innocent amoralism, Camus writes: 'In the days of innocence I did not know that morality existed. I now knew that it did, and could not live up to it.'[6] The love that rescues us from despair is, or includes, not just a compassion for the suffering, but a basic joy in existence, which is what we experience when we experience beauty; a joy in being alive in this world. Camus testifies that, 'in the worst years of our madness, the memory of this sky had never left me. It was this which in the end had saved me from despair.'[7]

The thought that justice is ultimately dependent on love is one that Camus shares, interestingly, with Aquinas. (I am not suggesting any direct influence here.) According to Alasdair MacIntyre, Aquinas's view is that 'justice cannot flourish, cannot indeed ... even exist as a natural virtue, unless and insofar as it is informed by the supernatural virtue of *caritas*.'[8] But, although *caritas* is normally translated

---

[4] Camus, 'Return to Tipasa', in *SEN* 149 (*LCE* 164).
[5] 'Camus, 'Return to Tipasa', in *SEN* 152 (*LCE* 168).
[6] 'Camus, 'Return to Tipasa', in *SEN* 149 (*LCE* 164).
[7] Camus, 'Return to Tipasa', in *SEN* 152 (*LCE* 168).
[8] MacIntyre, *Whose Justice?*, 205. See Aquinas, *Summa Theologiae*, I–II, LXV, 2.

as 'love',[9] it certainly cannot just be identified with what Camus means by love. As MacIntyre says, *caritas* is, for Aquinas, a 'supernatural' or theological virtue, and this in two senses. First, *caritas* is primarily the love of God, though it also expresses itself in a love for God's creation. Secondly, it comes from God; it is 'a gift of grace', not something achievable through human moral education.[10] Camus's love is not supernatural. But there are still parallels to be found even in these differences. Love for Camus is not the love of God, but it is also, as we have seen, directed not just to humans, but to the whole wider order of the world. And I think one can properly say—I will defend this claim further later on—that for Camus this order is something sacred. It also seems entirely natural to say that the experience at Tipasa that Camus records in this essay was a moment of grace—though not in Aquinas's specifically theological sense.[11] It was something given to him, not something he could have willed, and something that saved him from despair. For Camus, what goes beyond, but is also necessary to ground, justice (and ethics generally) is not, of course, Christian theology. But there is at least a significant structural parallel between him and Christian thinkers like Aquinas (and Kierkegaard).

Joy in beauty and horror at suffering, contemplation and rebellion, have to be held together. 'Yes, there is beauty, and there are the humiliated. Whatever the difficulties the enterprise may present, I should like to never be unfaithful either to the second or the first.' However, Camus continues, 'but this still sounds like ethics, and we live for something that goes beyond them'.[12] From this remark it might seem that the love and beauty that are a necessary complement and balance to justice themselves still remain within the ethical sphere, broadly speaking. In which case, beauty would not be the 'something beyond' ethics that we might have supposed.[13] But surely 'what we live for' does have to do with the beauty that Camus experienced at Tipasa, and that gave him the conviction that 'there lay in me an unconquerable summer'?[14] One way to read this passage is to take the 'something beyond' as being something that expresses itself in the sensuous beauty of nature while still transcending it. Similarly, it expresses itself in the demand for justice while also transcending that. The need to be faithful to both beauty and justice (the aesthetic and the ethical) comes from a sense of something that lies beyond both. (A Kierkegaardian thought, of course.) Or, to put what I think is really the

---

[9] Or as charity, a word that is etymologically derived from *caritas* but that has acquired narrow connotations that make it inappropriate as a translation.

[10] MacIntyre, *Whose Justice?*, 205. See, e.g., Aquinas, *Summa Theologiae*, I–II, LXIII, 2.

[11] Camus makes the parallel himself: 'These are days of exile, dryness and dead souls. To live again, we need grace, forgetfulness of ourselves, or else a homeland' ('Return to Tipasa', in *SEN* 149 (*LCE* 164)).

[12] Camus, 'Return to Tipasa', in *SEN* 153 (*LCE* 169).

[13] We could perhaps put this in Kierkegaardian terms: what is best about the aesthetic—joy in beauty, sensuous happiness, love—is not abolished by the ethical, but taken up into it (and, so Camus is arguing here, has to be so taken up if the ethical itself is to be viable); but there is still something beyond this whole (aesthetically enriched) ethical sphere.

[14] Camus, 'Return to Tipasa', in *SEN* 152 (*LCE* 168).

108   THE PHILOSOPHY OF CAMUS

same point in a slightly different way, perhaps what 'still sounds like ethics' is the sense of an *obligation* to be true to both beauty and justice. Camus has no doubt that he has that obligation. But he seems to want to point to something that lies beyond the whole sphere of obligation.

One wants, of course, in any case, to ask what is that 'something beyond ethics'? Camus, in this essay, either admits an incapacity to say, or cautions against the inappropriateness of the attempt even to try: 'If we could name it, what silence would follow!' Twilight has come to Tipasa at this point in his meditation, and he (almost) concludes the essay: 'What follows is mystery, the gods of night and what lies on the other side of pleasure. But how can this be expressed?'[15] What 'Return to Tipasa' does make clear is Camus's view that the ethical–political philosophy of *The Rebel*, while a crucial advance on the Absurdism of the *Myth*, does not by itself answer fundamental human questions, and is not even really self-sustaining. In the rest of this chapter, I shall explore some of the ways in which Camus tries to articulate an outlook that both goes beyond the ethical but is also necessary for the ethical itself to be viable.

II Back to the Greeks: Human Nature and Virtue Ethics

I will start with the first of the questions that I raised for Camus at the end of the previous chapter. This concerned the metaphysics underlying the phenomenological account of ethics that he gave in *The Rebel*. 'Analysis of rebellion leads at least to the suspicion that, contrary to the postulates of contemporary thought, a human nature does exist, as the Greeks believed' (*R.* 16). The phenomenological argument is powerful, but what exactly is this 'human nature' or human essence that it is supposed to reveal, and what, metaphysically, does Camus's belief in it commit him to? These are questions that he does not answer in any detail in *The Rebel*, although some of his commitments are clearly implied by his criticisms of Hegel, Marx, and Nietzsche. However, they need to be made more explicit in order fully to establish his ethical philosophy—as well as to answer critics such as Matthew Eshleman, who, in discussing the Sartre–Camus controversy, comments that Camus's 'strong view of human nature ... must have seemed as unsophisticated then as it does now'.[16] And the question is whether in order to do this, to provide a proper basis for the ethical, we will need to go beyond the ethical itself, or at least beyond the limits of the purely humanistic ethics that *The Rebel* articulates.

---

[15] Camus, 'Return to Tipasa', in *SEN* 153 (*LCE* 170).
[16] Eshleman, review of Aronson and of Sprintzen and Van den Hoven, 128. Eshleman does not, however, pause to explain what exactly he thinks is 'unsophisticated' about Camus's belief. I suspect that what he objects to in it is simply that a normative sense of human nature would set limits to the project of (collective or individual) self-creation, as discussed in the previous chapter. But this leaves his dismissive rhetoric a bit question-begging.

Although Camus did not give a detailed or explicit account of what exactly he meant by the idea of a universal human nature, we can proceed negatively by seeing what he rejects. By 'human nature' he certainly does not mean a purely biological account of the characteristics of *homo sapiens* (although, obviously, the biological facts about our species need to be seriously attended to if we are to think about 'human nature' philosophically). Camus consistently rejects all reductionist/objectivist accounts of human nature, according to which it would consist in some set of facts that are simply given. In *The Myth* he had argued that our self-consciousness, our capacity for reflection, prevents us from being simply identifiable with some given nature, like 'a tree among trees, a cat among animals' (*MS* 51). And in *The Rebel* he makes the striking comment that 'man is the only creature who refuses to be what he is' (*R*. 11). I have noted Kierkegaard's account of the human being as a synthesis of transcendent and immanent factors. And Camus seems, as I noted in the previous chapter, committed to a similar view. Our capacities for transcendence—self-consciousness, reason, free will (not necessarily in a metaphysically contentious senses, but in the sense of our being able to make decisions, to plot our course through life)—mean that we cannot simply be identified, as other organisms can be, with a fixed species-nature. We can step back from the basic biological imperatives of our being and choose, for example, not to reproduce; to suffer for a cause we consider worthwhile; or, indeed, to commit suicide.

So far, this might seem close to Sartre, according to whom 'existence precedes essence ... man first of all exists—and defines himself afterwards ... to begin with he is nothing, he will not be anything until later and then he will be what he makes of himself'.[17] But, as I noted back in the previous chapter, Camus clearly rejects Sartre's radical notion of self-creation, and his jab at the 'postulates of contemporary thought' is certainly aimed primarily at Sartre. Camus's position differs from Sartre's in two crucial ways. First, he does not identify the self solely with its capacities for transcendence, as Sartre does;[18] for who we are also includes our immanence, our finitude, our limits. Sartre, of course, recognizes and takes seriously what he calls our 'facticity'—our historical and biological givens. We are not, he insists, like the souls in Plato's Myth of Er,[19] who chose the bodies and the social circumstances into which they will be born.[20] But for him such things simply go to make up (in part) the situation that *we* (our free, self-conscious choosing selves) then need to respond to. They are not parts of who we are, for we are (in a sense) nothing; nothing but the stance that we take to the facts of the world,

---

[17] Sartre, *Existentialism and Humanism*, 28.

[18] Although Sartre, of course, denies that there is a human essence, one could put his point, a little paradoxically, by saying that for him it is our essence to have no essence. That is what is distinctive about humans, and what distinguishes them from other beings.

[19] See Plato, *Republic*, bk X, 617d–620d.

[20] Sartre, *Being and Nothingness*, 83.

110 THE PHILOSOPHY OF CAMUS

including those of our bodies and social circumstances. For Camus, by contrast, they really are aspects of us, parts of who or what we truly are, and they thus set limits to what we can choose to be—at least, without falling into self-destruction. So Camus rejects Sartre's radical libertarianism, as well as deterministic materialism; and, as we have seen, he rejects both the hubristic drive to self-creation *and* the loss of the self in a surrender to impersonal forces that he finds in both Nietzsche and Marx. His concern for a balance or synthesis of immanent and transcendent factors brings him much closer to Kierkegaard than to any of these other thinkers—again, whether or not he had Kierkegaard consciously in mind.

Secondly, it is clear that our shared human nature in Camus's sense is an essentially normative concept (as it also was for Kierkegaard). This is a repudiation both of Sartre, for whom the lack of a fixed human nature implies the lack of objective values, and of his own earlier Absurdism (to the extent that it ever really was his own, that is). But it is also a further reason for his rejection of the opposite extreme—biological reductionism. Even the Nazi doctors who performed horrific experiments on concentration camp inmates whom they considered sub-human, were not denying that their victims were of the same biological species; the point of the experiments, after all, was to gain knowledge of human anatomy, physiology, and so on, that could be used in treating 'Aryan' patients. The doctors were clearly failing to recognize something crucial about their victims, but it was not any specific biological fact. The 'common humanity' they failed (or chose not) to see is something essentially normative.[21] And, although our humanity cannot simply be identified with our transcendent capacities, they are still crucial for understanding the normative point. Our rationality, our self-consciousness—the fact that we are beings who can choose how to live our lives and reflect on how best to live them— explain why we are of more value than other beings.[22] (As Kant argued—that we can set ends for ourselves is what makes it wrong to treat us merely as means to another's ends.[23])

So Camus rejects both biological determinism and Sartrean libertarianism— both of which oppose the idea that there is a normatively relevant human nature. And, although he does not consider it explicitly, Camus would certainly be committed to rejecting another view, which has become widespread since his time: that of human nature as a social construction. This view—widely accepted in

[21] The point of the example, I should say, is not to claim that biological reductionism is, or leads to, Nazism; but to emphasize the difference between an essentially normative conception of human nature, like Camus's, and a purely biological understanding of human nature.

[22] A point that, to be fair, Sartre actually makes: 'But what do we mean to say by this [the priority of existence over essence], but that man is of a greater dignity than a stone or a table?' (*Existentialism and Humanism*, 28). But, although one (quasi-Kantian) strain in his thinking wants to make this the basis for an ethic of universal human dignity, his conviction that values have to be our own free creations ultimately wins out over this possible form of moral realism.

[23] It should, of course, be said that the mere capacity to suffer pain sets strict limits on what we can permissibly do even to subpersonal animals; even by way of potentially beneficial medical experiments.

Postmodern circles—also rejects the idea of human nature as something simply given by our biology or otherwise, but goes beyond that to argue that there is nothing more to 'human nature' than the ways it is thought of. How we think of and experience ourselves depends on the templates our cultures make available to us; and, since there are very different accounts of human nature given in different eras and different cultures, there just are very different ways of being human, and no transcultural 'human nature', which those ways may be more or less true to.[24] There are real insights lying behind this view. We are social beings, and, as such, shaped by particular societies (but this is itself a claim about what human nature essentially is); and we do tend to become what we think of ourselves as being (but this is also a universal human characteristic). But it does not follow that there are no cross-cultural universals; indeed, as my parentheses above have been intended to indicate, postmodern relativism covertly presupposes them.[25] Although Camus does not directly address the kind of relativistic historicism that would be propounded shortly after his death by Foucault, he would certainly have seen as it as being as ethically debilitating as the Messianic historicism of the Hegelian–Marxist tradition.[26]

Human nature is, then, a normative concept for Camus; to recognize another's humanity is to recognize limits to how he or she should be treated. But for Kierkegaard there is another, related, sense in which human nature is normative; it is the *telos* (goal) of 'the human being' to become a self—that is, properly to integrate the factors of transcendence and immanence. And a telos in this sense is not just something that one can, if one likes, choose to pursue, but is what one *should* pursue, and what one needs to attain in order to be fulfilled. The self for Kierkegaard is an unavoidably normative concept, and so, therefore, is 'the human being' for which selfhood is the *telos*. Moreover, according to Kierkegaard, the polarities of one's being can be integrated only if the self as a whole is properly related to 'the power which established it'—that is, God. And God, for Kierkegaard, is an essentially normative concept too; whatever else God may be for Kierkegaard,

---

[24] For a particularly influential version of such claims, see Foucault, *The Order of Things* (*Les Mots et les choses*).

[25] Foucault argues that the idea of the self as a synthesis of transcendent and immanent factors— what he calls the idea of 'Man' as an 'empirico-transcendental doublet' (*The Order of Things*, 318)—is of relatively recent origin and is probably on its way to being erased by the rise of the Structuralist view of the subject as an effect of sign-systems (*The Order of Things*, 386–7). But Foucault's own history of the rise and fall of various different conceptual frameworks (*epistemes*) presupposes not only human immanence (we are constrained in our thinking by the world views of our societies) but also human transcendence—for Foucault himself is able to write his history by taking up a position (at least apparently) outside all *epistemes*. (And, even if he is instead writing from within the supposed oncoming Structuralist *episteme*, the fact that he is *aware* of writing from within it still shows his at least partial transcendence of it.)

[26] Forms of historical relativism, albeit rather different from Foucault's, were, of course, popular in Camus's day (e.g. Spengler); it may be reasonable to think of them as underlying, at least in part, the nihilistic attitude of Camus's fictional 'German Friend' in his 'Letters to a German Friend'. (And, indeed, Heidegger's relativistic historicism does appear to have been a significant influence on Foucault.)

112   THE PHILOSOPHY OF CAMUS

He is the (Platonic) Good—the eternal, absolute normative standard; *the* Good from which all lesser goodness derives.

This may all sound far too metaphysical and theological for Camus. I am not suggesting that he found Kierkegaard's specifically Christian or even theistic views acceptable. But Camus, in rejecting 'the postulates of contemporary thought', does explicitly align himself with ancient Greek thinking: 'a human nature does exist, as the Greeks believed.' He does not go into more detail about his alignment with Greek thinking at this point, but the Platonic and Aristotelian conceptions of the essential human nature were strongly normative and teleological and fitted into their essentially normative and teleological conceptions of reality as a whole. For Plato, though things in the physical world cannot fully or adequately embody the pure Forms, their imitation of or participation in the Forms is what gives them whatever coherence and comprehensibility they do have, and it is the Forms that are the standards against which their excellences or failings are to be measured. Everything good or intelligible ultimately derives from the Form of Good and it is only by the light provided by the Good that we can live well. Aristotle abandons Plato's separated Forms, but still sees everything in nature teleologically, as striving to realize as fully as possible the potentials that constitute its essential nature. And this is the basis of his ethics; the good life for a human being is the one in which he (or she—although for Aristotle, basically, he) can fulfil the potentials that constitute the nature of humans as rational social beings. Various questions emerge at this point. How much, exactly, did Camus want to take from 'the Greeks'? And can one, in any case, formulate a normative conception of human nature, and use that as the basis for ethics, as Camus does, without some broader metaphysics of normativity? Is a normative conception of human nature necessarily a teleological one? If so, what teleology is involved in Camus's account of human nature? And, if one does have a teleological understanding of human nature, can that be divorced from a teleological conception of the wider, non-human world?

The attempt to return to 'the Greeks'—to an ethics based on an essentialist account of human nature—has been an important part of Anglophone philosophy since the mid-1950s. It has taken a variety of forms.[27] But they share the idea that ethics should start not from the notion of a moral rule, but from a consideration of what is the good life for a human being—a life in which the potentials characteristic of a human are fulfilled. These theories then consider what are the virtues—the states of character necessary for the living of a good life. (And not just instrumentally necessary; the idea, derived from Aristotle, is that, for example, courage and

---

[27] See, in particular, Anscombe, 'Modern Moral Philosophy'; Foot, *Virtues and Vices*; Midgely, *Beast and Man*; McDowell, 'Virtue and Reason'; MacIntyre, *After Virtue* and *Dependent Rational Animals*. Also important, although a bit of an outlier, as she favours a Platonic rather than an Aristotelian approach, is Iris Murdoch; see her *The Sovereignty of Good* and *Metaphysics as a Guide to Morals*. For more recent work in these traditions, see, e.g., Brewer, *The Retrieval of Ethics*, and McPherson, *Virtue and Meaning*.

justice are constitutive of a good, well-lived life, not merely liable on the whole to *lead* to such a life.) Moral rules do not drop out of the picture, but are subordinated to, and perhaps derived from, the notions of virtue and the good. The right thing to do is what the virtuous person would do in this particular situation.

I think Camus would have had a good deal of sympathy with this approach to ethics. He is consistently hostile in his attitude to a 'morality based on formal principles'.[28] Though he nowhere discusses the virtues systematically, he does frequently allude to states of character he finds admirable. As Matthew Sharpe notes:

> Each of the key lyrical essays in the 1954 collection *L'Ete*, in this vein, defends one or more such virtues: strength of character ('Almond Trees'); courage wed to intelligence ('Prometheus in the Underworld'); humility and friendship ('Helen's Exile'); humility and fidelity to self, despite the vicissitudes of fame ('The Enigma'); and the love of beauty and a chastened *philanthropia* everywhere.[29]

Sharpe also notes two states of character that might be considered master-virtues for Camus: intelligence (considered not simply as intellectual cleverness, but the capacity to think clearly and honestly about what matters; akin to *phronesis* in Aristotle[30]) and moderation (*mesure*), the capacity to control and balance one's passions (akin to the Greek *sôphrosunê*). We have already noted the idea of moderation—crucial to Camus's later philosophy—in a political context and will be looking at it in more detail in what follows.

Camus's emphasis on virtues over rules certainly does not mean that he rejects the idea that there are moral rules, or indeed that there are absolute moral obligations. (Aristotle and most of his recent Anglophone followers have also insisted that there are such obligations, and that virtues do not simply displace rules.) In *The Rebel* Camus insists that there is an obligation not to kill; but he also insists that we have the obligation sometimes to break that rule so as to protect victims of violence. As I noted in the previous chapter, he has sometimes been criticized for not giving a decision procedure to allow us to determine when violence and killing are permissible. Although, as we saw, he does provide some guidelines, I think he *deliberately* refrains from trying to provide such a procedure. Only the true Rebel (one who combines the virtues of a commitment to justice and an abhorrence of violence) can decide what should be done in the particular circumstances. Jean-Baptiste Clamence's cynical dictum from *The Fall*—'When one has no character, one *has* to apply a method' (*F.* 14)—could be taken as a back-handed motto for

---

[28] *CD* 13 (also in *RRD* 254 and—under the title 'The Artist and his Age'—in *SO* 233). See also, e.g., R. 123–4, 283.

[29] Sharpe, *Camus, Philosophe*, 360. Sharpe's whole discussion of Camus on the virtues (pp. 359 ff.) is very helpful.

[30] Sharpe, *Camus, Philosophe*, 363–6.

114 THE PHILOSOPHY OF CAMUS

'virtue ethics'. Conversely, if you really do have (ethical) character, you do not need a 'method' to tell you what to do.[31]

Some of the modern proponents of virtue ethics have presented it as a form of ethical naturalism—a theory that is able to provide an objective basis for morality without relying on any putative non-natural metaphysical facts or entities. Their hope is that we can develop a neo-Aristotelian ethics, without having to take on board what MacIntyre called Aristotle's 'metaphysical biology' or other Aristotelian–Platonic metaphysical commitments.[32] And this might seem attractive to Camus. Central to this project is the idea is that a term like 'good' could be both evaluative and straightforwardly descriptive—contrary to the prevailing mid-twentieth-century dogma of a strict distinction between 'facts' and 'values' (and the tendency to think of the latter as merely expressions of subjective preference or emotion). Naturalistic virtue theorists such as Philippa Foot and Rosalind Hursthouse like to use organisms as examples. A good wolf, for instance, is one that has its natural species characteristics fully developed—it is fast, has sharp teeth, a warm coat, and cooperates with other wolves in its pack. And this enables it to flourish, qua wolf. So too with human beings. We, of course, differ from other organisms; our needs and our characteristic way of life are much more complex. But we can still say that a human needs virtues such as courage, temperance, and justice in order to lead a flourishing human life. No non-naturalistic metaphysics is required to make sense of this, although, of course, an essentialism about species and their typical characteristics is needed. This is a teleological outlook, but the teleology it involves is a purely natural one, and the normativity that derives from this account is a 'natural' normativity.[33]

Attractive though this account may be, it does have serious problems. Although it is not simple biological reductionism, the worry is that it still exaggerates our immanence and underplays our transcendence. Philosophers like Foot insist that they are concerned with the conditions of our flourishing as *rational* animals, not as beings bounded by simple biological needs. But our rationality (or more broadly our capacities for transcendence—self-consciousness, personhood, and so on) do not simply add greater complexity to our animality; in a sense they allow us—though of course never completely—to transcend the merely biological sphere altogether. But, if this is the case, then the analogies between evaluating humans and evaluating other organisms seem to become too remote to be helpful.

---

[31] By a nicely malicious twist of fate, *The Fall* was published in the same year as Sartre's *Question de methode*, translated into English as *The Search for a Method*. And, of course, Sartre does deny, not only that humanity as a whole has an essential nature, but also that individuals have determinate characters.

[32] See MacIntyre, *After Virtue*, 148, 162–3. Since the (1981) first edition of *After Virtue*, MacIntyre has come to accept that his neo-Aristotelian ethics needs to be grounded in both metaphysics and biology, although still not in Aristotle's metaphysical biology. See the prologue to the third (2007) edition of *After Virtue*, p. xi.

[33] The classic modern statement of this view is Foot, *Natural Goodness*; see especially ch. 2, 'Natural Norms'. See also Hursthouse, *On Virtue Ethics*.

One obvious but crucial point is that wolves are not subject to moral assessment, although they can be evaluated as 'good' or 'bad'. But humans may be judged to be morally bad, even though they are apparently flourishing by criteria of health, subjective happiness, and even cooperative social engagement. And, indeed, the best way to flourish (in any obviously naturalistic sense) may often be to be complicit in evil or at least to turn a blind eye to it.[34] Judging a human being as good or bad in an ethical sense just seems too far removed from what is involved in judging a wolf—or a human being—to a be good or bad instance of its species, in the sense of merely natural normativity.[35] Not only do we have a much wider repertoire of behaviours than a wolf, but many of the ways of acting that seem to be natural to us (and therefore part of the basis on which we can make judgements of natural normativity) are also ethically wrong. As Anna Lannstrom puts it:

If we were trying to ground ethics in human nature, we would not start with the fact that we are the only animal that makes war on its own, or that we often are jealous, that we torture other human beings, or that we often are selfish. Rather, we might note that we are rational, that we are social and that we can form close friendships. That is, we would select good facts about [our] nature. In order to be able to do that, we need a distinction between good and bad already in place.[36]

Our conception of human nature must already be a normative, ethical one, for us to draw recognizably ethical conclusions from it.

Of course, these are only notes towards an argument against a purely naturalistic neo-Aristotelian approach to ethics.[37] But I hope to have indicated that there are grounds for scepticism about the project, and these are doubts that I think Camus, with his concern to do justice to human transcendence as well as immanence, would have shared. But, if a purely naturalistic reading of Aristotelian essentialism and teleology is not enough to get us to anything more than merely 'natural' (wolflike) normativity, then it seems that the project of going 'back to the Greeks' for an ethically adequate account of human nature will have to involve taking on board more of a metaphysical outlook than the 'postulates of contemporary thought'—in Camus's day or ours—would be comfortable with. However, as I have tried to indicate already, and will aim to show in more detail in the next section, this more metaphysical perspective would not have been so alien to Camus.

[34] Foot is aware of the problem and does try to address it—see *Natural Goodness*, ch. 6. But, although what she says there is interesting, and even moving, I do not think it is adequate to show how moral heroism, and even self-sacrifice, can be fitted into her naturalistic schema.
[35] Which is part of what Nietzsche meant by contrasting the value polarities 'good and bad' and 'good and evil' (although Nietzsche is not really a consistent ethical naturalist either).
[36] Lannstrom, *Loving the Fine*, 99.
[37] For more detailed arguments against that project, see McPherson, *Virtue and Meaning*; see also the discussion of Foot and Hursthouse in Rudd, *Self, Value and Narrative*, 117–25.

116   THE PHILOSOPHY OF CAMUS

III Back to the Greeks: A Metaphysics of Limit

In this section, while continuing the argument about what metaphysical backdrop is necessary for an ethics based on an appeal to 'human nature', I will also address the second Kierkegaardian worry that I raised at the end of the last chapter, about whether an entirely non-religious outlook can meet deep human needs. I have already noted Camus's conviction that there is an order of objective value to be found in the non-human world, one that is expressed most immediately to us in the beauty of nature. This is something beyond the merely ethical, although—as we saw in 'Return to Tipasa'—it needs to be recognized to prevent the ethical from collapsing into either fanaticism or despair. There Camus had said that justice needs to draw on something beyond itself in order to keep from shrivelling up. A few years earlier, in 'Helen's Exile', he had put it rather differently, by suggesting that proper human justice is an aspect or reflection of a wider cosmic justice, a principle of balance, order and limit:

> At the dawn of Greek though, Heraclitus had already conceived justice as setting bonds to the physical universe itself. 'The sun will not go beyond its bounds, for otherwise the Furies which watch over justice will find it out.' We, who have cast both the universe and the mind from their proper orbit, laugh at such threats. We light up in a drunken sky what suns we please. But the bounds nevertheless exist, and we know it.[38]

By setting aside these bounds, turning away from nature and beauty, we have turned justice from a recognition of proper limits into something that aspires to be absolute and that therefore becomes destructive. 'Equity for them [the Greeks] supposed a limit, while our whole continent is convulsed by a justice which it sees as absolute.'[39] But the fight for true justice, as distinct from its fanaticized simulacra, is based on a concern for recognizing and respecting proper limits, and as such it is not really distinct from the passion for true beauty (harmony, proportion).[40] 'All those who are fighting today for liberty are in the final analysis fighting for beauty.'[41] Here, as also in 'Return to Tipasa', as we have seen, the truly ethical and aesthetic are aligned, and are both expressions of something that is more basic still; the fundamental principle of limit and order that Heraclitus called *Logos* and saw as pervading the universe.

Hubris brings nemesis, Camus asserts: 'Our Europe ... eager for the conquest of totality, is the daughter of excess ... In its madness it pushes back the eternal

---

[38] Camus, 'Helen's Exile', in *SEN* 136–7 (*LCE* 149).
[39] Camus, 'Helen's Exile', in *SEN* 136 (*LCE* 149).
[40] As distinct, perhaps, from certain merely glib or flashy simulacra.
[41] Camus, 'Helen's Exile', in *SEN* 139 (*LCE* 151). For Camus, of course, true liberty involves and includes justice (and *vice versa*).

limits and at once dark Furies swoop down upon it to destroy. Nemesis is watching, goddess of moderation, not of vengeance. All those who go beyond the limit are by her pitilessly chastised.'[42] The danger of a self-deifying hubris is, as we have seen, a major theme of *The Rebel*. And Nemesis was, of course, to have been the theme of the third of Camus's cycles. But one cannot think in terms of hubris and nemesis without thinking teleologically. Hubris involves going beyond one's proper limits, stepping outside one's proper place in the world. But this presupposes that there is such a proper place, a right way for humans to live in relation to one another and to the rest of the world.[43] It is our *telos* (goal) properly to occupy that place and live that way. It is our *goal*, not just something that happens naturally and spontaneously, because we have the capacities for transcendence, which enable us to choose to go beyond our limits. And it has to be emphasized that those capacities are not just a threat to order and harmony; they are themselves essential aspects of human nature, so the properly human life has to be one that involves them. So keeping to our proper place cannot, for a human, simply involve unconsciously filling an ecological niche, since the life that is proper for a human includes rational deliberation. That a human may, as Camus says, 'refuse to be what he is' may, as he also worries, 'lead to the destruction of himself and others' (*R.* 11); if it is not to do that, our capacities for transcendence need themselves to recognize both their proper sphere and their necessary limits.

One might try to 'naturalize' this talk of hubris and nemesis by reducing it to historical or natural causality. A conqueror, such as Napoleon or Hitler, by refusing to limit his aggression, may unite so many enemies against him as to bring about his own downfall. Or, unrestrained human production or consumption will lead to climate change, with devastating consequences for human beings. Here the warning against hubris becomes an essentially prudential one. But, even from the fragmentary evidence that we have, Camus clearly intended more than that. For him, the issue is a fundamentally normative one. We *do wrong* to overstep our proper limits; doing so is an act of arrogance, and there is something fitting and deserved about the nemesis we thus bring on ourselves. When he speaks of Nemesis watching and chastising, he is, of course, speaking imagistically—he is not thinking of nemesis operating through conscious supernatural providence. But I do not think the imagery is just a literary flourish. Nemesis operates though natural and historical causality. But what is expressed in its operations is a basic normative order in the world, and in our own nature, which is not something that we can or should simply shape according to our own (individual or collective) will.

These ideas about limit and balance, hubris and nemesis, are strikingly similar to those of another passionate Hellenophile among Camus's contemporaries—

---

[42] Camus, 'Helen's Exile', in *SEN* 136 (*LCE* 148–9).
[43] For a contemporary argument for the importance of respecting such limits on our willing and desiring, see McPherson, *The Virtues of Limits*.

118   THE PHILOSOPHY OF CAMUS

Simone Weil. Camus, as an editor at the Gallimard publishing house, was responsible for the posthumous publication of many of Weil's writings, and he very much admired her, describing her as 'the only great mind of our times'.[44] In her remarkable essay on the *Iliad*,[45] Weil claims that 'force' is the real protagonist of the poem, a sort of autonomous power that the rulers and warriors of the epic think they can deploy for their own purposes, but that will, sooner or later, turn and crush them. But, she suggests, this is not just a way of talking about the grim folly of war, but expresses a deep metaphysical truth:

> retribution, which has a geometrical rigour, which operates automatically to penalize the misuse of force, was the main subject of Greek thought. It is the soul of the epic. Under the name of Nemesis, it is the mainspring of Aeschylus' tragedies. To the Pythagoreans, to Socrates and Plato, it was the jumping-off point of speculation on the nature of man and the universe.[46]

However, the modern West 'no longer even has a word to express it in any of its languages: conceptions of limit, measure, equilibrium, which ought to determine the conduct of life, are, in the West, restricted to a servile function in the vocabulary of technics'.[47] This, perhaps, is not entirely true; in any case, I think we can see Camus as aiming, in his use of terms such as 'limit' and 'moderation', to restore this vocabulary, so as to make it express something of that same Greek sense with which Weil was concerned. But, as I noted at the end of the last chapter, he was well aware that terms like 'moderation' would be misunderstood; taken to connote weakness or woolly-mindedness, rather than a summons to a demanding ethical task. Weil, it should be stressed, was aware that human life is not possible without the exercise of force in some sense; what is needed is not to abandon it for a state of pure passivity—the kind of high-minded, ineffectual idealism of which Camus was often unfairly accused. But, Weil notes, 'a moderate use of force, which alone would enable man to avoid being enmeshed in its machinery, would require superhuman virtue'.[48] As Camus also emphasized, the effort to retain balance, to respect limits, is hard; it is much easier to abandon oneself to force and let it carry one blindly to an extreme (*R*. 301). Or, perhaps, to try and stand back from the whole realm of force and adopt an attitude of quietism (the attitude of the yogi, as contrasted with the commissar). But, as Weil notes, the attempt to escape the world of force still leads one to become emmeshed in it; it is the lucidly attentive

---

[44] See Dunaway, 'Estrangement and the Need for Roots', 35.
[45] Weil, 'The *Iliad*'. This was one of the few works that Weil did publish in her lifetime (1941); it was republished in a collection edited by Camus, *La Source grecque*, in 1953.
[46] Weil, 'The *Iliad*', 195.
[47] Weil, 'The *Iliad*', 195.
[48] Weil, 'The *Iliad*', 199.

engagement with the world of power and action that enables one to avoid being controlled by it.

Whatever influence Weil may have had on Camus's thinking, the idea of limit and its importance for ancient Greek thought had been on his mind long before he encountered her writings. In his dissertation, *Christian Metaphysics and Neoplatonism*, he discusses the principle of Horus (Limit). In the Gnostic system of Valentinus, the *archon* Sophia foolishly creates the world as a formless mass. 'But God took pity on her and again created a special principle, the principle of Horus or limit. Limit, coming to the aid of Sophia, will restore her to her original nature and cast the world out of the pleroma, thus reestablishing the original harmony.'[49] A little later he observes that Horus is a specifically Greek, rather than a Christian or 'Oriental' element in the Gnostic synthesis (or agglomeration) of ideas: 'Greece introduced the notions of harmony and order into morality as into aesthetics. If Prometheus has suffered, it is because he has cast off his human nature. Sophia acted likewise, and it is by returning to the place which she was assigned that she once again finds peace.'[50] Again, we see the idea of limit as fundamental to both ethics and aesthetics and thus as establishing a connection between them. But the idea is also (as it was for Weil) a crucial metaphysical and epistemological—as well as a religious—one. In Valentinius' system, Limit is what gives the world whatever intelligibility and, in a sense, whatever being it may have, as well as whatever beauty. Christianity, Camus goes on to remark, broke up this synthesis:

> For the Christian who separates Reason and Beauty, the Truth of Beauty, Reason is reduced to its role of logical legislator. And thus conflicts between Faith and Reason become possible. For a Greek, these conflicts are less acute, because Beauty, which is both order and sensitivity, economy and the object of passion, remains a ground of agreement.[51]

In the Platonic tradition, the Good, the Beautiful, and the True go together—as does Reason, the faculty in us which aligns us with truth. And Camus takes this to license the thought that reason may proceed artistically, as a search for significant form, and that philosophical truth may be appropriately expressed in images. At least, he interprets Plotinus in these terms: 'To a certain extent, Plotinian Reason is already the "heart" of Pascal. Plotinus' philosophy is an artists' point of view. If things are explained, it is because the things are beautiful.'[52] A little later he comments: 'In this dialogue between the heart and Reason, truth can only be expressed through images.'[53] I noted in the Introduction Camus's concern to philosophize

[49] *CMN* 78.
[50] *CMN* 83.
[51] *CMN* 91.
[52] *CMN* 90.
[53] *CMN* 111.

120   THE PHILOSOPHY OF CAMUS

imagistically; it is fascinating to see here, at the start of his intellectual career, how this concern, which found expression in his whole life's work, began in his meditations on Greek and especially Neoplatonic thinking. It is certainly worth considering whether the literary flavour of his philosophizing expresses not—as is still often assumed—a lack of intellectual rigour, but a conscious choice based on certain philosophical commitments that he had derived from his study of Greek philosophy.

In this dissertation, Camus is concerned with exegesis rather than presenting his own substantive ideas. But his work there seems to have served as a foundation for many of his subsequent invocations of Greek thinking, in which he does clearly reveal his own views. In a significant *Notebook* entry from 1951, Camus admonishes himself: 'Go back to the passage from Hellenism to Christianity, the true and only turning point in history.' He adds: 'Essay on fate (Nemesis?).'[54] It is interesting that he uses the term 'fate' for the projected third cycle essay, while only tentatively suggesting 'Nemesis' (which, as we have seen, he generally uses elsewhere). But this is a very helpful indication of where his thought was heading. In talking of 'going back' to the theme of the transition from Hellenism to Christianity, he is clearly referring to his dissertation, which is precisely about that transition. But presumably his intention was to return to the material he had studied in this academic, exegetical exercise—early Christianity, Gnosticism, Plotinus, and St Augustine—in order to make an argument about its contemporary relevance. The basic direction that the argument would have taken is made clear from a number of remarks, such as the following: 'If, to outgrow nihilism, one must return to Christianity, one may well follow the impulse and outgrow Christianity in Hellenism.'[55] 'I feel closer to the values of the classical world than to those of Christianity. Unfortunately, I cannot go to Delphi to be initiated!'[56] He mentions again a theme that had already been important in *The Rebel* as one he wants to return to: 'Nemesis. Profound complicity of Marxism and Christianity (to develop). This is why I am against both.'[57] A little later he suggests a rather different emphasis: 'The world moves towards paganism, but it still rejects pagan values. They must be restored, to paganize belief, Graecize Christ and restore balance.'[58] Is he suggesting that Christianity, rather than being discarded, should itself be Graecized? Or that a suitably Graecized Christ can be rescued from Christianity? Camus does have a positive view of Jesus: 'I have a great deal of admiration for the first Christian. I admire the way he lived, the way he died. My lack of imagination keeps me from following him any further.'[59] A good deal of modern theology has

[54] *NB* II, 267.
[55] *NB* II, 183.
[56] 'Encounter with Albert Camus' (1951), from 'Three Interviews' (*LCE* 357).
[57] *NB III*, 192.
[58] *NB III*, 203.
[59] Camus, 'On Faulkner: Excerpts from Three Interviews', in *LCE* 320.

played off the supposedly Greek, metaphysical idea of Christ as the incarnation of the pre-existent Logos against the supposedly more Hebraic, biblical idea of Jesus as prophet, to the latter's favour. But there can be little doubt that, whatever Camus might have meant by 'Greacizing' Christ, this would not have involved retreating from the concrete human sphere to a metaphysical realm; on the contrary, the result would surely have been a very human figure.[60]

In any case, a schematic view of Western history becomes apparent in these remarks.[61] Modernity tends towards nihilism (there are no values, except those we choose to project or impose) or Marxism. But Marxism is an offshoot of Christianity, inheriting the historicism that Christianity had itself taken over from Judaism, but had somewhat softened, owing to the Greek influence on it.[62] By abandoning that softening, and embracing uncompromising historicism, Marxism itself becomes a thinly disguised nihilism, according to which values come to be in the course of a deterministic historical process. For Camus, what is needed now is not to abandon modernity (how would we even start to do that?) but to combat its nihilistic tendencies by looking back behind Christianity to Greek wisdom.[63] (As I will suggest below, it would be too simple to identify Camus *wholly* with this agenda, but it does represents the central trajectory of his later thought.)

Camus considers the attitude that he wants to promote to be not just Greek, but, more broadly, characteristically 'Mediterranean'. In *The Rebel* he writes:

The profound conflict of this century is perhaps not so much between the German ideologies of history and Christian political concepts, which in a certain way

---

[60] Weil would very likely have been relevant here. In the *Iliad* essay she claims that 'the Gospels are the last marvellous expression of the Greek spirit, as the Iliad is the first' (Weil, 'The *Iliad*', 212). Distaining both Roman and Hebrew civilizations as based on the belief that might makes right, she wanted to rescue the 'Greek' spirit of Christianity from what she saw as the Hebraic–Roman distortion of it that had largely prevailed in the history of the Church. However, she did come to believe in Christ as the incarnation of God, while Camus, as we have seen, drily noted that he 'lacked the imagination' to do more than admire the human life of Jesus.

[61] Although he focuses on the dialectic between Greek, Christian, and Modern thinking in the West, Camus is not without awareness of, or interest in, non-Western traditions. Apparently, he had once contemplated writing his dissertation on Hindu thought, on which his mentor, Jean Grenier, was an authority (see Todd, *Camus*, 43). And a very interesting 1957 entry in his *Notebooks* runs: 'Buddhism is atheism that became religious. Renaissance *originating from* nihilism. Unique example, I believe, and priceless to reflect on for us who are wrestling with nihilism' (*NB III*, 189). Whether he would have made more of this thought in his Nemesis essay, we cannot of course know.

[62] In his dissertation, Camus claims that 'the philosophy of history, a notion foreign to the Greek spirit, is a Jewish invention. Metaphysical problems are incarnated in time ...' (*CMN* 52). Later, in 'Helen's Exile', he sees Christianity as standing between this Hebraic historicism and the Greek notion of an eternal order. He does not, however, suggest that this is a stable synthesis, or, at least, one that is recoverable for us now. 'Christianity at least referred to a spiritual nature, and consequently maintained a certain fixity. Now that God is dead, all that remains is history and power' ('Helen's Exile', in *SEN* 138 (*LCE* 150)).

[63] Camus is quite clear that learning from ancient Greek wisdom cannot be a matter of antiquarian reconstruction: 'We cannot go back ... to Greek temples. When we speak about Hellenism, I do not think any of us wants to create an agora where we would stroll about in short tunics' ('The Future of European Civilization', in *SO* 161).

122   THE PHILOSOPHY OF CAMUS

are accomplices, as between German dreams and Mediterranean traditions ... in other words, between history and nature ... historical absolutism has never ceased to come into collision with an irrepressible demand of human nature, of which the Mediterranean, where intelligence is intimately related to the blinding light of the sun, guards the secret. (R. 299, 300)[64]

It is easy enough to criticize this system of stark dualisms—Greek/Modern, Mediterranean/German, nature/history, sun/darkness. The Roman Empire, which Camus loathed, was an essentially Mediterranean operation, with only some outlying provinces in northern Europe; in his own time, Italy was the home of Fascism, and right-wing nationalism was at least as characteristic of, and powerful in, Spain, and France too, as 'libertarian socialism' was. One might also note that he has almost nothing to say about the role of Islam or the Arabs in his 'Mediterranean' world view,[65] and that the enormous importance of Christianity in the Mediterranean world makes his wish to align it with 'German Ideology' and against the Mediterranean a bit implausible. But the problem with such criticism, in a way, is precisely that it is *too* easy; it is, after all, hardly as if Camus was unaware of all these things, or all the many others that would complicate his stark contrasts. What he is presenting is not really intended as a historical thesis; it is exactly an example of what he called his 'thinking in images'. 'The Mediterranean' being invoked here is not so much an empirical historical reality, but a kind of symbolic geography; a sort of semi-poetic image in which his perception of (aspects of) ancient Greek thought and cultural sensibility blend with his own deeply felt personal experience of growing up in Algeria, in a space marked by sharp, intense contrasts of sunlight, sea, mountains, desert. It is a world of hash beauty, unconsoling and even tragic, but free from illusions and self-deception:

The Mediterranean has its sunlit tragedy which is not that of the mists. On certain evenings, on the sea, at the foot of the mountains, night falls on the perfect curve of a little bay, and an anguished fulness arises from the silent waters. We realise in such places that, if the Greeks experienced despair, it was always through beauty and its oppressive quality ... Our own time, by contrast, has nourished its despair in ugliness and in convulsions. That is why Europe would be ignoble, if grief could ever have this quality.[66]

---

[64] See also his youthful and, it does have to be said, rather naive essay, 'The New Mediterranean Culture', in LCE. In *The Rebel* he does rather uncomfortably add to the passage just quoted, 'Naturally it is not a question of despising anything, or of exalting one civilization at the expense of another ...' (R. 300), even though he does seem to have been doing precisely that!

[65] A point that has, naturally enough, been noted by his 'postcolonial' critics.

[66] Camus, 'Helen's Exile', in SEN 136 (LCE 148).

In Camus's symbolic geography, even European (as opposed to Mediterranean) cities as beautiful as Prague and Amsterdam appear sinister, disorienting.[67] In *The Outsider*, Meursault, in Algiers, does not lie to himself (and only occasionally does so to others); in *The Fall*, Clamence, in Amsterdam, does nothing (perhaps) but lie.

These symbolic geographies are intensely personal, but they can be communicated to, and move, even those who do not have the same particular experience of or deep love of the place, the climate, or the landscape in question; their symbolic weight can be felt and appreciated even by those who cannot inhabit those forms of sensibility directly.[68] There is, I think, something admirable about Camus's willingness to accept vulnerability by attempting to express a political outlook that is supposed to be universal in terms that were so meaningful to him, but also so personal. But his doing so did, I fear, seduce him into some oversimple rhetoric that tended to divert attention from his serious points, and that sets up some distracting dissonances. One could, for instance, point out that, historically, parliamentarianism and religious and political toleration have tended to flourish more in northern Europe—in Britain, the Netherlands, and Scandinavia—than around the Mediterranean. (Perhaps fogs and the blurring of sharp outlines are more suited to a politics of compromise, to the avoidance of fanaticism?[69]) But Camus is struggling to connect his personal sense of place with his politics and ethics. And one connection, even for those who do not share his intense feeling for that particular environment, is simply that it *is* particular and personal. The very feeling for a particular place, with its climate, its landscape, with the constraints they place on human life and the opportunities they afford, is itself a form of resistance to the homogenizing pressure of grand totalizing schemes.[70]

IV Beyond Disenchantment: 'A Sense of the Sacred'

Can we say a little more about these key notions of limit, moderation, and balance and the role they played in Camus's later thinking? In *The Rebel*, as I discussed

---

[67] See his account of his own experiences in Prague in 'Iron in the Soul' (*SEN* 47-56 (*LCE* 40–51)) and the thinly fictionalized version of them in *A Happy Death*, pt two, ch. 1; and the role Amsterdam plays in *The Fall*.

[68] One might compare Camus's sense of the 'Mediterranean' essence with a very different writer's very different symbolic geography: C. S. Lewis's, 'Northerness': 'A vision of huge, clear spaces hanging above the Atlantic in the endless twilight of Northern summer, remoteness, severity ...' (Lewis, *Surprised by Joy*, 73), which Lewis connected with Norse mythology and the Norse sagas.

[69] A notion hauntingly explored in Kazuo Ishiguro's novel *The Buried Giant*, set in Dark Ages Britain.

[70] Madeline Bunting speaks of 'the placelessness which capitalism requires in order to ensure that the flows of capital, people and resources can be ordered to achieve economic efficiency. Local belonging, which impedes or slows down those flows, has to be undermined and eventually eliminated. The dystopian endpoint is that everywhere becomes a sort of anywhere, all distinctive characteristics erased. Metropolitan elites who determine cultural status subject the local and the parochial to dismissive contempt ...' (Bunting, *Love of Country*, 250).

124   THE PHILOSOPHY OF CAMUS

in the previous chapter, he showed their political relevance, and also developed a strikingly Kierkegaardian account of the need to balance properly the transcendent and immanent aspects of our being in order to navigate between the extremes of radical self-creation, and the abandonment of the self to impersonal forces (whether of biology or of history). Towards the end of the book, though, he makes some brief remarks about balance or limit as a basic metaphysical and epistemological principle, and indeed introduces the figure of 'Nemesis, the goddess of moderation and the implacable enemy of the immoderate' (R. 296) as symbolizing limit in this sense. Epistemologically, Camus still holds in a way to the maxim 'truths but no Truth'. He now cites Jaspers on 'the impossibility of man's grasping totality, since he lives in the midst of this totality' (R. 289). Applying this thought to the philosophy of history, he continues: 'history, as an entirety, could only exist in the eyes of an observer outside it and outside the world. History only exists, in the final analysis, for God' (R. 289). The thought here is very similar to Kierkegaard's (Climacus') claim, cited back in Chapter 1, that reality is a system for God, but cannot be apprehended as such by finite minds who are immersed in the reality they are trying to understand. (Jaspers was deeply influenced by Kierkegaard.[71]) Of course, Camus means the point hypothetically; if totality could be grasped, it could only be by God. Metaphysically, this would still seem at least to leave open the possibility that 'totality' exists, even if there is no God and therefore no one at all who can grasp it. For Jaspers, the idea of the world as a whole is a necessary limit-concept, one that is unavoidably presupposed in our thinking, even if we can never actually understand the world as a whole.[72] And Camus seems to be following him in this: by insisting that we cannot grasp the totality because we exist within it, Camus seems to be presupposing that the 'totality' is real, although it eludes our grasp. (In this he distinguishes himself from radical idealists or antirealists who take the idea of a reality in principle beyond our capacity to know it to be empty or meaningless.)

The principle of moderation or balance leads Camus to reject the 'absolute rationalism', which supposes that it can grasp reality completely, as a system, while insisting that this should not lead us to abandon a more modest rationalism—the conviction that we can obtain genuine, even if limited and relative, knowledge of the world around us by careful thinking and observation (R. 289 n.). With an admittedly vague reference to modern physics, he argues that science itself is reconizing its own inability to occupy an absolute point of view, so that 'our real knowledge ... only justifies a system of thought based on relative discoveries' (R. 295). He wants to reject scientism, without denying that science really can tell us truths about the world, without writing it off as merely ideology or social construction. But nor does he simply reject metaphysics, although for him

---

[71] See Czako, 'Karl Jaspers'.
[72] See Jaspers, *Philosophy*, i. 120–45.

legitimate metaphysics would have to be a considerably more modest enterprise than that of 'absolute rationalists' such as Spinoza or Hegel.[73] Camus does make some brief metaphysical claims of his own, again intended to illustrate the principle of balance. Being, for instance, can be thought of neither simply as essence, nor simply as existence (*R*. 296). Although he probably deploys this terminology to contrast his thinking with Sartre's, his point seems to be that we should reject both radical Platonism and nominalism. 'Essence' cannot exist in a separate transcendent realm—'where could one perceive essence except in the realm of existence and evolution?'—but that 'realm of existence' itself is not merely a chaos of sheer particularity and change, but is governed by 'essential' principles of order.

As in 'Helen's Exile', Camus invokes Heraclitus, 'the discoverer of the constant change of things', who also held that a limit was set to these changes by the underlying order (*logos*) by which they were governed. 'Being can only prove itself in development and development is nothing without being. The world is not in a condition of pure stability, nor is it only movement. It is both movement and stability' (*R*. 296). While taking a transcendent realm of pure essence to be both unknowable and unnecessary to postulate, he does now seem confident enough that there is an immanent order in things, of which we can have at least some knowledge; he thus abandons the (epistemological, if not necessarily ontological) nominalism of *The Myth*. This order is not something we can grasp fully or absolutely, but aspects of it become manifest to us in scientific enquiry (which necessarily postulates some rational order in what it investigates, this postulation being justified by the success of science in finding such order); in morality, where I find the humanity present in all of us setting limits to how I can legitimately treat others; and in the experience of both natural and artistic beauty.

In all these cases, what I experience is a constraint, something that places a limit on my willing or my fantasies; a sense of an independent reality, but one that is not simply a brute facticity against which I may have to bang my head, but something that requires respect and acknowledgement. The scientist, though an active enquirer who needs to ask the right questions, is seeking to explore the contours of a world that has its own independent form and coherence. The Camusian Rebel is someone who recognizes that the reality of others places limits on his or her freedom simply to do as he or she pleases (*R*. 284). And artists know that, however original, however creative, they may be, they are nonetheless constrained by the demands of proper form, that not everything goes, that the developing work itself makes demands on the artist for how it should be continued.[74] In all

---

[73] In this again I think he is close to Kierkegaard; see Evans, 'Realism and Anti-Realism', which defends the idea of Kierkegaard as a 'modest' metaphysician against the view of him as a wholly anti- or 'post'-metaphysical thinker.

[74] There may be many kinds of 'proper form' of course—but even an artwork intended to subvert some traditional notion of form will generate its own formal demands; that sort of subversion cannot be done just anyhow.

126   THE PHILOSOPHY OF CAMUS

these spheres—we might say, those of the True, the Good, and the Beautiful—we encounter a reality that does not allow us simply to do as we please. But this reality is not the stubborn, unreasonable surd that we, with our hunger for intelligibility and meaning, ran up against in *The Myth*. It is a normative reality, which, properly, we *should* welcome.

But can such a Neo-Hellenic vision of a normative cosmic order really be credible in a world that has been 'disenchanted', in Weber's famous phrase, by the rise of modern science? Does not science show us that the world is purposeless and valueless, a matter of brute contingent fact, operating according to blind mechanistic laws? Sharpe, following James Goss, considers this objection and a related one, according to which Camus himself is inconsistent, because he is committed to both the modern scientific picture of the world *and* the Neo-Hellenic normative cosmos, which are contradictory.[75] According to Sharpe, any charitable reading must 'assume that Camus thought that his acceptance of something like the modern scientific worldview was in no way truly inconsistent with a contemplative, normatively orienting sense of natural order and beauty that might answer the modern West's cultural angst'.[76] If we can show that Camus was *right* to think this, then we can answer the first objection as well as the second. Sharpe is correct to point out that Camus, being neither an irrationalist nor a radical social constructivist, accepted at face value the results of modern natural science.[77] But I do not think Camus would have been happy with talk about 'the modern scientific worldview'. Perhaps Sharpe is just using the term as a shorthand for the accepted results of science. But 'worldview' suggests a comprehensive, systematic philosophy, and Camus, as we have seen, precisely denies that science can give us any such thing. It can give us truths within its own particular fields, but not The Truth. Not only are there truths of human motivation and feeling that are not reducible to any scientific (for example, neurological) understanding; there are also truths about the natural world, such as those Camus encountered at Tipasa, that are irreducible to the truths of the natural sciences, though they do not contradict them.

Camus accepts science but rejects scientism, the attempt to build a comprehensive 'worldview' out of the results of the natural sciences alone. Modern science is a way of looking at the world that considers only its quantifiable and measurable aspects, and sets aside any questions of purpose, meaning, value. But it does not follow that those aspects of reality as we experience it are unreal, simply because our apprehension of them is non-scientific. The world as considered by science is an abstraction from a richer, broader reality, although what it thus considers in abstraction is (*pace* the social constructivists) perfectly real. And, as Sharpe rightly points out, even the abstract scientific world is a rational, ordered one.[78] Indeed, in

[75] See Sharpe, *Camus, Philosophe*, 308–17; Goss, 'Camus, God, and Process Thought', 114–28.
[76] Sharpe, *Camus, Philosophe*, 310.
[77] Sharpe, *Camus, Philosophe*, 312–13.
[78] See Sharpe, *Camus, Philosophe*, 312–13.

its own austere way, it is a beautiful one, and many scientists have testified to their awe at the mathematical beauty of the laws of nature. 'Disenchanted' naturalism—the vision of a meaningless, value-free world—is not itself a deliverance of science; it is a metaphysical theory, and one can consistently reject it, while continuing to accept the results of scientific investigations.

Goss, while himself rejecting the disenchanted world view (and indeed doing so more radically than Sharpe does), thinks Camus is still guilty of self-contradiction, arguing that, despite his attraction to a Neo-Hellenic vision of normative order, *The Myth of Sisyphus* shows that he is also committed to a kind of Cartesian dualism, one that sees the physical world as merely inert, alien, and unresponsive to the human need to feel at home in the world.[79] But, although I think this is largely true of *The Myth*, that book is not typical, in this respect, of Camus's work generally. Its bleak vision of the natural world is very different from the outlook of both the 'Lyrical Essays' that preceded it, and the explicitly Neo-Hellenic works that followed it. Even in *The Myth*, the basic love of life that (rather than any logical argument) keeps 'the absurd man' from suicide, can be seen as an instinctive affirmation that life is *worth* living. It has a value we must recognize, even if it does not satisfy our desire for intellectual 'clarity'. In any case, as I have argued, the Absurdism of *The Myth* is best understood as a thought-experiment that may never have completely represented Camus's own considered opinion; and, if he ever did hold it for himself, he had definitely rejected it by the time he wrote 'Helen's Exile' in 1948.

As we have seen, in 'Return to Tipasa' Camus speaks of love in connection with both justice and the beauty of the world. Simone Weil once wrote: 'The mind is not forced to believe in the existence of anything (subjectivism, absolute idealism, solipsism, skepticism ...). That is why the only organ of contact with existence is acceptance, love.'[80] The Camus of *The Myth* would have disagreed; we encounter reality, as distinct from our fantasized projections on to it, when we encounter it as alien, as frustrating our longings. But in his post-Absurdist thinking he seems to have become more open to the idea of love as a positive recognition and acknowledgement of the reality of what we need to relate to in order really to be ourselves. As Iris Murdoch, another philosopher (and novelist) much influenced by Weil, put it: 'Love is the extremely difficult realization that something other than

---

[79] Goss suggests that Camus should have resolved this contradiction by abandoning his quasi-Cartesianism and embracing some richer metaphysical account of non-human nature—his own preference being for a version of Whitehead's process philosophy. Although Whitehead's philosophy is one good example of a thoroughly non-disenchanted metaphysics that is nonetheless consistent with (and indeed partly inspired by) modern science, I think Camus was far too sceptical to have had much interest in following metaphysical speculations along Whitehead's lines. His own positive or 'enchanted' vision of nature remained phenomenological—that is, grounded in common human experience of the natural world.

[80] Weil, *Gravity and Grace*, 56–7.

128   THE PHILOSOPHY OF CAMUS

oneself is real. Love, and so art and morals, is the discovery of reality.'[81] Perhaps it is moving too fast to assimilate Camus's thought too closely to Weil's or Murdoch's at this point. Certainly, doing so would involve some extrapolation from the very brief and undeveloped metaphysical comments in *The Rebel*. But those comments are of interest mainly because they do at least give a clue to what his projected later essay on Nemesis might have said. And we know that he did connect the themes of Nemesis and love: 'the third stage is love: The First Man, Don Faust, the Myth of Nemesis.'[82] And this might seem puzzling; for, although Camus insists, as we have seen, that Nemesis is the goddess of moderation, not of vengeance, he also describes her operations as 'pitiless'.[83] But genuine love—as opposed to possessive or infatuated desire—recognizes and delights in the independent reality of the beloved, and the limits which that reality sets for oneself. Nemesis, we might say, is what comes on those who overstep the limits set by love. Had Camus lived to write it, I think the connection between love and the proper perception of reality might well have been central to the projected *Myth of Nemesis*.

It is certainly true that Camus recognized both ethics and art as having a metaphysical significance. In moral and aesthetic experience we are not just projecting or expressing subjective feelings; they are, rather, ways in which we come into contact with reality. (Similarly, I think, with scientific experience, though that was obviously of less interest to Camus personally.[84]) And, for all his scepticism about systematic metaphysics, I do not think Camus distained the desire to connect all these forms of experience, or to follow them back to an ultimate source. (The *logos* from which both beauty and justice derive, as I tentatively suggested above.) I quoted at the end of the previous chapter a passage from *The Rebel* where, in a political context, he mentions that 'the absolute is not attained, nor, above all, created, through history. Politics is not religion.' But, although this quest cannot be political, 'perhaps everyone is looking for this absolute on behalf of all' (*R*. 302). The desire for the absolute may be an ineradicable part of our being human—a thought that is also perhaps expressed in a striking passage from *The First Man*, the autobiographical novel (and the first work in the projected Nemesis cycle) on which Camus was working when he died. Describing his thinly fictionalized alter ego, Jacques Cormery, Camus writes:

> All that was left was this anguished heart, eager to live, rebelling against the deadly order of the world that had been with him for forty years, and still struggling against the wall that separated him from the secret of all life, wanting to go further,

---

[81] Murdoch, 'The Sublime and the Good', 215.
[82] *NB III*, 72.
[83] Camus, 'Helen's Exile,' in *SEN* 136 (*LCE* 149).
[84] Weil certainly saw science—and intellectual disciplines generally—in that light. See her 'Reflections on the Right Use of School Studies'.

to go beyond and to discover, discover before dying, discover at last in order to be, just once to be, for a single second but for ever.

He looked back on his life, a life that had been foolish, courageous, cowardly, willful, and always straining towards that goal which he knew nothing about.[85]

This concern for the 'secret of all life', for the 'absolute', Camus recognizes as, broadly speaking, religious. (That is the point of declaring it out of bounds to politics, on the basis that 'politics is not religion'.) And, although Camus's Neo-Hellenic outlook clearly refuses the Christian terminus of Kierkegaard's thought, it does not follow that it is not itself in some sense a religious view, or that it has no interesting parallels to Kierkegaard's religious stage. Camus himself was sometimes willing to use explicitly religious language to describe his own outlook. Back in Chapter 1 I quoted his 1942 remark: 'Secret of my universe; believing in God without human immortality.'[86] I think the 'God' in question here is the God sensed in the beauty and mystery of the world; but Camus is refusing the personal consolations of religion, the idea that there is a God who cares about individuals. Here he rejects the idea of a God who provides us with eternal life beyond this world; *The Rebel*, with its passionate concern for the suffering of the innocent, and its critique of the idea of a providence (divine or secularized) working itself out in history, also rejects the idea of a personally caring God operating *in* this world. In a 1956 remark, which I quoted at the end of the previous chapter, but which will also stand requoting, he stated: 'I don't believe in God, that's true. But I am not an atheist, nonetheless ... there is something vulgar ... yes ... worn out about being against religion.'[87] This might seem to be a statement of agnosticism—a refusal to choose between theism and atheism. That is certainly part of it. But I think it involves something more personal or existential than just an intellectual scepticism about the issue. Asked in 1959 to comment on his earlier statement about believing in God, but not in immortality, he replied simply: 'Yes. I have a sense of the sacred and I don't believe in a future life, that's all.'[88] If believing in God is equivalent to having a sense of the sacred, then that is compatible with not believing in the God of Christian theism (which is presumably why he was willing to say in different contexts both that he did and that he did not believe in God). But I think he refuses the label of atheism, not just because of a sceptical discomfort with affirming even negative positions, but in order positively to affirm this 'sense of the sacred'.

What does he mean by that, though? I think he is clearly referring here to the 'something beyond' mentioned in 'Return to Tipasa'—the basic cosmic order of 'Helen's Exile'. The sacred for him is primarily experienced in and through the

[85] *FM* 21.
[86] *NB II*, 12.
[87] Camus, 'On Faulkner: Excerpts from Three Interviews', in *LCE* 320. The second and third ellipses appear in the text of the interview.
[88] Camus, 'Replies to Jean-Claude Brisville' (1959), in *LCE* 364.

130   THE PHILOSOPHY OF CAMUS

beauty of nature. I quoted back in Chapter 1 from his early lyrical essay, 'Nuptials at Tipasa'. The essay begins: 'In spring, Tipasa is inhabited by gods and the gods speak in the sun and the scent of absinthe leaves, the silver-armoured sea, the blue glare of the sky, the flower-covered ruins and the light in great bubbles among the heaps of stone.'[89] The erotic imagery already present in the title runs throughout the essay; love is consummated, not only between Camus and the world around him, but between elements of that world—nature and the sea, the ruins and spring-time.[90] Although he says at one point: 'I leave others to concern themselves with order and moderation'[91]—terms that would become more positive for him later—he is finding an order—a proper way of being—in the world at Tipasa, an order in which he can feel deeply at home: 'It is not so easy to become what we are, to rediscover our deepest measure. But ... I was learning to breathe, I was fitting into the world and fulfilling myself.'[92] In doing so, in experiencing the deep joy at his 'nuptial' harmony with nature, he feels 'I had played my part well. I had performed my task as a man.'[93] I think, then, as James Woelfel puts it,

> It is not saying too much ... to describe the Camus of *Nuptials* as almost a nature-mystic. He experiences his profound feeling for that natural environment which is the vast, seemingly changeless context of all our human strivings in terms that are familiar from the vocabulary of the Western mystic—erotic love, experienced grace, ineffable union.[94]

One needs to be careful, of course. Having invoked the gods at the start of the 'Nuptials' essay, Camus goes on to suggest that they are dispensible images: 'Those who need myths are indeed poor ... what need have I to speak of Dionysus to say that I love to crush mastic bowls under my nose?'[95] But the sense of the sacred is there, whether or not one uses specific cultural images to invoke it; and, indeed, Camus refers again to the gods in the penultimate paragraph of the essay. This pantheistic spirituality is experienced with deep joy and fulfilment in 'Nuptials at Tipasa', but, if it is a religion, it is one that offers no consolation, and the young Camus is as much attuned to the harshness as to the sensuous beauty of nature. The companion essay, 'The Wind at Djemila', describes a visit to another ruined city, on a windswept plateau, whose 'arid splendour' leads Camus into a meditation on 'death without hope'. There is still a pantheistic sense of identification with the world of nature, but here he feels himself almost dissolving into the fierce wind and the lifeless world of rock and ruined stone through which it blows, reduced to

---

[89] Camus, 'Nuptials at Tipasa', in *SEN* 69 (*LCE* 65).
[90] See Camus, 'Nuptials at Tipasa', in *SEN* 70 (*LCE* 66).
[91] Camus, 'Nuptials at Tipasa', in *SEN* 70 (*LCE* 66).
[92] Camus, 'Nuptials at Tipasa', in *SEN* 70 (*LCE* 67).
[93] Camus, 'Nuptials at Tipasa', in *SEN* 74 (*LCE* 70–1).
[94] Woelfel, *Camus*, 19.
[95] Camus, 'Nuptials at Tipasa', in *SEN* 71 (*LCE* 68).

'a stone among stones', left 'defenceless against the slow forces within me that were saying no.'[96]

Camus's use of erotic imagery in 'Nuptials at Tipasa' to express a deep and intimate connection to the natural world is, as Woelfel notes, characteristic of much mysticism. It is found again, in a more intense and explicit form, in a much later work, the story 'The Adulterous Wife' from his 1957 collection *Exile and the Kingdom*. In this story, the protagonist, Janine, is accompanying her husband on a business trip he is taking into the far desert interior of Algeria. She is tired and oppressed by the heat, feeling estranged from her husband, who is too focused on his business dealings to pay much attention to her. Towards the end of the story, she slips away from her sleeping husband and goes up to an old fort—but not for the assignation the title has set us up to expect (at least not in the sense that we are expecting)—and stares at the night sky:

No breath, no sound, except at times the muffled cracking of stones being reduced to sand by the cold, came to disturb the solitude and silence that surrounded Janine. After a moment, however, it seemed to her that a kind of slow gyration was sweeping the sky above her. In the depths of the dry, cold night, thousands of stars were formed unceasingly, and their sparkling icicles, no sooner detached than they began to slip imperceptibly toward the horizon. She was breathing deeply, she forgot the cold, the weight of beings, the insane or static life, the long anguish of living and dying. After so many years fleeing from fear, running crazily, uselessly, she was finally coming to a halt. At the same time, she seemed to be recovering her roots and the sap rose anew in her body, which was no longer trembling. Pressing her whole belly against the parapet, leaning towards the wheeling sky, she was only waiting for her pounding heart to settle down and for the silence to form in her ... Then, with an unbearable sweetness, the waters of the night began to fill Janine, submerging the cold, rising gradually to the dark center of her being and overflowing wave upon wave to her moaning mouth. A moment later, the whole sky stretched out above her, as she lay with her back against the cold earth.[97]

Here, despite her lack of satisfying relations with other people, the night, the desert, and the stars give Janine peace, free her from her fear and anguish, her sense of futility and aimlessness; and they do so with a gentleness that is nonetheless overwhelmingly and literally erotic.

In a late essay, written as an introduction to a book by his mentor, Jean Grenier, Camus writes a little more explicitly or analytically about his sense of the sacred:

---

[96] Camus, 'The Wind at Djemila', in *SEN* 77 (*LCE* 75).
[97] Camus, 'The Adulterous Wife', in *EK* 24–5.

132   THE PHILOSOPHY OF CAMUS

Grenier, like Melville, ends his voyage with a meditation on the absolute and on God. Speaking of the Hindus he writes of a port that can neither be named nor situated in any particular place, of another island, but one forever distant, and in its own way deserted.

Once again, for a young man brought up outside traditional religions, this prudent, allusive approach was perhaps the only way to direct him to a deeper meditation on life. Personally, I had no lack of gods: the sun, the night, the sea ... But these are gods of enjoyment; they fill one, then they leave one empty. With them alone for company I should have forgotten the gods in favor of enjoyment itself. I had to be reminded of mystery and holy things, of the finite nature of man, of a love that is impossible in order to return to my natural gods one day, less arrogantly. So I do not owe to Grenier certainties he neither could nor wished to give me. But I owe him instead a doubt which will never end and which, for example, has prevented me from being a humanist in the sense that it is understood today—I mean a man blinded by narrow certainties.[98]

The 'gods of enjoyment' are the ones he encountered in his youth at Tipasa. In 'Nuptials', as we saw, he was ambivalent about whether the language of 'gods' was more than a, perhaps rather pretentious, literary flourish; why not just talk about the palpable, sensuous reality of the natural world? Here he analyses that early ambivalence. There is something not merely enjoyable, but mysterious, numinous, about the sun, the night, the sea; something that demands reverence—a demand that, however, we are tempted to ignore in our 'arrogant' quest to use them merely for our enjoyment. What enables us to resist that temptation, Camus claims, is a deeper sense of underlying mystery and holiness, from which the particular striking natural phenomena—the 'gods of enjoyment'—stand out. If Camus hints at a theology here, it is a resolutely negative one; the 'port', which is the ultimate *telos* of our spiritual journeying, cannot be named or located; the love that drives the journey is 'impossible'. He ends in a kind of agnosticism, expressing gratitude for doubt rather than certainty, but it is, one could say, a reverent agnosticism, the sense of a mystery before which our finite nature is properly humbled. Camus refuses the label of 'Humanist' as he had earlier refused 'Atheist'. Man is not the measure of all things, and, noble and essential though the humanistic ethic of *The Rebel* and *The Plague* is, there is indeed 'something that goes beyond' it, as Camus had said in 'Return to Tipasa'.

I do take the discussion so far in this chapter to have established that there is in Camus something at least somewhat analogous to, or comparable with, Kierkegaard's religious sphere; something that transcends the ethical, but in doing so also underpins it. I am thinking more of the generic 'Religiousness A' in Kierkegaard, rather than Christianity specifically ('Religiousness B', the

---

[98] Camus, 'On Jean Grenier's *Les Iles*' (1959), in *LCE* 327–8.

NEMESIS   133

paradox-religion). To be sure, there are large differences even here. The Kierkegaardian religious sensibility (even in Religiousness A) is directed towards the transcendent and eternal, while Camus finds the sacred in the sensible world. Camus's attitude to the transcendent remains, I think, agnostic; he is not committed to a dogmatic denial of it, and I have suggested there are occasional hints of his openness to its possibility, but what I think we can fairly call Camus's religious sensibility is basically pantheistic, this-worldly. As we have seen, in 'Helen's Exile' Camus criticizes Christianity for turning from 'the contemplation of nature' to 'the tragedy of the soul',[99] and it might seem that Kierkegaard, with his passionate concern for subjectivity and inwardness, and his subtle explorations of anxiety and despair, would be a natural target for this complaint. Certainly, the popular image of Kierkegaard suggests anguished introspection, rather than delight in natural beauty, and it is undoubtably true that Kierkegaard's main concern was to encourage serious ethical and spiritual self-examination in his readers. But it is not the case that he was indifferent to the world around him, or thought that interest in it was merely characteristic of the aesthetic stage. On the contrary, the Knight of Faith in *Fear and Trembling* delights in all the everyday sights and sounds of the sensible world around him—'a rat scurrying under a plank across the gutter, children playing'[100]—for 'he has felt the pain of renouncing everything ... and yet the finite tastes just as good to him as to one who never knew anything higher ... he has the security which makes him delight in it as if finitude were the surest thing of all.'[101] This is from a pseudonymous work, but, writing in his own name, Kierkegaard insists that we should delight in the beauty of the natural world as a gift from God; we should not become blasé but find it a cause for rejoicing

> that you can see ... that you can hear, that you can smell, that you can taste, that you can feel; that the sun shines for you and for your sake, that when it becomes weary, the moon begins to shine, and the stars are lit; that winter comes, that all nature disguises itself, plays the game of stranger, and in order to delight you; that spring comes, that the birds return in great flocks, and in order to give you joy ...[102]

Not only is nature *given* by God, it is itself a theophany; a revelation of God:

> In nature everything is unconditional obedience. The sighing of the wind, the echoing of the forest, the murmuring of the brook, the humming of the summer,

---

[99] Camus, 'Helen's Exile', in *SEN* 138 (*LCE* 151). Of course, he complains that secular Modernity is even worse, abandoning concern for the soul but failing to regain a sense for nature. It is a symptom of this that 'one seeks in vain for landscapes in major European writers since Dostoevsky' ('Helen's Exile', in *SEN* 138 (*LCE* 151)).

[100] *FT* 40.

[101] *FT* 40.

[102] Kierkegaard, 'The Lily of the Field and the Bird of the Air', in *WA* 39–40.

134   THE PHILOSOPHY OF CAMUS

the whispering of the leaves, the rustling of the grass, every sound, every sound you hear is all compliance, unconditional obedience. Thus you can hear God in it, just as you hear him in the harmony that is the movement of the celestial bodies in obedience.[103]

This is not pantheism; God expresses Himself in the world, but is not to be identified with it. But is also anything but a world-denyingly Gnostic, or self-absorbed, spirituality. And, if Kierkegaard finds God in the beauty of nature, so too, as we have just seen, for Camus 'the gods of enjoyment'—the observable, beautiful phenomena of nature itself—need to be seen as expressive of a deeper underlying holiness. Certainly, the two thinkers' positions and their sensibilities are, in important ways, quite different. But even these differences are not quite as stark as one might have supposed.

V Affirmation and Denial: Camus's Tragic Sense of Life

There is, then, in Camus, both early and late, 'a sense of the sacred'. And it is important to note that, although Camus rejects a pure humanism, and although he experiences the sense of the sacred intensely in and through the natural world (when that is apprehended with proper reverence), he also sees the sacred as present in humanity too. This, indeed, is the ultimate source of the Rebel's conviction that some things just cannot (morally) be done to other persons; that human persons have a worth or value that places demands on others to recognize and respect it. To regard something as sacred is to draw boundaries around it; to recognize certain actions towards it as violations. Positively, it is to see reverence—and perhaps 'a strange kind of love'—as appropriate attitudes towards it. The 'religious horror' produced by murder in ancient times (R. 279) testified to a sense of the sanctity of human life; and it is this that Camus is shocked that we have lost. In the age of bureaucratically administered mass murder, 'our tragedies stink of offices, and the blood they run with has the colour of dirty ink'.[104] It is true that *The Rebel* does, as I noted in the previous chapter, at one point explicitly present rebellion and sacredness as exclusive alternatives between which we have to choose. But, as I also argued there, and as I hope this chapter has made clearer, this cannot be Camus's own final judgement. For, if nothing is sacred, then human life is not sacred, and the founding conviction of rebellion itself—that certain actions violate the worth of humanity—becomes absurd.

However, if Camus does not in the end side with rebellion against the sacred, he nevertheless sympathizes strongly with the Metaphysical Rebel's protest against a

[103] WA 25.
[104] Camus, 'Helen's Exile', in SEN 137 (LCE 150).

world of suffering and death. The Metaphysical Rebel rejects the idea of a sacred order in the world out of a proper moral outrage at innocent suffering but is then (as we saw) left with the question of what justifies that moral outrage itself. If we are in a merely naturalistic universe,[105] then suffering and 'evil' are themselves simply natural phenomena. From what perspective, then, can we condemn them morally? In *The Rebel* itself, having identified the problem, Camus shifts to looking at 'Historical Rebellion' in order to argue that the revolt against particular social and political injustices needs to recognize its own proper limits and, in particular, that it needs to avoid turning into a secular pseudo-religion. But what then of Metaphysical Rebellion itself? Can *it* be rescued from the threatened self-undermining collapse into moral cynicism that Camus identified? In this chapter so far, I have tried to flesh out his 'Hellenic' outlook, arguing that he is committed to affirming some kind of normative order in the world, which is present to us in aesthetic as well as in moral experience. But this is the same world order that is filled with such unmerited suffering. And nor can this be blamed simply on 'history' rather than 'nature'; in addition to the needless cruelties we inflict on one another, there is all the suffering caused to creatures of all kinds, including humans, simply through the operation of natural processes. (Having written a novel about a plague, Camus was well aware of that, although 'natural evil' does not feature very much as an explicit topic in his theoretical work.) But how then can we affirm this order of the world without affirming all the pain and suffering it brings? The sacred provokes rebellion, which, through its rejection of the sacred, ends by undermining itself. But this does not invalidate its initial protest. Is there a way out of these circles, in which it seems both necessary and impossible to affirm both rebellion and the sacred?

As I noted in the previous chapter, the problem of evil arises for an immanent or pantheistic outlook at least as much as it does for theism (and it is one of Camus's philosophical merits to have recognized this). Both the attitudes between which Camus himself was torn—the 'Greek' affirmation of a harmonious world order, and the quasi-Gnostic revolt against this order of suffering and death—are, of course, in their own ways, religious responses to the world; neither would make much sense to an untroubled secularist or conventional naturalist. But I hope it is clear by now that, whatever Camus was, it was not that. And I hope it is also now clear that the tension between affirmation and denial of life is indeed central to Camus's work and sensibility as a whole. In his first publication, *L'Envers et l'endroit*, he wrote: 'There is no love of life without despair of life.'[106] In the new preface to that collection, which he wrote near the end of his life, in 1958, he quotes that remark and, although he judges he had made the point 'rather pompously', he nonetheless affirms the substance of it: 'I did not know at the time how right I

---

[105] In the sense of disenchanted naturalism; a universe without inherent value or meaning.
[106] *SEN* 60 (*LCE* 55).

136   THE PHILOSOPHY OF CAMUS

was."[107] His love of life leads to his Hellenic pantheism, his sense of a beautiful and harmonious world order that provides a proper locus for, and sets proper limits to, human strivings. The despairing horror at life leads to his quasi-Gnostic Metaphysical Rebellion—his revulsion from a world of suffering and death, his haunting sense that they are not natural, but somehow *should* not be. As Camus was well aware, Christianity offers a sort of synthesis or a middle way between Greek and Gnostic views. The world is a divine creation and is therefore good in its essential order; but it is fallen and in need of redemption. As the contemporary theologian David Bentley Hart puts it:

> it is clearly the case that there is a kind of 'provisional' cosmic dualism within the New Testament: not an ultimate dualism, of course, between two equal principles; but certainly a conflict between a sphere of created autonomy that strives against God on the one hand and the saving love of God in time on the other.[108]

Camus, though, rejects this attempt to explain how the essential goodness of the world can be compatible with the evil that pervades it. This is partly due to his metaphysical scepticism, but also to a moral as well as intellectual rejection of the idea of Christ's sacrificial and atoning death, and to the complex of ideas associated with judgement and punishment in historical Christianity. But he is clearly preoccupied with the problem for which Christianity attempts to provide a solution and is looking for some alternative response to it.

We know some of the routes he did not take. As well as Christianity, he explicitly rejects Nietzsche's 'absolute affirmation' with its yes-saying to the world and all the suffering that is integral to it. And (as we have also seen) he rejects the more conventional naturalism that would see no sense in taking any overall attitude to the world, but that would also recognize suffering as integral to life, and cruelty and aggression as among the natural attributes of our species. Such a view could be compatible with a kind of Humean conventionalism in morality but not (as I argued in the previous chapter) with the sense that murder, torture, and rape are violations of something sacred—which is fundamental to the attitude of the Rebel, and thus to Camus's whole ethical philosophy. I have noted at various points above Camus's interest in Gnosticism, which would write this world off as evil and locate the real source of value in a different realm. But, although there is certainly something Gnostic in the mindset of his Metaphysical Rebel, Camus's love of the physical world and its beauty made anything akin to a Gnostic solution impossible for him. One Platonic solution would be to recognize the beauty and order of the world as indicative of its connection to, or participation in, the world of pure Forms, while also recognizing that it could embody them only in a limited and

---

[107] *SEN* 24 (*LCE* 13).
[108] Hart, *The Doors of the Sea*, 62–3.

imperfect way, owing to the recalcitrance of the matter they had to inform. But, although not Gnostic,[109] this view still seems too other-worldly for Camus, with his love of the sensual immediacy of the world, as well as his explicit rejection, as we have seen above, of a transcendent world of pure essences.

Perhaps some modified—maybe drastically modified—version of a Platonic or Plotinian view might have emerged in the projected essay on Nemesis. Camus was certainly interested in the contrast between the Judeo-Christian view, which starkly distinguished between the all-powerful God and His creation, and the Greek view of a graduated cosmos, in which 'there were not gods on one side and men on the other, but a series of stages leading from one to the other' (R. 28). But the clearest hints at where he was going can be found—interestingly— in his writings on aesthetics: the chapter on 'Rebellion and Art' in *The Rebel*, his 1955 'Lecture on the Future of Tragedy', and his 1957 Nobel prize lecture 'Create Dangerously!' (I should note though that my current interest is not primarily in Camus's aesthetics *per se*, but in what his aesthetic writings tell us about his attitude to the problem of evil. Accordingly, I shall not try to pursue the many very interesting purely aesthetic questions that these writings do raise.) In the 'Rebellion and Art' chapter, Camus argues that the artist necessarily both rejects the world (by trying to create a new world that will have the coherence and unity that the actual world lacks) but also continues to affirm it: 'Artistic creation is a demand for unity and a rejection of the world. But it rejects the world on account of what it lacks and in the name of what it sometimes is' (R. 252). To accuse the world of lacking something is to presuppose that the world *ought* to have had that something. (As in *The Myth*, the world appears as absurd only in contrast to the stubborn conviction that it *ought* to have a Meaning.) And, Camus adds here, the world, at least partially or 'sometimes', does display something of that unity or Meaning that the artist denounces it for lacking.

The artist thus protests against the world because its empirical reality (of suffering and injustice) fails to accord with its own essential normative order. Camus goes on to cite a remark by Van Gogh to the effect that this world is one of God's 'sketches that have turned out badly'. Camus comments: 'Every artist tries to reconstruct this sketch, and to give it the style it lacks' (R. 256).[110] Putting it (slightly) less imagistically, one might say that the artist finds the essential order of how things should be, that can be dimly intimated as underlying the empirical actuality of the world, and creates so as to make this order perspicuous. In 'Create Dangerously!', Camus notes that artists are 'incapable of rejecting what is real, yet [are] still devoted to challenging the ever unfinished aspects of reality'.[111] 'Unfinished' suggests incomplete, failing fully to embody some pattern or idea. Thus a great

---

[109] Camus notes Plotinus' critique of the Gnostics at *CMN* 67, 91.

[110] Some such perception is presumably why Stanislas Fumet, a Catholic critic cited by Camus, claims: 'Art, whatever its aim, is always in sinful competition with God' (R. 259).

[111] *CD* 32 (also in *RRD* 264; *SO* 231).

138   THE PHILOSOPHY OF CAMUS

artist is able to create a work that achieves a completeness and unity that is lacking in the world, but that we somehow all vaguely sense should be there. Such a work accordingly 'awakens in everyone ... the insistent yet fleeting image of a reality that we recognize without having ever experienced it'.[112] The last remark appears to be an allusion to the Platonic theory of recollection, and the discussion so far may make it seem that Camus's aesthetics is a version of the—ultimately Neoplatonic—Classicism according to which art finds the ideal in the empirical.[113] As Schopenhauer put it, the true artist is someone who 'understands nature's half-spoken words'[114] and is thus able to create forms more beautiful than any actually found in nature itself. I think there is a sense in which Camus's aesthetics is basically Classical, and he firmly rejects a merely empirical, naturalistic realism in art. But he does not think that the artist should escape into a world of pure form or 'ideal' beauty; let alone that the artist should falsify reality by creating a sentimental world of happy endings and inspirational propaganda.[115] The artists' created world *is* still this this actual world, with all its pain and ugliness; but stylized, so that everything in it expresses more completely what it essentially is. Referring specifically to the novel, he says,

> the world is undoubtably the same one that we know. The suffering, the illusion, the love, are the same. The heroes speak our language, have our weakness and our strength. Their world is neither more beautiful nor more enlightening than ours. But they at least pursue their destinies to the bitter end ... they complete things that we can never consummate. (*R.* 263)

Art thus appears as a response to the absurdity—the lack of 'unity' (fulness, coherence, Meaning)—of the experienced world that was diagnosed in *The Myth*. But Camus has moved on from Absurdism, and it is because the world is not simply without 'unity', is not simply an agglomeration of disconnected phenomena, but exhibits, however imperfectly, an essential order, that art can be a celebration of reality, rather than a defiant counter to it (see *R.* 258). Not only does art—even formalist art—necessarily draw its elements, its raw materials, from reality (*R.* 269), but—although Camus does speak of 'the mind that gives reality its form' (*R.* 371)— the form that organizes these materials cannot be an arbitrary imposition (as in Surrealism, which he criticizes in *R.* 88–104) but is a making perspicuous of a form

---

[112] *CD* 34 (*RRD* 265; *SO* 242).

[113] As he had noted in his dissertation, 'Plotinus' philosophy is an artist's point of view' but 'it is not the appearances that Plotinus seeks, but the inside of things [the essential natures of things, the norms to which they are striving to conform] that is his lost paradise' (*CMN* 90).

[114] Schopenhauer, *The World as Will and Representation*, i. 222.

[115] Camus treats formalism and naturalistic realism as the opposite pitfalls that good art needs to avoid. 'Socialist Realism' gets the worst of both worlds by both denying any transcendent ideals *and* sentimentally falsifying the 'natural' world it purports to depict. See *R.* 268–72; *CD* 11–29 (*RRD* 252–63; *SO* 232–40).

NEMESIS   139

dimly perceived in reality itself (Schopenhauer's 'half-spoken words'). And even a work that presents us with a world of grief and suffering 'still creates a form of salvation' because 'to talk of despair is to conquer it' (R. 263).[116]

The artist, Camus insists, offers a model for how a Metaphysical Rebel can avoid falling into a self-undermining nihilism—by holding world rejection and world acceptance together in tension. The artist does so through an act of creation, but artistic creation is a special case of a universal impulse, for 'everyone tries to make his life a work of art' (R. 261). We all, Camus suggests, have a drive to find a kind of unity or coherence in our own lives, even in our failures and sorrows. 'It is therefore justifiable to say that man has the idea of a better life than this. But better does not mean different, it means unified. This passion, which lifts the mind above the commonplaces of a dispersed world, from which it nevertheless cannot free itself, is the passion for unity' (R. 262). In The Myth, this was, to borrow Sartre's phrase, 'a useless passion,'[117] though one that Camus then recommended we continue to live defiantly with. Now, he seems to suggest, it is a passion that can find a partial satisfaction, though perhaps more in art than in life. Even great art though does not offer any solution to the problem of life; it does not resolve the contradiction between affirmation and denial. 'It is both rejection and acceptance, at one and the same time, and that it why it can be continually and perpetually torn apart.'[118] But it may perhaps teach us how to live with this contradiction.

If this is true of art generally, it may be all the more true of tragedy in particular. In the 'Lecture on the Future of Tragedy', Camus wonders whether modernity can produce genuine tragedy. The loss of the sense of the sacredness of life has meant that in our day 'the most monstrous wars have not inspired a single tragic poet.'[119] He claims that only two eras of tragic drama have existed in Western history—that of the ancient Greeks (Aeschylus to Euripides) and that of early modern Western Europe (Shakespeare, the Spanish Golden Age, Corneille, and Racine). Both, he claims, occurred on the cusp of a movement from a religious to a humanistic culture, when 'the pendulum of civilization is half-way between a sacred society and a society built around man.'[120] This analysis is obviously—as

---

[116] For Camus, a 'literature of despair' is a contradiction in terms, since to seek to find the proper form for expressing despair is already to have taken on a meaningful task, and thus to have transcended the despair ('The Enigma', in SEN 145 (LCE 158-9)).

[117] Sartre, Being and Nothingness, 615. I am applying Sartre's phrase here in a slightly different sense from that in which he used it, though these senses are related.

[118] CD 32 (RRD 264; SO 341).

[119] Camus, 'Lecture on ... Tragedy', in SEN 200 (LCE 306). Camus is concerned in this lecture with the prospects for a revival of tragedy in contemporary French theatre; elsewhere he does find a genuine tragic sensibility present in some modern prose writers—notably Melville and Faulkner. See Camus, 'Herman Melville', in SEN 180 (LCE 291-2), and 'William Faulkner', in SEN 183-4 (LCE 315-16). (Camus adapted Faulkner's Requiem for a Nun for the French stage, as part of his contribution to trying to revive a genuinely tragic drama.)

[120] Camus, 'Lecture on ... Tragedy', in SEN 199 (LCE305). Though I am not going to do so here, it would be interesting to compare this analysis with the essay on 'The Tragic in Ancient Drama Reflected in the Tragic in Modern Drama', which appears in the first volume of Kierkegaard's Either/Or, ascribed

140   THE PHILOSOPHY OF CAMUS

Camus acknowledges—indebted to Nietzsche's *The Birth of Tragedy*; but he adds to it a theme from Hegel; that tragedy is about the clash of two antagonists, or conflicting principles, both of which have right on their side, but neither of which can recognize what is right about the other. 'The perfect tragic formula would be "All can be justified, no one is just."'[121] As a result, 'the constant theme of classical tragedy ... is the limit that must not be transgressed. To make a mistake about this limit, to try to destroy the balance, is to perish.'[122] Putting the two themes together, he argues that, in true tragedy, we have the clash between, 'on the one hand, man and his desire for power, and on the other, the divine principle that is reflected by the world.'[123] The tragic hero rebels against the sacred order of the world, and it crushes him; but there is something right about both his rebellion and his destruction. When this balance, this tension, is destroyed, tragedy ceases to be possible. In a firmly religious culture, where the goodness of the divine order is taken for granted, there may be dramas of sin and repentance, but no tragedy.[124] But likewise, if the sense of a hidden sacred order that sets limits to human endeavour is lost, if all is decided by human will and reason, limited only by brute facticity, then too there can be no tragedy. 'The denial of the mystery of existence, once again destroys tragedy. Atheistic or rationalist tragedy is thus equally impossible.'[125]

There are plenty of literary and historical questions that could be raised about this analysis (as with most theories of tragedy, it seems we can find examples of paradigmatic tragedies that do not obviously fit this definition). But my concern here is with the general philosophical implications of this account of tragedy. Of course, in this lecture Camus is talking directly about art, not life. But tragedy for him is important, because it expresses an attitude to life. The lesson of tragedy is that the 'divine' order of the universe should simultaneously be affirmed and denied. The rebel against it is justified in protesting against its injustice, but always and necessarily presupposes that the universe is not simply morally chaotic, and thus presupposes the validity of that same divine order.[126] So 'Prometheus is both just and unjust, and Zeus, who pitilessly oppresses him, also has right on his side.'[127] Hence tragedy calls us to the attitude of moderation and balance that I have discussed above, but it is a reminder that what that moderation involves is not some

---

to the aesthetic pseudonym 'A' (*E/O* i. 139–64). The main theme of this essay (which may or may not reflect Kierkegaard's own considered views) is the greater reflectiveness and inwardness of modern tragedy, which, indeed, renders it problematic as drama.

[121] Camus, 'Lecture on ... Tragedy', in *SEN* 196 (*LCE* 301). Intentionally or otherwise, this formula recalls *The Myth*'s 'There are truths but no truth'.

[122] Camus, 'Lecture on ... Tragedy', in *SEN* 196 (*LCE* 302).

[123] Camus, 'Lecture on ... Tragedy', in *SEN* 197 (*LCE* 302).

[124] See Camus, 'Lecture on ... Tragedy', in *SEN* 197–8 (*LCE* 302–3).

[125] Camus, 'Lecture on ... Tragedy', in *SEN* 198 (*LCE* 303).

[126] Here is the difference between tragedy and Gnosticism: the Gnostic condemns the evil of this world order by reference to another different one; the tragic hero has no other order to appeal to but the one he or she also attacks.

[127] Camus, 'Lecture on ... Tragedy', in *SEN* 196 (*LCE* 301).

NEMESIS 141

tepid compromise, but the holding in tension of apparently incompatible extremes that nonetheless continue to depend on one another: 'What can I long for ... except the power to exclude nothing, and learn to weave from strands of black and white one single rope that is stretched to breaking point?'[128]

A critic might respond at this point that, in trying to 'exclude nothing', Camus is calling us to accept a contradiction, and that contradictions cannot (should not) be accepted. He is telling us that the basic world order is good and should be accepted and celebrated; *and* that it is bad and should be rejected. Is there a way to reconcile these claims, and, if there is, can he tell us what it is, philosophically and not mythologically or imagistically? As I noted in the previous chapter, Camus in *The Rebel* attempted to deal with various apparent contradictions (between justice and freedom, and between non-violence and the (moral) requirement for effective action to protect the vulnerable). His response (as we saw) was that 'these contradictions only exist in the absolute. They suppose a world and a method of thought without mediation' (*R*. 288). In the abstract, absolute freedom and absolute justice are perhaps irreconcilable, but the task of practical politics is to provide a proper balance, so that each limits and restrains the other. This seems both commonsensical as well as a bit Hegelian (as the term 'mediation' might suggest). Here we can have Both–And, rather than Either–Or, so long as neither antithesis is pressed to an extreme. The question of non-violence, as we also saw, is actually more problematic for Camus, since he was not willing to renounce the absolute moral demand for non-violence, but also insisted that we are morally required sometimes to abandon that demand. Practically speaking, he does allow for a compromise solution— use violence only to the minimum degree necessary, only against aggressors, no capital punishment, and so on—but this compromise is something that, although (morally) unavoidable, still ought to leave us morally uncomfortable. To kill, even when it would have been morally wrong not to, is still to do something terribly wrong. Hence, 'the Rebel can never find peace' (*R*. 285). This would seem to constitute a genuinely tragic situation in his sense—although there are better and worse ways of living with a tragic situation of this sort.

Can the apparently contradictory stance of the tragic hero in general (both affirming and denying the order of things) be handled in either of these ways? Camus does indicate that full-blown tragedy occurs when the limits formed by the necessary tension between order and rebellion are crossed; when each, one might say, is pushed to an abstract extreme. This happens when the hero forgets the true complexity and tension of the situation, and thus becomes merely negative in his or her attitude to the world order; and when the divine powers (personifications of that order) then simply crush the rebel without acknowledgement of the legitimacy of his or her initial protest. Camus attributes the hero's transgression to

---

[128] Camus, 'Return to Tipasa', in *SEN* 153 (*LCE* 168).

142   THE PHILOSOPHY OF CAMUS

pride or even to stupidity (Ajax),[129] and this would seem to imply the possibility at least of averting tragedy by stopping short of the limit; the possibility for the tragic hero of holding in tension together both the recognition of the legitimacy of the order and the protest against it, without taking either too far. (As with the proper tension between freedom and justice.) At moments, though, Camus seems to suggest that a sort of tragic necessity may prevail: it is not simply that the hero is justified in protesting so far but no further; rather, that he is justified in pressing his rebellion all the way, but that in doing so he also justifies his own destruction. 'The more justified this revolt and the more necessary this order, the greater the tragedy that stems from the conflict.'[130] This might seem more like the dilemma between violence and non-violence, where it seems we will be both guilty *and* justified whatever we do, with no fully satisfactory midpoint to be found between the competing claims on us.

Perhaps the best response to the apparent contradiction between affirming order and rejecting it would be to recognize that, although they cannot be reconciled theoretically, in the abstract, they can—with difficulty—be lived together. We are too much 'in the midst' of the world order to survey it as if in a 'view from nowhere'[131] and explain how it all hangs together, how the experienced goodness of the world order can be compatible with its evils. But we can, nevertheless, live with both a joy in the order of the world, and a horrified revolt against the suffering it involves, while seeing both responses as genuinely grounded in the nature of things, rather than being merely subjective reactions in us to a morally neutral universe.

The chorus draws the lesson, which is that there is an order, that this order can be painful, but that it is still worse not to recognize that it exists. The only purification comes from denying and excluding nothing, and thus accepting the mystery of existence, the limitations of man—in short, the order where men know without knowing.[132]

If we combine, as Camus did, a properly modest estimation of what human thought can achieve with a disinclination to reject what we experience as real but cannot grasp theoretically, then we may perhaps respond to the challenge I posed above by saying that there *are* things that can be expressed only mythologically or imagistically, which abstract philosophical reasoning cannot grasp. The insights of the great tragedies may not be translatable without remainder into the language

---

[129] Camus, 'Lecture on ... Tragedy', in *SEN* 197 (*LCE* 302).
[130] Camus, 'Lecture on ... Tragedy', in *SEN* 197 (*LCE* 302).
[131] In the evocative term that Thomas Nagel has made familiar (see Nagel, *The View from Nowhere*).
[132] Camus, 'Lecture on ... Tragedy', in *SEN* 122 (*LCE* 304).

NEMESIS 143

of systematic or analytical philosophy, but they may still offer us the best language
that we have for responding to the fundamental challenges of human life.[133]

In making this tentative elaboration on some of Camus's remarks I have drawn
(silently) on Kierkegaard a good deal. But I do not think I have been reading
Kierkegaard into Camus. They share a moderated philosophical scepticism, a distrust (which is not to say a rejection) of abstract thinking; a conviction that our
experience—personal, aesthetic, moral, religious—can legitimately lead us beyond
the limits of what can be proved, or even precisely articulated theoretically. One
might perhaps say that the Camusian Rebel, like the Kierkegaardian Knight of
Faith, lives by paradox. Not, to be sure, by the same paradox. For the pseudonym
Johannes *de silentio*, Abraham's paradox lies in his utterly individual, ultimately
incommunicable relationship to God; for Kierkegaard himself, in the end, the
paradox is the Lutheran one that we are at once wretched sinners and justified by
God; saved by free grace, but bound to strict obedience; and that this is because
of the sacrificial death of the innocent man who was also God, the impossible
'God in time'.[134] It is precisely the impossibility of thinking through the paradox,
its absolutely repelling effect on rational thought, that pushes us away from seeking to *understand* it (which involves holding it at an intellectualizing distance),
and forces us instead to *live* in the light of it.

> Suppose that Christianity does not at all want to be understood; suppose that,
> in order to express this and to prevent anyone, misguided, from taking the road
> of objectivity, it has proclaimed itself to be the paradox. Suppose that it wants to
> be only for existing persons, and essentially in inwardness ... which cannot be
> expressed more definitely than this: it is the absurd, adhered to firmly with the
> passion of the infinite.[135]

This is why 'Christianity is not a doctrine but an existence-communication'.[136] For
Camus, the paradox is that we live in a world that we rightly affirm as embodying beauty and value while also protesting against the evil of this world order;
although the protest would collapse without the affirmation that it nonetheless
seeks to undermine. It is certainly a different paradox, and even a different type of

---

[133] Kierkegaard's pseudonym Johannes *de silentio* claims that one speech from Shakespeare's *Richard III* is worth more than all the systems of ethics, which have 'no intimation of the nightmares of existence' (*FT* 105). This can be applied religiously too; the passion stories in the Gospels do not pose a puzzle that needs to be solved by an explanatorily satisfactory 'theory of the atonement'; they already contain a far richer content than any such theory does.

[134] See *CUP* i. 570–81.

[135] *CUP* i. 214. The *Postscript* is a pseudonymous work, whose supposed author, Johannes Climacus, denies being a Christian. Kierkegaard, writing in his own name, never describes Christianity as 'absurd', though he insists that it is paradoxical and inaccessible to intellectual understanding. When looked at purely intellectually, without faith, it appears absurd, but for faith, which takes it up and lives it, existentially, it is not absurd. See the remarks from Kierkegaard's *Journals*, quoted in *CUP* ii. 98–9.

[136] *CUP* i. 570.

144   THE PHILOSOPHY OF CAMUS

paradox. None of its individual components is inherently paradoxical as the 'God in time' is. Indeed, the beauty of the world and its horrors are both apparent; the difficulty is with holding those perceptions together. But this paradox too can, it seems, be lived, even if we are unable to unravel it intellectually.

Perhaps it would not be pushing it too far, however, to suggest that, underlying this Camusian paradoxical attitude, too, is a kind of faith, a belief that somehow it *does* all cohere; that there is an 'absolute', a 'secret of life', beyond our ability to formulate, which makes both affirmation and revolt appropriate attitudes to the same single reality, but which gives affirmation the final word. For, if there is not, in the end, a normatively good underlying order to the world, however obscurely it shines through the empirical phenomena, then it seems we would fall into the self-stultification with which the Metaphysical Rebel is threatened; the moral revolt against suffering and evil would lead to a nihilism that undermines the basis for the revolt. Hence the remark in a very early (1938) essay: 'a consent lay sleeping at the heart of my revolt.'[137] The sensible empiricist (from whom we have heard at various points already) might again ask at this point whether such a claim is melo-dramatic or excessive. Why not just say that there are good things about the world and bad things, and leave it at that? Why adopt any total attitude—of affirmation or negation—to the world as a whole? The empiricist might even cite Camus: 'One cannot say that nothing has any meaning ... nor that everything has a meaning, because the word "everything"' has no meaning for us' (R. 296). Exegetically, I think that the material I have considered in this chapter so far shows that Camus did have a sense of reality as a whole, or 'nature' as an appropriate object of a global attitude; or, rather, a sense of an underlying order that can be affirmed without leading us to a Nietzschean affirmation of 'everything', of all phenomena.[138] The empiricist is right, of course, that we should affirm some phenomena and deplore others, but we need to note that there is a logical priority to the affirmation; we are appalled by plagues and massacres *because* we take human life to be of value. (And, as I have argued above, it makes no sense to think of humanity as the only thing of value in an otherwise valueless universe.) But to be able to judge about the goodness or badness of particular phenomena in a non-arbitrary way, we need a standard of goodness that is rooted in reality, not just in a demand for formal consistency or something like that.

'"You're right," said Cormery, "I've loved life. I'm hungry for it. At the same time, life seems horrible to me, it seems inaccessible. That is why I am a believer, out of scepticism. Yes, I want to believe, I want to live, forever." Cormery fell silent.'[139] Here it seems that life is 'horrible' not just because there is—of course—so much

---

[137] Camus, 'The Desert', from *Nuptials*, in *SEN* 101 (*LCE* 106).
[138] This is how I think we should interpret the remark I had the 'sensible empiricist' quote from Camus above; as a defence of our right to make both affirmative and negative judgements about particulars without being able to grasp all phenomena as a 'totality'.
[139] *FM* 28.

NEMESIS 145

suffering in it, but because there is something about it—something fundamental about it—that is 'inaccessible'. Cormery loves life, but also suffers from an unappeasable hunger for a fulness or completion that our life intimates but cannot fully embody—the state that Camus's writings on aesthetics seem to assume is basic to humanity, and that art can at best partially assuage. Presumably, then, the desire to live forever that he expresses is a desire not merely for this painful tension to continue without end, but for an eternal life in which the fulness for which he hungers can be realized. The thought is striking, especially when we recall that, in *The Myth*, it was the denial of immortality, rather than the denial of God as such, that was essential for the sense of the absurd. Close though Cormery is to Camus, one cannot assume from this passage from a draft of a fictional work that Camus had abandoned his long-standing disbelief in immortality. Indeed, I have already quoted above an unequivocal statement from an interview Camus gave in 1959, when he would have been working on *The First Man*, and in which he states simply: 'I don't believe in a future life.'[140] He has moved beyond Absurdism, but it seems that life remains, for him, if not absurd, then still tragic. We are torn between the love of life and a horror of it, and, if we are given hints of a possible fulness or underlying 'unity', these remain only hints, which will leave us permanently dissatisfied if—as Camus continued to believe—there is no other life in which this fulness can be experienced.[141]

In an essay on the French novelist Roger Martin du Gard, whom he much admired, Camus raises the question:

Can the community of men, which sometimes helps us to live, also help us to die? This is the question underlying all Martin du Gard's work, which creates its tragic quality. For if the reply is negative, the situation of the modern unbeliever is temporarily madness, even if a tranquil madness. This is doubtless why so many men today proclaim with a kind of fury that the human community keeps us from dying. Martin du Gard has never said this, because in truth he does not believe it.[142]

The sense of human solidarity underling the political ethics of *The Rebel* is of crucial importance for Camus, and may 'help us to live', but it still leaves us to confront the deaths that each of us must die for ourselves. Camus, like Martin du Gard (and Kierkegaard), rejects the specious immortality conferred by the continuity of human society, as he rejects the substitution of Utopian political dreams for a future life. Human community cannot help us avoid death, but can it help us die?

---

[140] Camus, 'Replies to Jean-Claude Brisville' (1959), in *LCE* 364.
[141] Here again Camus comes close in a way to Aquinas, who argues that no finite, temporal goods can fully satisfy us, and so human life *would* be tragic, unfulfilled, without the promise of resurrection and the beatific vision. See Aquinas, *Summa Theologiae*, II–I, Q 1–5.
[142] Camus, 'Roger Martin du Gard' (1955), in *LCE* 269.

146   THE PHILOSOPHY OF CAMUS

It is striking that Camus assumes here that the unbeliever who honestly confronts death and who cannot find any 'help' in human solidarity would be in a condition of madness. (There is a very strong contrast here with Meursault, who hopes for a crowd shouting abuse at him as he is led to his execution—unless that could count as a negative way in which human community can help us die?[143]) The questions that Camus raises here at any rate indicate an awareness that there is a serious issue as to whether we can confront death honestly and non-self-deceptively, but without religious hope, without falling into despair or madness—even if a 'tranquil madness'.[144] But is it the very raising of this question, or the suspicion that it might have a negative answer—or that it might perhaps be undecidable—that constitutes the 'tragic quality' that Camus finds in Martin du Gard's work?

VI Finding a Language

Camus offers us a tragic world view in which we have to live an unresolvable tension between affirmation and denial, while at the same time providing at least hints that affirmation is more fundamental. Cormery fell silent after his statement of quasi-belief. For Camus, too, perhaps one has to fall silent before this final mystery. But it may be that, between silence and an all-too-confident theoretical-explanatory loquacity, there are other options; which may be why, as I noted at the start of this chapter, Camus was considering writing aphorisms or lyrical essays, perhaps as alternatives to a conventionally discursive work. There is a significant *Notebook* entry from 1953, headed 'For Nemesis':

> Excess in love, indeed the only desirable, belongs to saints. Societies, they exude excess only in hatred. This is why one must preach to them an intransigent moderation. Excess, madness, ruin, they are secrets and risks, for some, and one must say nothing of them or at most barely suggest.
>
> For this reason poetry is the eternal nutrient. One must entrust it to guard the secrets. As for us, who write in the language of all, we must know that there are two kinds of wisdom, and sometimes pretend to be unaware that one is higher.[145]

This is fascinating in various ways. Having defended moderation so passionately (and, as I have insisted, moderation for Camus is a passion and a demanding task); having apparently endorsed the Greek view that 'the only definite crime [is] excess' (*R.* 28); Camus now makes one crucial exception: love. To say that excess in love is

---

[143] *O.* 120.
[144] See the comment by Julian Young (who is himself a Heideggerian pantheist and rejects orthodox theism): 'the idea of ... absolute annihilation is one we cannot face with equanimity ... someone who believes that death is absolute extinction ... whatever they may say, cannot but inhabit a mood of fundamental anxiety' (Young, 'Death and Transfiguration', 139).
[145] *NB III*, 67, 68.

desirable is of course paradoxical, since the term 'excess' implies *too much*; really his point must be that there can be no excess, no 'too much', in love.[146] This is not intended to endorse any old passion or infatuation; Camus does say that Heathcliff's love for Cathy in *Wuthering Heights*, for which he 'would kill everybody on earth', shows 'strength of character' (*R.* 3), but a love that leads to an indifference to the lives of others is not something he could see as acceptable. (It would be at best one of the conflicting forces that make up a tragedy—as of course it does in *Wuthering Heights*—because it goes beyond limits that must themselves be upheld.) The desirable 'excess' of love (better: the love that is not an excess, although it has no limits) is, as Camus says, for 'saints'. One need not, of course, take that term in its specifically religious sense. But there is again at least a structural parallel with Kierkegaard here. Moderation, limit, balance are the central themes, both of Camus's ethics, and of the quasi-pantheistic spirituality that goes beyond ethics but is necessary for it. But, just as, for Kierkegaard, Christianity ('Religiousness B') goes beyond both the ethical and the 'immanent' natural religious attitude (Religiousness A);[147] so too, for Camus, it seems, not only ethics but also the 'Greek' spirituality of limit and immanent order is transcended by an attitude of love. And, as we know, love, along with nemesis, was to have been the theme of his third cycle.

For Kierkegaard, Christianity transcends, but does not abolish, ethics and Religiousness A (or, indeed, the aesthetic); it takes them up into itself. Similarly, I think, for Camus, limit and moderation are not abolished by love. To love well—which perhaps only 'the saint' can do—requires one to attend well to all the demands on one, to balance them so as to 'exclude nothing'. Nonetheless, love here is seen as something that transcends the philosophy of limit. Does this mean that Camus is now seeing the Greek philosophy of limit as insufficient and—despite himself, maybe—turning to the Christian idea of love as the central virtue (however different his actual conception of love might have been from the Christian one)? Or is he really staying within the 'Greek' outlook, perhaps looking to something more like the Platonic *eros*—the divine madness that drives our 'ascent' to the absolute (that is, the Form of Beauty/Goodness[148])? Or are these Platonic and Christian conceptions of love reconcilable with one another?[149] Or does Camus have in mind a notion of a properly 'excessive' love that is neither Platonic nor Christian? We cannot really say with the material he left to us. We can be sure,

---

[146] Without wanting to make Camus out as a Thomist *malgré lui*, it is once more interesting to note a parallel with Aquinas, for whom the 'theological virtues' of faith, hope, and love are not to be understood (like the natural virtues) in an Aristotelian fashion as means between extremes of excess and deficiency; in these virtues there can be no excess. See Aquinas, *Summa Theologiae*, II–I, XLIV, 4.

[147] For which Kierkegaard, of course, also looks back to the Greeks and, above all, Socrates.

[148] See Plato, *Symposium*, 201d–212c. I am assuming that the Form of Beauty in the *Symposium* is identical to the Form of Good in the *Republic*.

[149] A strict distinction between eros and agape has sometimes been insisted on by theologians; for a classic instance, see Nygren, *Agape and Eros*. But the Platonic ascent had formed part of the basis for Christian mysticism for centuries; Platonic eros, as Camus was well aware, was central to the thought and sensibility of St Augustine. See *CMN*, ch. 4.

148   THE PHILOSOPHY OF CAMUS

though, that, whatever philosophical connection Camus envisaged between love and sanctity or higher wisdom, the love he was concerned with would have been such as to find direct down-to-earth expression in our attitudes to the people and places around us. The only work from the Nemesis/love cycle of which he left a substantial fragment is *The First Man*; most of what we have of it is a luminous evocation of Camus's childhood. It is not 'about' love, but is constantly expressive of it—of his love for his mother, his teachers, the whole social and physical world in which he grew up. In the 1958 preface to his early essays, *L'Envers et l'endroit*, he notes that 'there is more genuine love in these clumsy pages than in all the others that have followed them' and that he dreams of a new work that 'in one way or another ... will be like [*L'Envers et l'endroit*] and that it will speak of a certain form of love'.[150] *The First Man*, with its intense sensuous evocation of concrete detail, was, I think, intended to be that work.

Returning to the *Notebook* entry, its insistence that, although moderation needs to be preached, there is something further or higher, might suggest that the 'Albert Camus' of *The Rebel* and other works may indeed function similarly to a Kierkegaardian pseudonym. (So it is not just that the voice of the Metaphysical Rebel that is heard there, is, as I have already suggested, akin to a pseudonym, but that there could be something pseudonymous, in the Kierkegaardian sense, about even the main authorial voice of *The Rebel* as a whole.) While *The Myth* sets out an Absurdist view that Camus probably never entirely held, and that he certainly came to repudiate, *The Rebel* is undoubtably expressing some of Camus's strongly held convictions; but there he is not saying all of what he took to be the final truth.[151] The truth of 'excess', of madness even, is a secret, which would be dangerously misunderstood if it were to be openly spoken of; therefore it can only be hinted at. At least this is true for those who write 'in the language of all', which must be clear, simple, intended to communicate, to facilitate dialogue. 'The mutual understanding and communication discovered by rebellion can survive only in the free exchange of conversation. Every ambiguity, every misunderstanding leads to death; clear language and simple words are the only salvation from this death' (*R.* 283). Although Camus's target here is obviously the obscurantist jargon of totalitarianism and the philosophies that enable it, this might also seem to require a repudiation of poetic, ironic, ambiguous, playful, inventive language; of Modernist literature, for one thing. The ethical concern for universal communication trumps the aesthetic concern for playful, personal, experimental usage. That this is not Camus's final intention is, I think, clear, but the *Notebook* entry that I quoted above does show some of the tension he felt. It is notable that he contrasts 'the language of all' with 'poetry', whose allusive, non-literal, personal language guards the secrets

---

[150] Camus, 'Preface ...', in *SEN* 18, 25 (*LCE* 6, 14).

[151] Again, we should remember that several of Kierkegaard's pseudonyms—Johannes Climacus, for instance—are very close to Kierkegaard and express many of his deeply held views, while not sharing what Kierkegaard himself takes to be the ultimate truth. (Climacus is not a Christian.)

NEMESIS 149

while allowing the higher wisdom of love and excess (of which perhaps Camus was 'pretend[ing] to be unaware' in the passage just quoted from *The Rebel*) nonetheless to find its expression.[152] Again, it seems that he was struggling with the form that his essay on Nemesis would take—whether it could have been written in a conventionally philosophical manner, or whether he could find a suitably 'poetic' style to give proper expression to what he needed to say there.[153]

Some other remarks from the *Notebooks*, in which Camus seems to have been trying out ideas for the Nemesis essay, show that he had by no means rejected the ideal of moderation: 'N: power in moderation is the highest power.'[154] This seems to hark back to Simone Weil's idea that the 'moderate' use of force is the only way to avoid become emmeshed by it. Another remark seems to hint, enigmatically, at what he might mean by the idea of excluding nothing. It too points to the idea of a 'Higher word' or higher wisdom, but breaks off tantalizingly:

> N. realized. Multiplication of experiences but controlled, oriented towards the greatest belief and the highest epoch, but extreme freedom but according to discipline—and the life risked without truce, like a permanent sanction—and accepted and *prodigal* solitude, bowing only before the human being, secretly. Say no more but do make meaning of a higher word and speak only according to ...[155]

Another, long, entry from December 1959, very near the end of Camus's life, certainly seems to be finding a 'poetic' style, very different from the classic lucidity of *The Myth* and *The Rebel*, and very different even from the 'Lyrical Essays':

> *For Nemesis* (at Lourmarin, December '59).
> Black horse, white horse, a single hand of man controls the two passions. At breakneck speed, the race is joyous. Truth lies, frankness hides. Hide yourself in the light.
> The world fills you and you are empty: plenitude.
> Soft sound of foam on the morning beach; it fills the world as much as the clatter of fame. Both come from silence.

---

[152] One might worry that there is something deceitful or manipulative about this attitude; similar concerns have been expressed about Kierkegaard's techniques of 'indirect communication'. See, e.g., Aumann, *Art and Selfhood*, ch. 7. Such critiques raise deep issues about the ethics of communication. I think Kierkegaard (and Camus) can be defended, but it would take me too far afield to go into these issues here.

[153] Similar issues are raised in Kierkegaard's corpus; especially in *Fear and Trembling*, where the aesthetic is the sphere of ambiguity and concealment, whereas the ethical (and the lower forms of religious existence) demand clear, open communication that can be understood by all. But faith cannot make itself understood, based as it is on an utterly personal relationship between the individual and God, and therefore may be indistinguishable to an outsider from a reversion to the aesthetic. See especially Problema III (*FT* 82–120).

[154] *NB III*, 185.

[155] *NB III*, 186. The final ellipsis is in the original and marks the point where the remark breaks off.

150   THE PHILOSOPHY OF CAMUS

The one who refuses chooses himself, who covets prefers himself. Do not ask nor refuse. Accept surrender.

Flames of ice crown the days; sleep in the motionless fire.

Equally hard, equally soft, the slope, the slope of the day. Back at the summit? A single mountain. The night burns, the sun creates darkness. O earth, that suffices at everything. Freed of everything, enslaved to yourself. Enslaved to others, freed of nothing. Select your servitude.

Behind the cross, the devil. Leave them together. Your empty altar is elsewhere.

The waters of pleasure and of sea are equally salty. Even within the wave.

The exiled individual reigns, the king is on his knees. In the desert, solitude ceases.

On the sea, without truce, from port to island, running in the light, above the liquid abyss, joy, as long as very long life.

You mask yourself, here they are naked.

In the brief day that is given to you, warm and illuminate, without deviating from your course. Millions of other suns will come for your rest.

On the flagstones of joy, the first slumber.

Sowed by the wind, reaped by the wind, and creative nonetheless, and proud to live a single instant.[156]

Clearly the theme of balance, of holding apparent opposites in a creative tension, is central to this passage; so is the piling-up of paradoxes, which gives it an almost Daoist flavour. At the moment of greatest tension, the opposites cross over into one another. Resonant imagery from throughout Camus's career returns: sun, desert, exile, sea, the mountain summit to which Sisyphus repeatedly rolled his stone. His agnostic non-Christian spirituality is affirmed again; cross and devil are left behind together in favour of an 'empty altar'.[157] Has Camus passed beyond philosophy in this extraordinary prose–poetry? We do not of course know whether the proposed essay on Nemesis would have read anything like this, or whether Camus was here capturing thoughts and images on the wing, as it were, and would have worked them into a more conventional discursive prose. But, in any case, he is still responding to what are recognizably philosophical questions, while struggling to find a language that will not betray the insights it seeks to express. In this he is perhaps comparable with the later Heidegger, and even the later Merleau-Ponty, who

[156] NB III, 255–6.
[157] I suspect there is a reference here to the Athenians' altar 'to an unknown god' on which St Paul commented (Acts 17:23).

were both struggling to find a language that would take them beyond the limits of conventional philosophical discourse—without abandoning their philosophical concerns, but precisely in order to remain true to where their philosophical itineraries had taken them.

VII Radical Evil? Reading *The Fall*

I have discussed Camus's response to the problem of evil—how we can affirm the goodness of existence in the face of its horrors. But there is another problem of evil to be considered—concerning the evil within ourselves. This is the third of the Kierkegaardian problems that I raised for Camus at the end of the previous chapter. Once we recognize that we are subject to non-negotiable moral constraints—that we are obligated to respect the worth and dignity of all persons, and that this sets clear limits to what we can and cannot do to them—then we are also faced with the fact that human beings in general seem very bad at doing what they are morally obligated to do. And each of us, if we are honest, has to face the first-personal fact that *I* am very bad at living up to *my* moral obligations. I may not be guilty of murder, torture, genocide—although Camus was very aware of how many ordinary unremarkable human beings ended up becoming guilty of such things—and I may even seem to do reasonably well morally compared to many of those around me. But, the more seriously I take the demands of morality, the more I am liable to realize how far I fall short of living by them. And these demands are unconditional: I cannot shrug off my not being very good at morality as I can shrug off my not being very good at mathematics. But, if ethics makes demands on us that we are unable to fulfil, then the ethical stage would seem to be radically unstable. It would be liable to powerful criticisms, both from a kind of Nietzschean amoralism, which would see ethical demands as stifling, repressive impositions on a human nature to which they are not suited; and from a Kierkegaardian religious perspective that emphasizes the need of humans for divine forgiveness and grace. Can Camus defend an ethical perspective from these criticisms, while retaining an honest, unillusioned view of human moral failure?

Some commentators have argued that this is a problem that Camus did not really see clearly until quite late in his career, when he finally confronts it in his last published novel, *The Fall*. Phillip Rhein claims:

> The action of *La Chute* [*The Fall*] emphasizes certain aspects of human behavior that have not hitherto been investigated by Camus. In all of his writings from *L'Envers et l'endroit* to *L'Homme revolte*, there has been an underlying assumption of human innocence ... evil was always considered an outside force ... Realising the one-sidedness of his argument up to this time, Camus sought to correct his reasoning in *La Chute* ...The laws of logic dictate that, if all are innocent, there

152   THE PHILOSOPHY OF CAMUS

can be no human-created evil to resist. Obviously evil does exist and people exist who create the conditions against which the rebel revolts ... His concern with the guilty evildoer Jean-Baptiste Clamence, as opposed to the innocent rebels who up to this time have been his primary concern, represents a turning-point in his thought and a progression to a more complete, if less optimistic, understanding of human nature.[158]

I think Rhein is onto something here, though I do not think Camus was ever par-ticularly inclined to a naive optimism about human benevolence and altruism. The 'human innocence' on which he does insist in the Absurdist phase is not a judgement that humans are morally admirable; it is, rather, the consequence of his refusal to think in moral terms at all. Meursault does not complain that he is the victim of a miscarriage of justice, nor does he appeal from the French legal sys-tem of his day to purportedly higher standards of 'true' justice; he simply does not think in terms of justice, injustice, responsibility, at all. Camus's realization that this amoral thinking was untenable in the face of the massive human-created evil of war and totalitarianism was what led him to his ethical phase. He has some-times been accused of a certain evasion in *The Plague*, since the evil against which his characters struggle there is a natural rather than a humanly produced one, so the novel does not have to confront issues of guilt and responsibility.[159] But *The Rebel* is, of course, directly concerned to address the problem of human evil on a massive scale. Rhein claims that Camus still failed to come to terms there with the deeper causes of evil, seeing it as a consequence of intellectual error; he claims that Camus 'blamed the crimes committed in the name of communism upon the philosopher Hegel'.[160] I do not think Camus was ever as naive as that. (And, although his concern in *The Rebel* is to trace the *intellectual* roots of modern political murderousness, he never denies the historical importance of economic, social, and political factors.) It is true, though, that he did sometimes seem inclined to a certain kind of intellectualism about evil, stating, for instance, 'I would think— much like Socrates—that a person does not think badly because he is a criminal, but is a criminal because he thinks badly'.[161] Underlying this statement is a concern with the ways in which people who are not simply monsters can be manipulated by propaganda and various forms of corrupt thinking into committing monstrous acts. But it does still seem to express, we might say, a relative optimism; the invo-cation of Socrates is an implicit denial of the Christian idea of original sin (and its secular analogues) according to which wrongdoing is an effect, not of ignorance, but of a corrupt will.

[158] Rhein, *Albert Camus*, 87–8.
[159] He tries to respond to this charge in his open letter to Roland Barthes; see *SEN* 220–2 (*LCE* 338–40).
[160] Rhein, *Albert Camus*, 87.
[161] Camus, 'The Individual and Freedom' (1946), in *SO* 44.

Kierkegaard explicitly considers the 'Socratic definition' of 'sin as ignorance' according to which 'if a person does what is wrong, he has not understood what is right'.[162] Despite his deep admiration for Socrates, Kierkegaard firmly rejects such intellectualism. 'The intellectuality of the Greeks was too happy, too naïve, too aesthetic, too ironic, too witty—too sinful—to grasp that anyone could knowingly not do the good or knowingly, knowing what is right, do wrong.'[163] Although 'sin' (not the term Camus used, of course) does, according to Kierkegaard, typically involve ignorance, it is, for him, a kind of motivated ignorance; we know what is right, but we repress that knowledge because we do not *want* to act on it. The ultimate problem, then, is not ignorance but the corruption of the will: 'sin is not a matter of a person's not having understood what is right, but of his being unwilling to understand it, of his not willing what is right.'[164]

This seems to be a sharp rejection of the position that Camus was defending in the remark I quoted from him above, about criminality being the result of bad thinking. However, Camus's view may itself be a bit more complex than that remark by itself may make it seem. In the 'Letters to a German Friend' he tells his imaginary Nazi addressee: 'I am fighting you because your logic is as criminal as your heart. And in the horror you have visited on us for four years, your reason plays as large a part as your instinct.'[165] Here 'bad thinking' is not just lazy, sloppy, or intellectually inept thinking; it is morally corrupt ('criminal') thinking. And, if reason itself can be corrupted, then virtue cannot follow as a matter of course from reason dispelling ignorance.[166] Moreover, 'criminal' thinking surely presupposes a 'criminal heart'; it is the intellectual expression of a basically corrupt existential orientation or attitude to life. On this view, 'thinking badly' is not simply intellectual error, curable by a pure, neutral rationality; it is corrupt *existential* thinking, a kind of thinking that is itself one aspect of the corruption of the whole person. It is significant that, at the start of *The Rebel*, Camus announces that the story he will be telling is 'the history of European pride' (*R*. 11). It is a history not simply of intellectual errors, but of the expressions, on the intellectual plane, of a basic existential flaw—the hubris that rejects necessary limits. Kierkegaard and Camus are certainly in agreement that our thinking is one aspect of our existing; it is not something that takes place in a pure detached sphere of its own. (Kierkegaard, indeed, suggests that Socrates' real point may have been an ironical criticism of the

---

[162] *SUD* 95.

[163] *SUD* 90.

[164] *SUD* 95.

[165] Camus, 'Letters', in *RRD* 30.

[166] This would be a particularly naive version of the 'Socratic' view, and one that Plato, at any rate, did not hold. In the *Symposium*, he has Alcibiades explain at length how Socrates tries to persuade him to turn away from his unscrupulous pursuit of political ambition and turn towards the philosophical life. But he cannot bring himself to do what he knows is right: 'So,' he says, 'I refuse to listen to him; I stop my ears and tear myself away from him ... I know perfectly well I can't prove he's wrong when he tells me what I should do; yet, the moment I leave his side I go back to my old ways ...' (*Symposium*, 67 (216 a–b)). Clearly, Alcibiades' problem is more—or other—than just ignorance.

154   THE PHILOSOPHY OF CAMUS

idea that a purely intellectual, propositional knowledge of what is right is sufficient to bring about proper moral behaviour. If there is a truth to the idea that moral knowledge is what leads to moral behaviour, then the knowledge in question must consist in an existential appropriation, not merely an intellectual apprehension, of moral truths.[167])

Camus's critique, in *The Rebel*, of the philosophies that have excused or prepared the way for mass murder is in large part motivated by the perception that our capacity for moral choice may get eroded by the insidious effect of powerfully tempting but delusive ideas. The 'bad thinking' generated by those ideas can create a fog in which we may stumble into complicity with evil. But we are still responsible for doing so. In the 'Letters', Camus wants to understand how a certain intellectual climate may have contributed to the rise of Nazism, but he shows no inclination to excuse or forgive those whose 'criminal hearts' made them susceptible to the nihilism of the 'criminal logic' of their day. One of our moral responsibilities is to think clearly; not to let ourselves be bamboozled by 'bad thinking'—even and especially not the bad thinking of minds as brilliant and therefore seductive as Hegel's, Marx's, Nietzsche's, or Sartre's. (This indicates that the problem is not simply with obviously crude, inept, or foolish thinking; the most brilliant intelligence can lead us disastrously astray if we are not orientated by a basic ethical sense.) But, in *The Rebel*, Camus, while confronting the enormity and extent of human evil, and while he is at least not a *naive* intellectualist about it, still posits a philosophy of moral outrage, clear thinking, and respect for limits as an adequate response to that evil. However insidious the temptation to evil, it is something that we can avoid if we choose to do so. There can be a morally righteous Rebel (even though, as we have seen, the Rebel may not be able to avoid 'dirty hands' entirely). In the ethical world of *The Plague* and *The Rebel*, there can be people who are innocent, not in the Absurdist sense, but in the sense of being genuinely moral, just people. And, on this point, it seems, he does continue to disagree with Kierkegaard.

Is Camus's at least somewhat optimistic view really correct, though? Might even the best people still harbour some corruption within them? And, even if there are secular saints (like, perhaps, Dr Rieux in *The Plague*), it seems there are very few of them. And if I, on an honest self-examination (itself no easy task!), have to conclude that I am not one of them, what then? In 'Return to Tipasa', as we have seen, Camus bleakly remarks: 'In the days of innocence I did not know that morality existed. I now know that it did, and could not live up to it.'[168] In the 1958 preface to *L'Envers et l'endroit* he notes, even more bleakly: 'Man sometimes seems to me to be a walking injustice. I am thinking of myself ... I have doubtless never said that I was a just man. I have merely happened to say that we should try to

---

[167] See *SUD* 90–2.
[168] Camus, 'Return to Tipasa', in *SEN* 149 (*LCE* 164).

be just, and also that such an ambition involved great toil and misery.'[169] Does the ethical life require us to live with a constant burden of guilt, and a constant struggle towards heights that seem unattainable? Does it have anything to say to me except to keep repeating that I must try harder, even as I fail again and again? And is not this liable to lead either to a deep gnawing resentment against ethics and its demands; or to a hypocritical self-deception, as I pretend to myself that I have succeeded in living up to those demands; or to a sort of comfortable bourgeois moralism, in which I lower the demands of morality until I can feel comfortable with them? These are questions that Camus explores in his brilliant and disturbing novella *The Fall*. Since he does not discuss them in any detail in his theoretical works, I will be departing from my usual rule and considering *The Fall* rather more closely than I have his other literary works.

The Fall is the darkest and most ambiguous of all Camus's writings. Its protagonist, Jean-Baptiste Clamence, was once a successful Parisian lawyer, a defender of noble causes, handsome, charming, prosperous—and also a cynical and promiscuous womanizer. He now lives under what we discover is an assumed name, in a bare apartment in Amsterdam, where he provides informal legal advice to the shady clientele of the seedy bar that he frequents. The book consists of a series of monologues in which he explains this change in his life to an unnamed interlocutor. Back in Paris, a growing sense that there was something fraudulent about his existence started finding expression in a mysterious untraceable laughter that began to accompany him. One evening, although he loves to perform charitable actions when there is a crowd to observe them, he fails to do anything to save a young woman who has jumped into the Seine when there was no one else around. Growing ever more mordantly cynical about himself and the whole *milieu* in which he lives, he tries to destroy his own reputation for nobility and high-mindedness, and looks for oblivion in debauchery. When nothing works, he abandons his legal practice, moves to Amsterdam, and becomes 'Clamence'. There he buttonholes strangers such as his current interlocutor and charms them into hearing his confessions. But he is not exactly a penitent; rather, as he puts it, a 'judge–penitent'. The whole point of his narrative is to make his interlocutors see that Clamence's guilt is not personal to him, but universal; and, more particularly, to find a comparable vanity, hypocrisy, and egoism in themselves. The apparently damning self-portrait he constructs is really 'the image of all and of no one' (*F.* 139). He shows the portrait 'with great sorrow. "This, alas, is what I have become!" ... But at the same time the portrait I hold out to my contemporaries becomes a mirror' (*F.* 140). In this way, Clamence shrugs off his own personal guilt and self-hatred, and turns it into an instrument to dominate others. For, if we are all guilty, then those who realize their guilt are superior to those who do not. 'I am like them, to be sure; we are in the soup together. But I have a superiority in that I know it

---

[169] Camus, 'Preface', in *SEN* 24 (*LCE* 14).

156   THE PHILOSOPHY OF CAMUS

... the more I accuse myself, the more I have a right to judge you' (F. 140). Indeed, it transpires that Clamence too is ultimately seeking self-divinisation, albeit by a more twisted and devious route than the other figures Camus creates or considers: 'I am on the mountain, the plain stretches before my eyes. How intoxicating to feel like God the Father and to hand out definitive testimonials of bad character and habits' (F. 143).

This strange narrative has attracted a wide range of interpretations. Some have seen it in personal terms, either as disguised autobiography, a confession by Camus of his own sense of moral bankruptcy, or as an attack on Sartre and the fashionable leftist Parisian intellectual scene. There is no doubt something in both of these interpretations, nor need they be considered incompatible.[170] Certainly Camus's guilt about his marital infidelities and his insecurity about the status as a moral exemplar that he was for a time accorded by many of his contemporaries fed into the portrayal of Clamence. And Camus's *Notebooks* show that the key notion of the judge–penitent emerged from his bitter reflections on the controversy with Sartre: 'Existentialism. When they accuse themselves, one can be sure that it is always to crush others. Judge–penitents.'[171] But, beyond these personal references, how can we situate *The Fall* in the development of Camus's thought? Some Christian readers have seen in it an admission of the failure of humanistic ethics to acknowledge or respond adequately to the corruption of the human heart; a confession—whether consciously intended as such on Camus's part or not—of the need for divine grace. Unquestionably, *The Fall* is saturated with Christian images and references, starting with the title, but also including Clamence's chosen name, which alludes both to John the Baptist, the precursor of Christ, and the voice 'crying in the wilderness' from the Prophet Isaiah;[172] the comparison of Amsterdam with its concentric canals to the circles of Dante's Hell (Clamence notes that he lurks in the last and deepest circle—reserved in Dante for the traitors (see F. 14–15)); the reference to the doves (traditionally images of the Holy Spirit) hovering above the city, and Clamence's vision of their descent (F. 73, 145); and his election as 'pope' by his fellow-prisoners in a Wartime camp (F. 125). Clamence also discourses at some length explicitly about Christ and theology (F. 110–16). The question is what to make of all this.

Stephen Evans claims that '[i]n *The Fall* we see Camus' disillusionment over the possibility of morality in a world without God'.[173] Moral demands remain valid, but Camus, as Evans sees it, despairs of humans ever being able to live up to them. Another Christian writer, Bernard Murchland, argued, in an article written while Camus was still alive, that, after *The Fall*, 'the development of his work must, if it continues, culminate in some spiritual position ... It is quite possible that the novel

---

[170] See, e.g., Judt, *The Burden of Responsibility*, 104.
[171] *NB III*, 131. See Sharpe, *Camus, Philosophe*, 341–3, for a more detailed analysis.
[172] Isaiah 40:3.
[173] Evans, *Existentialism*, 39.

(*The Fall*) expresses a realization of sin and unworthiness—the dark night before the coming of grace ... it seems to be an authentic cry for salvation.'[174] He continues, though: 'But it would not do to force this conclusion. [*The Fall*] could conceivably be satirizing the whole notion of guilt and protesting its being used as a weapon for enslaving men and deadening their creative powers for self-transcendence.'[175] More recently, Robert Solomon has taken up this latter suggestion, arguing that *The Fall* should be read as a Nietzschean parable about how a strong, happy man was sadly brought down by his failure to rid himself of a lingering Christian sense of guilt.[176]

Srigley rejects Solomon's reading, but also sees *The Fall* as explicitly anti-Christian. Camus, on Srigley's interpretation, saw Nietzsche—like Marx and other influential Modern philosophers—not as offering an alternative to Christianity, but as continuing by other means its disastrous departure from Greek notions of harmony and balance. In his previous works Camus had tried to develop a critique of Modernity without wholly repudiating its aspirations and therefore without wholly repudiating the Christianity that lay behind them. This, Srigley thinks, leads to inconsistencies in both *The Myth* and *The Rebel*. With *The Fall*, the gloves were off. 'No more concessions to Modernity's good intentions, and no more conciliation in relation to Christianity, either.' Rather Camus extends his critique of Modernity 'to the very foundations of its apocalyptic aspirations, namely to the metaphysical unrest that is Christianity's central teaching.'[177] Sharpe, however, rejects Srigley's interpretation as too 'abstract'[178] and sees *The Fall* as more of an essay in moral psychology, which expresses Camus's continuing distrust of general, universalizing claims. Clamence's problem is that, instead of facing up to his own shortcomings and trying to live a better life, he generalizes so as to pretend that his guilt is really universal: 'we cannot accept any interpretation which suggests that Clamence's blanket decrial of universal guilt should be read as Camus' own.'[179] Sharpe therefore rejects Rhein's idea that *The Fall* shows a new and more pessimistic understanding of human evil, not present in the earlier work.

As we saw, Clamence warned us that his narrative turned into a mirror, so it is perhaps not surprising that commentators (and I have given only a sampling) look into *The Fall* and find it reflecting their own views back at them. Obviously, I run the same risks as anyone else in trying to come to terms with this brilliantly treacherous little book. It might be tempting to start by considering whether Clamence goes wrong by thinking himself guilty at all (Solomon); by generalizing from his

---

[174] Murchland, 'The Dark Night before the Coming of Grace?', 63.

[175] Murchland, 'The Dark Night before the Coming of Grace?', 63–4. However, he does go on to claim that, in his short-story collection, *Exile and the Kingdom*, Camus 'returns to the same redemptive themes' (p. 64) and that these stories would be harder to read ironically.

[176] See Solomon, *Dark Feelings, Grim Thoughts*, ch. 8.

[177] Srigley, *Camus' Critique*, 83.

[178] Sharpe, *Camus, Philosophe*, 338.

[179] Sharpe, *Camus, Philosophe*, 343.

158   THE PHILOSOPHY OF CAMUS

guilt to universal guilt (Sharpe); or by using his (valid) perception of universal guilt as a way to judge others. I think Solomon's interpretation is untenable, but, if Clamence does come to an accurate perception of the vanity and selfishness of his own life, is he right to extrapolate to others as he does? Sharpe quotes Clamence: 'After prolonged research on myself, I brought out the fundamental duplicity of the human being' (*F*. 84) and comments: 'as if a sample of one, looked at in the light of a wounded narcissism, were a valid basis to infer concerning human nature per se.'[180] But, if one does believe in a universal human nature (as Camus did), then it is not necessarily unreasonable to think that careful self-examination might bring truths about humanity as such to light. (Sharpe fails to note the difference between the Phenomenological method of intuition of essences and an empirical induction by enumeration. According to the crucial argument at the start of *The Rebel*, one case in which I witness a person being abused should be enough to make me realize that there is a universal humanity that the abuser is violating.[181]) But it may, in any case, be approaching things in the wrong way to ask (as I started to above) whether a literary work like *The Fall* makes a case for universal human guilt or not. In *The Fall*, Camus is not trying to construct a theory of human nature (whether or not on the basis of insufficient data); rather, by exposing us to Clamence's interrogation, he is challenging each of us, first-personally, to see if there is something of the Clamence in me too.

To see what Camus is attempting, it is helpful to consider the epigraph to *The Fall*, which Camus took from Lermontov. There Lermontov, speaking of his book *A Hero of our Time*, states that it 'is a portrait, but not of an individual; it is the aggregate of the vices of our whole generation in their fullest expression'. Presumably, Camus intended to suggest that *The Fall* does the same for his generation and its vices (and, if neither he nor Sartre was free of those vices, then both of them might indeed be recognized in it). But, as we have just seen, Clamence himself claimed to have painted just such a generalized portrait 'of all and of no one'—but one that then turned into a mirror. *The Fall* is written throughout in the second person (a remarkable feat of stylistic virtuosity); whoever Clamence's interlocutor is, or whether there even is one,[182] each of us, as the reader, is addressed personally. The book then is at least intended to be a critical portrait of the vices of its age, but presented, not with sociological detachment, but with the directness of a personal address. It challenges each of us to consider whether we find something like Clamence's vices in ourselves. 'Admit', he asks his interlocutor, 'that today you feel less pleased with yourself than you did five days ago?' (*F*. 141). And, of course,

---

[180] Sharpe, *Camus, Philosophe*, 345.
[181] See Kierkegaard's comment: 'If an observer will only pay attention to himself, he will have enough with five men, five women and ten children for the discovery of all possible states of the human soul' (*CA* 126).
[182] It is at least possible that the whole monologue is going on in Clamence's own feverish mind, or that it is his own past self that he is addressing.

it is the reader who is asked to admit that— or at least challenged seriously to consider it.

This procedure is very Kierkegaardian. In the introduction to *The Concept of Anxiety*, Kierkegaard argues that sin cannot be made the subject of any theoretical enquiry without distorting the concept; it can be properly grasped only in an attitude of personal concern. 'Sin does not properly belong in any science, but is the subject of the sermon, in which the single individual speaks as a single individual to the single individual.'[183] He goes on, though, to liken the sermon in this respect to the Socratic dialogue, which is also crucially about 'appropriation'[184]— that is, the individual being able to apply what is being said to his or her own life. And there is certainly something Socratic about Clamence's technique. Socrates ironically presented himself as ignorant, but in a way that served to reveal his interlocutors' ignorance (concealed behind misunderstandings and pretentions to knowledge). Similarly, Clamence's avowal of his own guilt and corruption bring to light his interlocutors' hidden shortcomings—although, of course, Clamence's own motives in doing this are themselves thoroughly corrupt. Kierkegaard insists on the Socratic character of his pseudonymous writings, as indirect communications intended to serve as occasions for self-examination on the part of each individual reader; and, if we ask why Camus invented Clamence, we can see that he functions very much like a Kierkegaardian pseudonym in this respect. Clamence is certainly not to be identified with Camus, and his often brilliantly cynical observations are not necessarily Camus's own (though many of them may be); but he acts as a stimulus, for each of us personally, to engage in serious self-examination.

Of course, one may worry that, in presenting a picture of vice in which his readers may find themselves too, Camus is himself playing Clamence's game. Or is he even doing Clamence one better, by showing that he has seen through, not only our quotidian vices, but also the efforts of Clamence-like 'judge–penitents' (such as Sartre as he saw him) to play God via self-abasement? But, if so, is he not still locked into the game of moral one-upmanship? Perhaps, then, we should not only see Jean-Baptiste Clamence as akin to a Kierkegaardian pseudonym, but also see even the 'Albert Camus' who appears as the author of *The Fall* as akin to a pseudonym, whom the real Camus intended us to see through as still being trapped in the Clamencian game. But if we, along with the posited 'real Camus', do see through the author of *the Fall*, then are *we* not still just taking one further step in an infinite regress of moral smugness? If our heads are starting to spin a bit at this point, perhaps we should take that as pointing us to a further dimension of *The Fall*'s message.

Whether moral corruption is universal or merely very widespread, there is no question that Clamence digs himself deeper into it by taking on the role of

---

[183] *CA* 16.
[184] *CA* 16.

160   THE PHILOSOPHY OF CAMUS

'judge–penitent'—avoiding facing up to his own guilt by finding it in others. He is really perverting the Gospel precept 'do not judge, so that you may not be judged'[185] and making it 'judge yourself in order to judge others' (see *F*. 138). And, just as we are being challenged by Clamence to see ourselves in his portrayal of his own first-order moral corruption, as we might call it, so we are also challenged by Camus to see ourselves in Clamence's higher-order corruption—that is, his eagerness to adopt a judgmental stance towards others. *The Fall*, I think, certainly contains a critique of a certain kind of moralizing—an eagerness to seek out and find guilt in others (although, as I noted above, it is hard to avoid the trap of moralizing against the moralizers). This moralizing may take the form of simple self-righteousness, or the more twisted way that Clemence embraces, of calling attention to one's own sins in order to demonstrate one's superior moral sensitivity. In any case, a later *Notebook* entry (June 1959) continues Camus's attack on 'Morals':

> I have abandoned the moral point of view. Morals lead to abstraction and to injustice. They are the mother of fanaticism. And blindness. Whoever is virtuous must cut off the heads. But what to say of those who profess morality without being able to live up to its high standards. The heads fall, and he legislates, unfaithful. Morality cuts in two, separates, wastes away. One must flee morality, accept being judged and not judging, saying yes, creating unity—and for the time being, suffering agony.[186]

Whatever this is, it cannot be a repudiation of ethics as such in favour of some kind of amoralism, for 'Morals' are being judged in explicitly ethical terms. In part it is a critique of a kind of social conformity.[187] But what is most striking is its rejection of the judgemental attitude. The 'virtuous' condemn others while living in hypocrisy with their own guilt. But the advice to 'flee morality' while 'not judging, saying yes, creating unity' and accepting suffering is itself moral advice.[188] One is reminded of Kierkegaard's distinction between a 'first' and a 'second' ethics. The first comes to grief with the realization of human sinfulness (our inability to live up to moral demands): 'Sin, then, belongs to ethics only insofar as upon this concept it is shipwrecked ... A category that lies entirely beyond its reach has appeared ...'[189] Kierkegaard goes on to note that 'all ancient [pre-Christian] ethics was based on

---

[185] Matthew 7:1 (New Revised Standard Version).
[186] *NB III*, 248.
[187] A slightly earlier note reads: 'For years I've wanted to live according to everyone else's morals. I've forced myself to live like everyone else ... And after all of this, catastrophe came. Now I wander amid the debris, I am lawless, torn to pieces and accepting to be so, resigned to my singularity and to my infirmities' (*NB III*, 246 (April 1959)).
[188] Or at any rate, ethical advice, if one wants to distinguish a narrow, rule-bound 'Morality' from a broader notion of 'Ethics', as some later philosophers do. See Williams, *Ethics and the Limits of Philosophy*, ch. 10; MacIntyre, *Ethics in the Conflicts of Modernity*, ch. 3.
[189] *CA* 17.

the proposition that virtue can be realized. Sin's skepticism is altogether foreign to paganism.'[190] This impasse can be solved only theologically ('dogmatically') with the concepts of original sin, forgiveness, and grace. On this basis, a 'second ethics' becomes possible: 'the new ethics presupposes dogmatics ... only the second ethics can deal with its [sin's] manifestation.'[191]

In terms of its content, this 'second ethics' would centrally involve love rather than judgement, and in his major (non-pseudonymous) work on Christian ethics, *Works of Love*, Kierkegaard argues that we have a duty to interpret other people's behaviour in the most generous light possible, while subjecting our own motives to the strictest scrutiny.[192] Although he believes in the universality of sin, Kierkegaard also thinks that the only sins that any person ought to be concerned with are his or her own. Hence his interpretation of the injunction mentioned above: 'Do not judge, so you may not be judged.' Kierkegaard notes that this is expressed as a warning of external consequences, so that it seems in principle 'as if at times one could judge without being judged in return. But', he continues, 'this is not the case ... to judge someone else is to judge yourself or to be disclosed yourself.'[193] When I judge another, one thing at least that I do is to 'disclose' or reveal myself as being willing to judge—as well as raising the question of whether the judgements I make of others can themselves be turned back on me. Camus, of course, does not accept Kierkegaard's theological assumptions, but his advice about 'not judging, saying yes' while also accepting suffering—the suffering of isolation, and of one-self being exposed to the judgement of others—seems strikingly Kierkegaardian. Camus too seems to have been looking beyond the ruins of 'Morality' to a non-judgemental 'second ethics'. And, of course. the third, Nemesis, cycle was to have centrally involved the theme of love.

Though it does not give a theory—much less a theological one—of human evil, *The Fall* inescapably raises the question of how to respond to it. Clamence ironically comments on Christianity: 'After all, it was a stroke of genius to tell us: "You're not a very pretty sight, that's certain! Well, we won't go into the details! We'll just liquidate it, once for all, on the cross!"' (*F.* 114). Camus certainly shares this scepticism about the idea of Christ's death as a redemptive vicarious sacrifice that frees us from the burden of sin. But, while rejecting the Christian solution to the problem of human corruption, Camus certainly take the problem itself seriously. And I think he clearly rejects the heroic humanism that supposes all we need to do is grit

[190] *CA* 19.
[191] *CA* 20, 21.
[192] See Kierkegaard, 'Love Believes All Things', in *WL* 225–43. How one combines that generosity with a realism about people's motives, and a willingness to take the moral attitude that one needs to take to a Hitler or Stalin (or to some other more everyday characters in one's social environment) is another question, of course. Kierkegaard does not address it in detail, but he does recognize that the 'servants of justice' do legitimately try to assess the guilt of others and to act accordingly towards them. (He is not an anarchist.) See *WL* 292–4.
[193] *WL* 233.

162 THE PHILOSOPHY OF CAMUS

our teeth and will to be good; that seems both unrealistic and liable to lead to the pathologies of moralism, as noted above. As for Clamence's own solution, it is clear enough that it is not really successful, even in its own terms; there is something desperately unconvincing in his cry 'I am happy, I tell you, I won't let you think I'm not happy! I am happy unto death!' (*F.*, 144).[194] At the end of the book, he does seem to feel a real longing for something that could rescue him from the dead-end of festering egoism in which he has trapped himself, as expressed in his wish for a second chance to rescue the young woman whom he let drown—although he also admits he does not *really* want that: 'It's too late now. It will always be too late. Fortunately!' (*F.* 147). Does this ambivalent longing for and fear of some kind of grace simply express (as on humanistic readings of *The Fall*) Clamence's weakness, his unwillingness to pull himself together by his own efforts? I think not; as we have seen throughout this chapter, Camus insists that, to prevent ethics 'shrivelling up', turning into something bitter, punitive, vindictive, we need to open ourselves to something larger than ourselves, something that goes 'beyond ethics'. Of course, for Camus, this is the logos, the harmonious order of the world that expresses itself in natural beauty. And natural beauty is, significantly, something that Clamence insistently forces himself to reject.

Amsterdam is a beautiful city; but it appears in *The Fall* as sinister, damp, fog-bound, disorienting—the opposite, of course, to Camus's beloved Mediterranean. At one point, Clamence takes his interlocutor out on the Zuider Zee in order to revel masochistically in

> that most beautiful negative landscape. Just see on the left that pile of ashes they call a dune here, the grey dike on the right, the livid beech at our feet and in front of us the sea the color of a weak lye-solution, with the vast sky reflecting the colorless waters. A soggy hell, indeed! Everything horizontal, no relief; space is colorless and life dead. Is not universal obliteration, eternal nothingness, made visible? (*F.* 72)

He does admit, however, that 'the sky is alive' (*F.* 73) and goes on to refer to those mysterious doves, which, he says, hover over Holland in their millions. 'They ... would like to come down. But there is nothing but the sea and the canals, roofs covered with shop signs, and never a head on which to light' (*F.* 73). He has placed himself in this negative landscape precisely because it offers no purchase to the doves of the Holy Spirit, no possibility for grace to descend.[195] On their return journey Clamence translates this traditional Christian symbolism into the terms of

---

[194] I suspect this is a reference to Kierkegaard's *The Sickness unto Death*, which is about the varieties of despair and the self-deceptions through which we try to hide them from ourselves.
[195] Although it is interesting that *the* dove, which traditionally symbolized the Spirit, here becomes millions of them—perhaps a suggestion that, even when Clamence (or Camus?) seems to come closest to Christianity, he feels the need to transpose its symbolism into a more polytheistic register.

NEMESIS 163

Camus's own symbolic geography, contrasting their 'soggy hell' where everything merges into everything else with 'the Greek archipelago' where 'new islands would appear on the horizon. Their treeless backbone marked the limit of the sky and their rocky shore contrasted sharply with the sea. No confusion was possible ... in our little boat ... I felt we were scudding along ... on the crest of the short, cool waves in a race full of spray and laughter' (*F.* 97). And then he breaks off: 'I am becoming lyrical! Stop me, *cher*, I beg you ... Do you know Greece? No? So much the better. What should we do there, I ask you? There one has to be pure in heart' (*F.* 97–8). The reference to Camus's own Mediterranean-themed 'Lyrical Essays' is unmistakable, and so too is Clamence's rejection of the secular grace, the 'unconquerable summer', that Camus had found in the beauty of Tipasa.

Clamence has chosen to cut himself off from grace, however conceived. In so doing, he seems to come close to Kierkegaard's category of those who despair in defiance by refusing to accept forgiveness or grace: 'in spite of or in defiance of all existence he wills to be himself with it [his despair], to take it along, almost flouting his agony. Hope in the possibility of help ... — no — that he does not want ... Rather than to seek help he prefers, if necessary, to be himself with all the agonies of hell.'[196] Clamence's despairing cynicism places him (as he sees it) in a position of superiority over others; and that is not something he is willing to give up. As Kierkegaard puts it, what he is most afraid of is that eternity 'will separate him from his, demoniacally understood, infinite superiority over other men, his justification, demoniacally understood, for being what he is.'[197] And, yet, there is still that something in Clamence that continues to long for a way out. At the end of the book, seeing the snow falling, he exclaims:

It must be the doves, surely. They finally made up their minds to come down, the little dears ... they are fluttering at every window. What an invasion. Let us hope they are bringing good news. Everyone will be saved, eh?—and not only the elect. Possessions and hardships will be shared ... The whole shooting match, eh? (*F.* 145)

It is a Christian apocalyptic vision, but one that has an immediate socio-political relevance (the sharing of possessions and, not an end to hardships, but a sharing of those too); and also modifies traditional Christian eschatology (so that 'everyone will be saved') in a way that deeply resonates with Camus's own outlook. But Clamence continues: 'Come now, admit that you would be flabbergasted if a chariot came down from heaven to carry me off or if the snow suddenly caught fire. You don't believe it? Nor do I' (*F.* 145–6). In the end he is left as he describes himself, 'an empty prophet for shabby times, Elijah without a messiah, choked with fever

---

[196] *SUD* 71.
[197] *SUD* 72.

164   THE PHILOSOPHY OF CAMUS

and alcohol ...' (*F.* 117). Where does that leave us? Not, I think, with Srigley's critique of Christianity and Modernity—though, no doubt, with a critique of some of their pathologies; and not just with a case study of a narcissistic personality, from which we can take away the reassuring reflection that at least we are better than that. It leaves each of us readers, individually, with a challenge: am I, in some way, like that? And, if I am, what, if anything, can I do about it?

For, whatever Clamence might think about the inescapable corruption of the human being, and his ambivalent longing for something like grace to rescue him, Camus is not, I think, intending *The Fall* to teach us any sort of fatalism. He does take seriously the deep-seated human tendency to egoism and injustice, while also rejecting the grim jaw-clenching moralism that supposes we can cure ourselves by some sheer act of will. But, in accordance with his general philosophy of moderation and balance, he does not think this should lead us to despair. We remain free agents, capable of taking responsibility for ourselves; and, as I have tried to suggest in previous sections, what he sees as the way out of self-absorbed egoism—including the egoism of wallowing in one's own sense of guilt—is love. Freedom is not about grabbing oneself by the scruff of the neck, but is exercised, as Weil said, in the difficult act of paying attention to what is real outside of oneself, and finding it worthy of admiration and love.[198] (Opening ourselves, we might say, to the grace that is there in the world around us, if we are willing to attend to it.) In 'Return to Tipasa', Camus spoke of 'two thirsts that cannot long be neglected if all our being is not to dry up, the thirst to love and the thirst to admire'.[199] Clamence is, precisely, someone who has dried up through neglecting those thirsts. And he has done so through the misuse of his own freedom.

Towards the end of *The Fall*, as he reveals more of his hand, Clamence gives us a sense of what he means by 'freedom': 'Once upon a time, I was always talking of freedom. At breakfast I used to spread it on my toast ...' (*F.* 132). Initially he used the rhetoric of freedom as an excuse for his egoism—especially in sexual matters: 'With that key word I would bludgeon everything that contradicted me; I made it serve my desires and my power. I would whisper it in the ear of my sleeping mates and it would help me to drop them' (*F.* 132). But it gradually dawns on him that freedom is, rather, 'a chore ... a long-distance race, quite solitary and very exhausting' (*F.* 133). So now, he tells us, he wants to give it up, surrender it to some tyrannical 'master' who will leave us without the painful burdens of choice and responsibility. 'On the bridges of Paris, I too learned that I was afraid of freedom. So hurray for the master, whoever he may be, to take the place of heaven's law ... When we are all guilty, that will be democracy ... All together at last, but on our knees and heads bowed' (*F.* 136). There can be no doubt that, at this point at

---

[198] See Weil, 'Reflections on the Right Use of Schools Studies' and 'Forms of the Implicit Love of God'. The idea is developed by Murdoch, especially in *The Sovereignty of Good*.
[199] In *SEN* 152 (*LCE* 167).

least, Camus is indeed engaged in a caustic satire on Sartre. 'At the end of all, free-dom is a court sentence', Clamence remarks (*F.* 133), paraphrasing Sartre's famous dictum: 'Man is condemned to be free.'[200] And, when Clamence describes himself as 'an enlightened advocate of slavery' (*F.* 132) who wants to throw that freedom away to ruthless 'masters', this is certainly a bitter verdict on Sartre's apologia for Stalinism.[201] From Camus's perspective, Sartrean freedom is an abstract egoism, divorced from any positive relations to others (who feature in Sartre's universe only as threats to my freedom). But such freedom is eventually exhausting, and then one tries to surrender it to History and its self-appointed agents—again, the lurching between extremes of transcendence and immanence.

But the problem is not just with Clamence's Sartrean misconception of freedom, for even the more modest sense of freedom that Camus himself advocates may still be experienced as a burden. Clamence testifies to his fear of freedom, and there is, I think, a suggestive parallel with Kierkegaard's dictum that 'anxiety is freedom's actuality as the possibility of possibility'.[202] The sense of ourselves as free, even when it is taken in a more modest sense than Sartre's, induces anxiety. What dis-turbs us in the state of anxiety (in Kierkegaard's semi-technical sense) is not any definite threat, but the sense of possibility itself, and the possibility of choosing either good or evil.[203] Hence, 'anxiety is the dizziness of freedom ... in anxiety there is the selfish infinity of possibility, which does not tempt like a choice but ensnar-ingly disquiets with its sweet anxiousness'.[204] Kierkegaard's *The Concept of Anxiety*, like *The Fall*, is full of images of vertigo, dizziness, and falling.[205] Clamence, as we just saw, associated freedom with power and control, but the recognition of one's freedom may also be what throws one off balance; to know that one *could* fall induces one into falling. (The fascination of the abyss.) This is why Kierkegaard thinks that, although (as we have seen) the fall into sin cannot be explained, the closest we can come to explaining it is through the understanding of anxiety.

Anxiety, however, also appears in the opposite condition: the 'demonic', which Kierkegaard defines as 'anxiety about the good'.[206] Human freedom means that the sinner always has the possibility of turning back to the good, but, for the demoniac, this prospect is itself unnerving. Like Clamence, therefore, he tries to persuade himself that it is 'too late' for that. 'The demonic is unfreedom that wants to close

---

[200] Sartre, *Existentialism and Humanism*, 34.
[201] This is not to suggest that Clamence is only or even primarily a parody of Sartre.
[202] *CA* 42.
[203] This is why Kierkegaard is careful to distinguish between anxiety and fear (which, for him, is always directed to some definite threat).
[204] *CA* 61.
[205] The parallels are striking enough (and *The Concept of Anxiety* is, in part, about the Fall, the story of Adam and Eve, and original sin) to make me wonder if Camus had been reading or rereading it (and *The Sickness Unto Death*, also) while he was working on *The Fall*. But the parallels are worth noting, whether or not that is the case.
[206] *CA* 118 ff.

166 THE PHILOSOPHY OF CAMUS

itself off.'[207] But it seems that, despite himself, Clamence cannot simply lapse into a state of contented corruption; hence his ambivalent longing for the descent of the doves. (Kierkegaard describes anxiety as '*a sympathetic antipathy* and *an antipathetic sympathy*.'[208]) The evildoer has in a sense lost his or her freedom—in the sense, not of 'an abstract *liberum arbitrium* [free will]',[209] which Kierkegaard rejects, but in the sense of the orientation to the good that characterizes a human being regarded as 'spirit'. But this loss can never be complete; hence Clamence's continuing uneasy recognition of the possibility of genuine penitence, which he tries to suppress through his strategy of turning his examination of his own short-comings into a means of dominating others. But this is itself a freely willed evasion, for 'unfreedom is a phenomenon of freedom'[210]—it is not simply something that happens to us. This is perhaps why Clamence—having mapped Amsterdam's geog-raphy onto that of Dante's Hell—makes a point of noting that he is in the last circle, reserved by Dante for the traitors. Clamence—though eminently untrustworthy in general—is primarily a traitor to himself.

[207] *CA* 123.
[208] *CA* 42.
[209] *CA* 49.
[210] *CA* 135n.

Conclusion

My aim in this book has been to provide a perspicuous overview of Camus's philosophical thought and—though without attempting a comprehensive evaluation—to argue that it is more rigorous, more defensible, and deserves to be taken more seriously, than has often been supposed. I hope to have shown that using the Kierkegaardian account of the aesthetic, ethical, and religious stages of life as a point of comparison has been helpful in this regard. I have also tried to show that Kierkegaard's account of the self as a synthesis of complementary but potentially conflicting factors held together by the self's orientation to a source of objective value can serve as a useful point of comparison for Camus's attempt to develop a view of human nature that would 'exclude nothing' and would stand as a corrective to the one-sided and therefore dehumanizing ideologies of his day. And I hope that the comparison with Kierkegaard's literary techniques—particularly his use of pseudonyms—can help us to understand better Camus's (more complex than has often been realized) relation to his own works. While these comparisons between Camus and Kierkegaard —and the more specific ones that I have made at various points in the book—are suggestive, I have not tried to make any detailed biographical case for Kierkegaard's direct influence on Camus. It may indeed have been greater than has usually been supposed, but the commonalities may also have been due simply to the convergence of Camus's independent thinking with Kierkegaard's. And, while I have stressed the commonalities, I have tried not to exaggerate them or to downplay the differences between the two thinkers. But a full investigation of those differences needs to be based on a recognition of the extent to which—as I said in the Introduction—Camus and Kierkegaard argued on common ground.

When I started this book, I was convinced that there was at least a clear structural parallel between Kierkegaard's and Camus's philosophical thinking, and that Kierkegaard's schema of the stages of life would thus prove a useful template for a systematic reconstruction of Camus's thought. In the course of writing the book, I was struck and even surprised to discover how extensive the more substantive parallels were, in particular, with respect to religious questions. In an early draft of the Introduction, I had written: 'I am not trying to suggest that Camus is a religious thinker.' I finished the book convinced that—and in a non-trivial sense—he really is. Certainly not quite in Kierkegaard's sense. Camus rejects the Christian terminus of Kierkegaard's religious thinking, although he continued to have an ambivalent fascination with Christianity. And there remain significant differences between Camus's 'sense of the sacred' and even Kierkegaard's non-Christian 'Religiousness A'. But I do think the key to Camus's work and sensibility is the duality of affirmation and negation that haunted him throughout his career. And these are both, as I have argued throughout, essentially religious attitudes ('Greek' and 'Gnostic') albeit non-Christian ones.[1] (The neo-Gnosticism might be considered only *quasi*-religious, in that it lacks the belief in a higher world that historical Gnosticism had. But that lack is precisely what makes for the radical

---

[1] Christianity (conventional theism in general) with its stress on divine transcendence is too other-worldly for the first view, and, with its doctrines of Creation and Providence, all-too worldly for the second.

168 CONCLUSION

instability in Metaphysical Rebellion that Camus diagnosed.) The tension between them is obvious, but for Camus they belong inescapably together. One cannot love life without being horrified at suffering and death; and one cannot feel that horror without presupposing the value of that vulnerable and suffering life. Insofar as Camus resolves the tension between them, it is through his discussion of the tragic world view. That might be understood as a way of living with the tension but without resolution; but I have suggested that we find in his work at least hints of a final reconciliation, the belief that, even in tragedy, conflict does not have the last word. He was haunted by the saying of Sophocles' Oedipus, that, in spite of everything he has done and suffered, 'all is well'.[2]

In the early Lyrical Essays, these attitudes of acceptance and negation coexist without much attempt at showing *how* they can do so. Camus's main concern is simply with being true to both sides of the coin (*l'envers et l'endroit*—obverse and reverse) to use his own image; with affirming the truth of all his experience, whether at Tipasa or at Djemila. In *The Myth* the neo-Gnostic attitude initially predominates, but Absurdism, as I have argued, carries with it the conviction that the world *should* exemplify the Meaning it denies, and so it remains in a way parasitic on the belief in world order that it rejects. As *The Myth* continues, it switches over to an affirmation of life despite, or in, its absurdity, which is, however, inseparable from a continued revolt against that absurdity. In *The Rebel*, the dialectic between the two attitudes is analysed more explicitly than before, and the false (but also quasi-religious) synthesis—treating rebellion as a stage leading to the creation of a Utopian, totally harmonious world order by human action in the future—is rejected. Already in *The Rebel*, and in the various later essays and fragments that I examined in Chapter 3, the notion of a sacred world order in nature is developed, while Camus continues to struggle to do justice to what is legitimate in the impulse to rebellion, and with the reality of evil in the human heart and suffering in the world.

The accident that killed Camus in 1960 deprived us of his third cycle, except for the fragment of *The First Man*. That by itself shows that he was still at the height of his literary powers; we can only regret deeply the loss both of that novel as a whole, and of the projected Nemesis essay. Camus's greatest work may well still have laid ahead of him; had he lived to complete it, we would have had a very different overall sense of Camus and of the significance of the finished writings that he did leave us. We can be grateful though for what we do have, and for how it can continue to challenge us to take on for ourselves the question of how the trajectory of this thinking can be continued; what responses we can find to the issues that Camus raised with such clarity and honesty.

---

[2] He quotes it even in *The Myth* (*MS* 122); and also in the 'Lecture on ...Tragedy' (*SEN* 199 (*LCE* 304–5)).

Bibliography

Works by Camus

These are cited by the following abbreviations:

CD   *Create Dangerously*, trans. Sandra Smith (New York: Vintage Books, 2019)

CMN   *Christian Metaphysics and Neoplatonism*, trans. Ronald Srigley (Columbia, MO: University of Missouri Press, 2007)

DR   'In Defence of *The Rebel*', in David Sprintzen and Adrian van der Hoven (eds), *Sartre and Camus: A Historic Confrontation* (Atlantic Highlands, NJ: Humanities Press, 2004)

EK   *Exile and the Kingdom*, trans. Carol Cosman (New York: Vintage Books/Random House, 2006)

F.   *The Fall*, trans. Justin O'Brien (New York: Vintage Books/Random House, 1991)

FM   *The First Man*, trans. David Hapgood (London: Hamish Hamilton, 1995)

HD   *A Happy Death*, trans. Richard. Howard (London: Penguin Books, 1973)

LCE   *Lyrical and Critical Essays*, trans. Ellen Conway Kennedy (New York: Vintage Books/Random House,1970)

LE   'Letter to the Editor of *Les Temps Modernes*', in David Sprintzen and Adrian van der Hoven (eds), *Sartre and Camus: A Historic Confrontation* (Atlantic Highlands, NJ: Humanities Press, 2004)

MS   *The Myth of Sisyphus*, trans. Justin O'Brien (New York: Vintage Books/Random House, 1991)

NB I   *Notebooks 1935–42*, trans. Philip Thody (New York: Marlowe and Co., 1996)

NB II   *Notebooks 1942–51*, trans. Justin O'Brien (New York: Marlowe and Co., 1996)

NB III   *Notebooks 1951–59*, trans. Ryan Bloom (Chicago: Ivan R. Dee, 2008)

O.   *The Outsider*, trans. Stuart Gilbert (Harmondsworth: Penguin Books, 1961)

OC iv   *Œuvres completes*, iv. *1957–1959*, ed. Raymond Gay-Crosier et al. (Paris: Gallimard, 2008)

P.   *The Plague*, trans. Robin Buss (London: Penguin Books, 2002)

R.   *The Rebel*, trans. Anthony Bower (New York: Vintage Books/Random House, 1991)

RRD   *Resistance, Rebellion and Death*, trans. Justin O'Brian (New York, Vintage Books, 1960)

SEN   *Selected Essays and Notebooks*, ed. and trans. Philip Thody (London: Penguin Books, 1970)

SO   *Speaking Out: Lectures and Speeches 1937–1958*, trans. Quintin Hoare (New York: Vintage Books, 2022)

Some essays are included in more than one collection; I have quoted from the versions in *SEN* where possible but have also given references to the equivalent passage in *LCE*.

170 BIBLIOGRAPHY

Works by Kierkegaard

I have referred throughout to the complete English edition, *Kierkegaard's Writings*, published by Princeton University Press under the general editorship of Howard and Edna Hong, using the standard sigla.

CA	*The Concept of Anxiety*, trans. R. Thomte (Princeton: Princeton University Press, 1980)
CI	*The Concept of Irony*, trans. H. and E. Hong (Princeton: Princeton University Press, 1989)
CUP i	*Concluding Unscientific Postscript*, i (text), trans. H. and E. Hong (Princeton: Princeton University Press, 1992)
CUP ii	*Concluding Unscientific Postscript*, ii (notes), ed. and trans. H. and E. Hong (Princeton: Princeton University Press, 1992)
E/O i	*Either/Or*, i, trans. H. and E. Hong (Princeton: Princeton University Press, 1987)
E/O ii	*Either/Or*, ii, trans. H. and E. Hong (Princeton: Princeton University Press, 1987)
FT	*Fear and Trembling* (published with *Repetition*), trans. H. and E. Hong (Princeton: Princeton University Press, 1983)
PC	*Practice in Christianity*, trans. H. and E. Hong (Princeton: Princeton University Press, 1991)
PF	*Philosophical Fragments* and *Johannes Climacus*, trans. H. and E. Hong (Princeton: Princeton University Press, 1985)
PV	*The Point of View*, trans. H. and E. Hong (Princeton: Princeton University Press, 1998)
SUD	*The Sickness unto Death*, trans. H. and E. Hong (Princeton: Princeton University Press,1980)
TA	*Two Ages*, trans. H. and E. Hong (Princeton: Princeton University Press, 1978)
UDVS	*Upbuilding Discourses in Various Spirits*, trans. H. and E. Hong (Princeton: Princeton University Press, 1993)
WA	*Without Authority*, trans. H. and E. Hong (Princeton: Princeton University Press, 2009)
WL	*Works of Love*, trans. H. and E. Hong (Princeton: Princeton University Press, 1995)

Works by Other Authors

Adams, Robert, *Finite and Infinite Goods* (Oxford: Oxford University Press, 1999).

Aquinas, St Thomas, *Summa Theologiae*. (The references I give to Parts, Questions, and Articles apply to any edition.)

Anscombe, Elizabeth, 'Modern Moral Philosophy', *Philosophy*, 33/124 (1958), 1–19.

Aron, Raymond, *The Opium of the Intellectuals* (New Brunswick, NJ: Transaction Publishers, 2009).

Aumann, Antony, *Art and Selfhood: A Kierkegaardian Account* (Lanham, MD: Lexington Books, 2019).

Ayer, A. J., 'Albert Camus: Novelist–Philosophers VIII', *Horizon*, 13 (1946), 155–68.

Berg, Eric, 'Albert Camus and Soren Kierkegaard', in Matthew Sharpe, Maciej Kaluza, and Peter Francev (eds), *Brill's Companion to Camus: Camus among the Philosophers* (Leiden and Boston: Brill, 2020), 113–35.

Berthold, Daniel, 'Kierkegaard and Camus: Either/Or?', *International Journal for Philosophy of Religion*, 73/2 (2013), 137–50.

Blackburn, Simon, 'How to Be an Ethical Anti-Realist', in Blackburn, *Essays in Quasi-Realism* (Oxford: Oxford University Press, 1983).

Brewer, Talbot, *The Retrieval of Ethics* (Oxford: Oxford University Press, 2009).

BIBLIOGRAPHY   171

Bunting, Madeline, *Love of Country: A Hebridean Journey* (London: Granta Books, 2016).

Carlsson, Ulrika, 'The Ethical Life of Aesthetes', in Adam Buben, Eleanor Helms, and Patrick Stokes (eds), *The Kierkegaardian Mind* (Abingdon: Routledge, 2019), 135–44.

Caroll, David, *Albert Camus the Algerian: Colonialism, Terrorism, Justice* (New York: Columbia University Press, 2007).

Churchland, Patricia, 'Epistemology in the Age of Neuroscience', *Journal of Philosophy*, 84/10 (1987), 544–53.

Churchland, Paul, 'Eliminative Materialism and the Propositional Attitudes', *Journal of Philosophy*, 78/2 (1981), 67–90.

Crowley, Martin, 'Camus and Social Justice', in Edward Hughes (ed.) *The Cambridge Companion to Camus* (Cambridge: Cambridge University Press, 2007), 93–105.

Cruickshank, John, *Albert Camus and the Literature of Revolt* (New York: Oxford University Press/Galaxy Books, 1960).

Czakó, István, 'Karl Jaspers: A Great Awakener's Way to Philosophy of Existence', in John Stewart (ed.), *Kierkegaard and Existentialism* (Kierkegaard Research: Sources, Reception and Resources, vol. 9: Farnham, Surrey, and Burlington, VT: Ashgate, 2011), 155–98.

Davenport, J., 'The Esthetic Validity of Marriage: Romantic Marriage as a Model for Ethical Will—A Defense of Judge Wilhelm', in Hermann Deuser and Marcus Kleinert (eds), *Kierkegaard's Entweder-Oder [Either/Or] Klassiker Auslegen* (Berlin: De Gruyter, 2017), 169–91.

De Beauvoir, Simone, *Force of Circumstance*, trans. Richard Howard (New York, Putnam's Sons, 1964).

De Beauvoir, Simone, *The Prime of Life*, trans. Peter Green (Harmondsworth: Penguin, 1965).

Del Noce, Augusto, *The Crisis of Modernity*, ed. and trans. Carlo Lancellotti (Montreal: McGill-Queen's University Press, 2015).

Del Noce, Augusto, 'Marx's "Non-Philosophy" and Communism as a Political Reality', in Del Noce, *The Problem of Atheism*, ed. and trans. Carlo Lancellotti (Montreal: McGill-Queen's University Press, 2022), 247–330.

Del Noce, Augusto, 'Marxism and the Qualitative Leap', in Del Noce, *The Problem of Atheism*, ed. and trans. Carlo Lancellotti (Montreal: McGill-Queen's University Press, 2022), 332–59.

Descartes, René, *Discourse on Method* and *Meditations on First Philosophy*, trans. Donald Cress, 4th edn (Indianapolis: Hackett Publishing, 1988).

Dostoevsky, Fyodor, *The Brothers Karamazov*, trans. Richard Pevear and Larissa Volokhonsky (New York: Farrar, Strauss and Giroux, 1990).

Dummett, Michael, *Thought and Reality* (Oxford: Oxford University Press, 2006).

Dunaway, John, 'Estrangement and the Need for Roots: Prophetic Visions of the Human Condition in Albert Camus and Simone Weil', *Religion & Literature*, Summer, 17/2 (1985), 35–42.

Dworkin Ronald, *Justice for Hedgehogs* (Cambridge, MA: Belknap/MIT Press, 2011).

Eshleman, Matthew, review of Ronald Aronson, *Camus and Sartre: The Story of a Friendship and the Quarrel That Ended It*, and David Sprintzen and Adrian van den Hoven (eds), *Sartre and Camus: A Historic Confrontation*, *Journal of French and Francophone Philosophy*, 14/2 (2004), 124–30.

Evans, C. Stephen, *Existentialism: The Philosophy of Despair and the Quest for Hope* (Grand Rapids, MI: Zondervan Publishing, 1984).

Evans, C. Stephen, *Kierkegaard's Ethic of Love: Divine Commands and Moral Obligations* (Oxford: Oxford University Press, 2004).

Evans, C. Stephen, 'Realism and Anti-Realism in Kierkegaard's *Concluding Unscientific Postscript*', in Evans, *Kierkegaard on Faith and the Self: Collected Essays* (Waco, TX: Baylor University Press, 2006), 29–46.

Evans, C. Stephen, *Kierkegaard on Faith and the Self: Collected Essays* (Waco, TX: Baylor University Press, 2006).

Evans, C. Stephen, *God and Moral Obligations* (Oxford: Oxford University Press, 2013).

172 BIBLIOGRAPHY

Ferreira, Jamie, 'One's Own Pastor: Judging the Judge', in Niels Cappelhorn, Hermann Deuser, and Brian Soderquist (eds), *Kierkegaard Studies Yearbook* (Berlin: De Gruyter, 2008), 200–15.

Foley, John, *Albert Camus: From the Absurd to Revolt* (Montreal and Kingston: McGill-Queens University Press, 2008).

Foot, Philippa, *Virtues and Vices and Other Essays in Moral Philosophy* (Oxford: Blackwell, 1978).

Foot, Philippa, *Natural Goodness* (Oxford: Oxford University Press, 2001).

Foucault, Michel, *The Order of Things* (London and New York: Tavistock Publications, 1970).

Frankfurt, Harry, 'Freedom of the Will and the Concept of a Person', in Frankfurt, *The Importance of What We Care About* (Cambridge: Cambridge University Press, 1988), 11–25.

Frankfurt, Harry, 'Identification and Wholeheartedness', in Frankfurt, *The Importance of What We Care About* (Cambridge: Cambridge University Press, 1988), 159–76.

Frankfurt, Harry, *The Reasons of Love* (Princeton: Princeton University Press, 2004).

Fried, Gregory, *Towards a Polemical Ethics: Between Heidegger and Plato* (Lanham, MD, and London: Rowman and Littlefield, 2021).

Friedman, Maurice, *Encounter on the Narrow Ridge: A Life of Martin Buber* (New York: Paragon House, 1991).

Furtak, Rick, *Wisdom in Love: Kierkegaard and the Ancient Quest for Emotional Integrity* (South Bend, IN: University of Notre Dame Press, 2005).

Gillespie, Michael, *Nihilism before Nietzsche* (Chicago: University of Chicago Press, 1995).

Gillespie, Michael, *Nietzsche's Final Teaching* (Chicago: University of Chicago Press, 2017).

Grenberg, Jeanine, *Kant's Defense of Common Moral Experience: A Phenomenological Account* (Cambridge: Cambridge University Press, 2013).

Goss, James, 'Camus, God, and Process Thought', *Process Theology*, 4/2 (1974), 114–28.

Habermas, Jurgen, *Moral Consciousness and Communicative Action*, trans. Christian Lenhardt and Shierry Nicholsen (Cambridge, MA: MIT Press, 1990).

Hannay, Alastair, *Kierkegaard* (London: Routledge, 1982).

Hannay, Alastair, *Kierkegaard and Philosophy: Selected Essays* (London: Routledge, 2006).

Hart, David Bentley, *The Doors of the Sea: Where Was God in the Tsunami?* (Grand Rapids, MI: Wm. B. Eerdmans Publishing Co., 2005).

Hefferman, George, 'Camus and Husserl and the Phenomenologists', in Matthew Sharpe, Maciej Kaluza, and Peter Francev (eds), *Brill's Companion to Camus* (Leiden and Boston: Brill, 2020), 177–98.

Hilderbrandt, Dietrich von, *Ethics*, trans. John Crosby (Steubenville, OH: Hilderbrandt Press, 2020).

Hursthouse, Rosalind, *On Virtue Ethics* (Oxford: Oxford University Press, 1999).

Husserl, Edmund, *Ideas Pertaining to a Pure Phenomenology and to a Phenomenological Philosophy: First Book*, trans. F. Kersten (The Hague: Martinus Nijhoff, 1982).

Ishiguro, Kazuo, *The Buried Giant* (London: Faber, 2015).

James, William, 'The Will to Believe', in James, *Pragmatism and Other Writings*, ed. Giles Gunn (London: Penguin Books, 2000), 198–218.

Jaspers, Karl, *Reason and Existenz*, trans. William Earle (New York: Noonday Press/Farrar, Straus and Giroux, 1955).

Jaspers, Karl, *Philosophy*, i, trans. E. B. Ashton (Chicago: University of Chicago Press, 1969).

Jonas, Hans, 'Gnosticism, Existentialism and Nihilism', in Jonas, *The Gnostic Religion* (London: Routledge, 1992), 320–40.

Judt, Tony, *The Burden of Responsibility: Blum, Camus, Aron, and the French Twentieth Century* (Chicago: Chicago University Press, 1998).

Kaluza, Maciej, 'Camus and his Hegel(s)', in Matthew Sharpe, Maciej Kaluza and Peter Francev (eds), *Brill's Companion to Camus: Camus among the Philosophers* (Leiden and Boston: Brill, 2020), 199–222.

Kant, Immanuel, *Critique of Pure Reason*, trans. Norman Kemp Smith (London: Macmillan, 1933).

Kant, Immanuel, *Groundwork of the Metaphysics of Morals*, trans. Mary Gregor (Cambridge, Cambridge University Press, 1997).

Koestler, Arthur, *The Yogi and the Commissar* (London: Hutchinson and Co., 1965).

Kolakowski, Leszek, *Religion* (London: Fontana, 1982).

Kolakowski, Leszek, *Husserl and the Search for Certitude*, 2nd edn (Chicago: University of Chicago Press, 1987).

Korsgaard, Christine, *The Sources of Normativity* (Cambridge: Cambridge University Press, 1996).

Korsgaard, Christine, *Self-Constitution: Agency, Identity and Integrity* (Oxford: Oxford University Press, 2009).

Lancellotti, Carlo, 'Translator's Introduction', in Augusto Del Noce, *The Crisis of Modernity*, ed. and trans. Lancellotti (Montreal: McGill-Queen's University Press, 2015), ix–xii.

Lannstrom, Anna, *Loving the Fine: Virtue and Happiness in Aristotle's Ethics* (Notre Dame, IN: University of Notre Dame Press, 2006).

Leiter, Brian, *Nietzsche on Morality* (Oxford and New York: Routledge, 2015).

Levinas, Emmanuel, *Totality and Infinity*, trans. Alphonso Lingis (Pittsburgh, PA: Dusquene University Press, 1969).

Levinas, Emmanuel, *Otherwise than Being, or Beyond Essence*, trans. Alphonso Lingis (Pittsburgh, PA: Dusquene University Press, 1998).

Lewis, C. S., *Surprised by Joy* (San Diego and New York: Harcourt, 1955).

Lippitt, John, 'Getting the Story Straight: Kierkegaard, MacIntyre and Some Problems with Narrative', *Inquiry*, 50/1 (2007), 34–69.

Luther, Martin, 'On Secular Authority', in *Luther; Selections from his Writings*, ed. John Dillenberger (New York: Anchor Books/Doubleday, 1961), 363–402.

McBride, Joseph, *Albert Camus: Philosopher and Litterateur* (New York: St Martin's Press, 1992).

McDowell, John, 'Virtue and Reason', in McDowell, *Mind, Value and Reality* (Cambridge, MA: Harvard University Press, 1998).

MacIntyre, Alasdair, *Whose Justice? Which Rationality?* (London: Duckworth, 1988).

MacIntyre, Alasdair, *Dependent Rational Animals: Why Human Beings Need the Virtues* (London: Duckworth, 1999).

MacIntyre, Alasdair, 'First Principles, Final Ends and Contemporary Philosophical Issues', in MacIntyre, The Tasks of Philosophy: *Selected Essays Vol. 1* (Cambridge: Cambridge University Press, 2006), 143–78.

MacIntyre, Alasdair, 'Philosophy Recalled to its Tasks', in MacIntyre, *The Tasks of Philosophy: Selected Essays Vol. 1* (Cambridge: Cambridge University Press, 2006).

MacIntyre, Alasdair, 'Truth as a Good', in MacIntyre, *The Tasks of Philosophy: Selected Essays Vol. 1* (Cambridge: Cambridge University Press, 2006), 197–215.

MacIntyre, Alasdair, *After Virtue*, 3rd edn (Notre Dame, IN: University of Notre Dame Press, 2007).

MacIntyre, Alasdair, *Ethics in the Conflicts of Modernity* (Cambridge: Cambridge University Press, 2016).

McPherson, David, *Virtue and Meaning: A Neo-Aristotelian Perspective* (Cambridge: Cambridge University Press, 2020).

McPherson, David, *The Virtues of Limits* (Oxford: Oxford University Press, 2021).

Marx, Karl, 'Towards a Critique of Hegel's Philosophy of Right: Introduction', in Marx, *Selected Writings*, ed. Lawrence Simon, (Indianapolis: Hackett, 1994), 27–39.

Merleau-Ponty, Maurice, *Phenomenology of Perception*, trans. Donald Landes (Oxford and New York: Routledge, 2012).

Midgely, Mary, Beast and Man: *The Roots of Human Nature* (London: Routledge, 1978).

Mumma, Howard, *Albert Camus and the Minister* (Brewster, MA: Paraclete Press, 2000).

Murchland, Bernard, CSC, 'The Dark Night before the Coming of Grace?', in Germaine Bree (ed.), *Camus: A Collection of Critical Essays* (Engelwood Cliffs, NJ: Prentice Hall, 1962), 59–64.

Murdoch, Iris, *The Sovereignty of Good* (London: Routledge, 1970).

Murdoch, Iris, *Metaphysics as a Guide to Morals* (London: Penguin Books, 1992).

174   BIBLIOGRAPHY

Murdoch, Iris, 'De Beauvoir's *The Ethics of Ambiguity*', in Murdoch, *Existentialists and Mystics: Writings on Philosophy and Literature*, ed. Peter Conradi (London: Chatto and Windus, 1997), 122–24.

Murdoch, Iris, 'The Sublime and the Good', in Murdoch, *Existentialists and Mystics: Writings on Philosophy and Literature*, ed. Peter Conradi (London: Chatto and Windus, 1997), 205–20.

Nagel, Thomas, 'The Absurd', in Nagel, *Mortal Questions* (Cambridge: Cambridge University Press, 1979), 11–23.

Nagel, Thomas, *The View from Nowhere* (Oxford: Oxford University Press, 1986).

Nehamas, Alexander, *Nietzsche: Life as Literature* (Cambridge, MA: Harvard University Press, 1985).

Nygren, Anders, *Agape and Eros*, trans. Philip Watson (New York: Harper, 1969).

Pattison, George, *The Philosophy of Kierkegaard* (London: Acumen, 2005).

Pfau, Thomas, *Minding the Modern* (Notre Dame, IN: University of Notre Dame Press, 2013).

Piety, M. G., *Ways of Knowing: Kierkegaard's Pluralist Epistemology* (Waco, TX: Baylor University Press, 2010)

Plato, *Republic*, trans. Robin Waterfield (Oxford, Oxford University Press, 2008).

Plato, *Symposium*, trans. Alexander Nehemas and Paul Woodruff (Indianapolis: Hackett, 1989).

Putnam, Hilary, *Reason, Truth and History* (Cambridge: Cambridge University Press, 1981).

Putnam, Hilary, *Renewing Philosophy* (Cambridge, MA: Harvard University Press, 1992).

Rawls, John, 'Kantian Constructivism in Moral Theory', *Journal of Philosophy*, 77/9 (1980), 515–72.

Rhein, Philip, *Albert Camus*, rev. edn (Boston, MA: Twayne Publishers, 1989).

Richardson, J., *Nietzsche's System* (Oxford: Oxford University Press, 1996).

Ricoeur, Paul, *Oneself as Another*, trans. Kathleen Blamey (Chicago: University of Chicago Press, 1992).

Rizzuto, Anthony, *Camus' Imperial Vision* (Carbondale, IL: Southern Illinois University Press, 1981).

Rorty, Richard, *Contingency, Irony and Solidarity* (Cambridge: Cambridge University Press, 1989).

Rudd, Anthony, 'Reason in Ethics Revisited: *Either/Or*, Criterionless Choice and Narrative Unity', in Niels Cappelhorn, Hermann Deuser, and Brian Soderquist (eds), *Kierkegaard Studies Yearbook* (Berlin: De Gruyter, 2008), 179–99.

Rudd, Anthony, 'The Skeptics: Kierkegaard and Classical Skepticism', in Jon Stewart and Katalin Nun (eds), *Kierkegaard and the Greek World*, ii. *Aristotle and Other Greek Authors* (Kierkegaard Research: Sources, Reception and Resources, vol. 2; London: Ashgate, 2010), 165–82.

Rudd, Anthony, *Self, Value and Narrative: A Kierkegaardian Approach* (Oxford: Oxford University Press, 2012).

Rudd, Anthony, 'Kierkegaard on the Self, and the Modern Debate on Selfhood', in Jeffrey Hanson and Sharon Krishek (eds), *The Cambridge Companion to Kierkegaard's 'The Sickness Unto Death'* (Cambridge: Cambridge University Press, 2022), 42–60.

Sartre, Jean-Paul, *Existentialism and Humanism*, trans. Philip Mairet (London: Methuen, 1948).

Sartre, Jean-Paul, *Being and Nothingness*, trans. Hazel Barnes (New York: Philosophical Library, 1956).

Sartre, Jean-Paul, *Sartre by Himself*, ed. and trans. R. Seaver (New York, Urizen, 1978).

Sartre, Jean-Paul, 'Reply to Albert Camus', in David Sprintzen and Adrian Van der Hoven (eds), *Sartre and Camus: A Historic Confrontation* (Atlantic Highlands, NJ: Humanities Press, 2004).

Scanlon, T., *What We Owe to Each Other* (Cambridge, MA: Harvard University Press, 1998).

Schopenhauer, Arthur, *The World as Will and Representation*, i, trans. E. F. J. Payne (New York: Dover Publications, 1969).

BIBLIOGRAPHY 175

Scheler, Max, *Formalism in Ethics and the Non-Formal Ethics of Value*, trans. Manfred Frings and Roger Funk (Evanston, IL: Northwestern University Press, 1973).

Sextus Empiricus, *Outlines of Pyrrhonism*, trans. Benson Mates, as *The Skeptic Way* (New York: Oxford University Press, 1996).

Shafer-Landau, Russ, *Moral Realism: A Defence* (Oxford: Oxford University Press, 2003).

Sharpe, Matthew, 'Restoring Camus as *Philosophe*: On Ronald Srigley's *Camus' Critique of Modernity*', *Critical Horizons*, 13/3 (2012), 400–24.

Sharpe, Matthew, *Camus, Philosophe: To Return to our Beginnings* (Boston: Brill, 2015).

Sharpe, Matthew, Maciej Kaluza, and Peter Francev (eds), *Brill's Companion to Camus: Camus among the Philosophers* (Leiden and Boston: Brill, 2020).

Shestov, Lev, *Athens and Jerusalem*, trans. Bernard Martin (Athens, OH: Ohio University Press, 1966).

Sokolowski, Robert, *Introduction to Phenomenology* (Cambridge: Cambridge University Press, 2000).

Solomon, Robert, *Dark Feelings, Grim Thoughts* (Oxford: Oxford University Press, 2006).

Sprintzen, David, *Camus: A Critical Examination* (Philadelphia: Temple University Press, 1988).

Sprintzen, David, and Adrian van der Hoven (eds), *Sartre and Camus: A Historic Confrontation* (Atlantic Highlands, NJ: Humanities Press, 2004).

Srigley, Ronald, *Camus' Critique of Modernity* (Columbia, MO: University of Missouri Press, 2011).

Stan, Leo, 'Albert Camus: Walled within God', in Jon Stewart (ed.), *Kierkegaard and Existentialism* (Kierkegaard Research: Sources, Reception and Resources, vol, 9; Farnham, Surrey, and Burlington, VT: Ashgate, 2011), 63–94.

Strawson, Galen, 'Real Materialism', in Strawson, *Real Materialism and Other Essays* (Oxford: Oxford University Press, 2008), 19–52.

Street, Sharon, 'Coming to Terms with Contingency: Humean Constructivism about Practical Reason' in James Lenman and Yonatan Shemmer (eds), *Constructivism in Practical Philosophy* (Oxford: Oxford University Press, 2012), 40–59.

Taylor, Charles, *Sources of the Self* (Cambridge: Cambridge University Press, 1989).

Tiswald, Justin, and Bryan Van Norden (eds), *Readings in Later Chinese Philosophy* (Indianapolis: Hackett, 2014).

Todd, Olivier, *Albert Camus: A Life*, trans. Benjamin Ivry (London: Vintage/Random House, 1998).

Trawny, Peter, *Freedom to Fail: Heidegger's Anarchy*, trans. Ian Moore and Christopher Turner (Cambridge: Polity Press, 2015).

Turner, Jeffrey, 'To Tell a Good Tale: Kierkegaardian Reflections on Moral Narrative and Moral Truth' in John Davenport and Anthony Rudd (eds), *Kierkegaard after MacIntyre* (Chicago: Open Court, 2001), 39–57.

Weil, Simone, *Gravity and Grace*, trans. Emma Craufurd (London: Routledge and Kegan Paul, 1963).

Weil, Simone, 'Reflections on the Right Use of School Studies with a View to the Love of God', in Weil, *Waiting on God*, trans. Emma Craufurd (New York: Harper and Row, 1973), 105–16.

Weil, Simone, 'Forms of the Implicit Love of God', in Weil, *Waiting on God*, trans. Emma Craufurd (New York: Harper and Row, 1973), 137–215.

Weil, Simone, 'The *Iliad*, or the Poem of Force', trans. Mary McCarthy, in Sian Miles (ed.), *The Simone Weil Reader* (London: Virago, 1986).

Wietzke, Walter, 'Narrativity and Normativity', in John Lippitt and Patrick Stokes (eds), *Narrative, Identity, and the Kierkegaardian Self* (Edinburgh: Edinburgh University Press, 2015).

Williams, Bernard, *Descartes: The Project of Pure Inquiry* (Harmondsworth: Penguin, 1978).

Williams, Bernard, 'Persons, Character and Morality', in Williams, *Moral Luck* (Cambridge: Cambridge University Press, 1981), 1–19.

Williams, Bernard, *Ethics and the Limits of Philosophy* (Cambridge, MA: Harvard University Press, 1985).

Woelfel, James, *Camus: A Theological Perspective* (Nashville and New York: Abingdon Press, 1975).

Young, Julian, 'Death and Transfiguration: Kant, Schopenhauer and Heidegger on the Sublime', *Inquiry*, 48 (2005) 131–44.

Young, Julian, *Nietzsche's Philosophy of Religion* (Cambridge: Cambridge University Press, 2006).

Zaretsky, Robert, *Albert Camus: Elements of a Life* (Ithaca, NY, and London: Cornell University Press, 2011).

Index

For the benefit of digital users, indexed terms that span two pages (e.g., 52–53) may, on occasion, appear on only one of those pages.

Absurd, the; Absurdity, 15–16, 23–58; *see also* Absurdism; Absurdist

Absurdism; Absurdist, 7–9, 16–20, 28–33, 36–74, 127–128, 152–154; *see also* Absurd, the; Absurdity

Adams, Robert, 73–74 nn.41–42

Algeria, 21 n.69, 40–41 n.60, 59, 93–94, 105–106, 122, 131

Anscombe, Elizabeth, 112–113 n.27

Aquinas, St. Thomas, 106–107, 144–145 n.141, 146–147 n.146

Aristotle, 62, 112–115, 146–147 n.146

Aron, Raymond, 38, 96–97 n.105

Aumann, Antony, 148–149 n.152

Ayer, A.J., 47

Bakunin, Mikael, 97–98 n.109

Berg, Eric, 2 n.5, 16

Berlin, Isaiah, 102–103 n.120

Berthold, Daniel, 25–26

Blackburn, Simon, 76–77 n.50

Brewer, Talbot, 112–113 n.27

Buber, Martin, 70 n.31

Buddhism, 121 n.61

Bunting, Madeline, 123 n.70

Camus, Albert
  Status as philosopher, 1–3
  And Existentialism, *see* Existentialism
  And classical Greek culture, 1–2, 18–20, 45–46, 62–71, 80, 83–88, 112–122, 135–140, 146–148
  Literary works of, *see* On literature and literary style
  Political engagements of, 21–22, 71, 80–108, 123–124, 145–146
  "cycles", 15–17, 18–19, 104–105, 116–117
  Attitudes to his own writings, 4–9
  And religion, *see* Religion
  On the absurd, *see* Absurd, the; Absurdity; Absurdism; Absurdist
  On knowledge and its limits, 23–30

  On morality (ethics), 36–37, 50, 63–66, 73–77, 92–95, 100–103, 106–115, 160–162 *see also* On the ethical
  And Gnosticism, *see* Gnosticism, Gnostics
  On the sacred, *see* Sacred, the
  On slave revolt, 62–63, 67
  On the ethical, 105–115 *see also* On morality (ethics)
  And Levinas, *see* Levinas, Emmanuel
  And Foucault, *see* Foucault, Michel
  And postmodernism, *see* Postmodernism
  On Metaphysical Rebellion, *see* Rebellion, Metaphysical
  Critique of Nietzsche, 18, 82–83
  Critique of Marxism, 18, 82–83
  Quarrel with Sartre, 21, 89–90, 93 n.95
  On Stalinism, 85–86 n.77, 93–97
  On syndicalism, 97–98
  On humanism, 59–60, 81–82, 102–103, 134, 161–162
  On atheism, 19–20, 32–33, 45–46, 69, 72–74, 81–82, 101–103, 129, 132
  On human nature, 12–13, 18, 39, 62–65, 68, 80, 98–102, 108–121, 151, 157–158
  Hellenism of, 68–70, 120–121, 167
  On moderation and limit, 69, 98–100, 113, 116–119, 123–130, 140–141, 146–149
  On love, 40–42, 43–44, 105–108, 127–138, 144–148, 164
  On nature and natural order, 41–44, 82–88
  On literature and literary style, 1–8
  On tragedy, *see* Tragedy
  On human goodness and evil, 68–74, 94–103, 134–145, 151–154

Carlsson, Ulrika, 10 n.33

Caroll, David, 21 n.69

Churchland, Patricia, 42–43 n.66

Churchland, Paul, 42–43 n.66

Christianity, 18–20, 32–37, 46–47, 67–71, 86–88, 119–122, 132–133, 135–137, 143–144, 146–148, 157, 161–162, 163–164, 167–168

Clamence, Jean-Baptiste (Camus character), 113–114, 123, 151, 155–166

Communism, 21, 84–86, 96–98, 152
Confucianism, 39–40
Crowley, Martin, 95 n.100
Cruickshank, John, 7–8 n.25, 45–46 n.75
Czako, Istvan, 123–124 n.71

Davenport, John, 100 n.117
De Beauvoir, Simone, 38, 93–94
Del Noce, Augusto, 86–87
Descartes, Rene, 5, 7–8, 60–61
Dostoevsky, Fyodor, 2, 32–34, 50, 55–56, 72,
    78–81, 132–133 n.99
Dummett, Michael, 30–31 n.34
Dunaway, John, 117–118 n.44
Dworkin Ronald, 75

Empiricism, Empiricist, 30–31, 33–34, 40–41,
    47–50, 63, 77–79, 144
Eshleman, Matthew, 108
Essence, essentialism, 30–31, 39–40, 62, 63–65,
    74–75, 80, 108–110, 114–115, 124–125
Evans, C. Stephen, 4–5 n.13, 73–74 nn.41–42,
    124–125 n.73, 156–157
Existentialism, 3, 18, 80, 82–83 n.71, 156

Fascism, 81–82 n.65, 84–85, 86–87, 122
Ferreira, Jamie, 100 n.117
Foley, John, 21 n.69, 23–24, 64–65
Foot, Philippa, 112–113 n.27, 114–115, 114–115
    n.34, n.37
Francev, Peter, 1 n.3
Frankfurt, Harry, 79–80
Fried, Gregory, 91
Friedman, Maurice, 70 n.31
Foucault, Michel, 26, 64–65
Furtak, Rick, 100 n.117

Gillespie, Michael, 79 n.53, 81–82 n.65
Gnosticism, Gnostics, 19–20, 47–48, 57–58,
    68–70, 74–75, 119–121, 134–137, 140–141
    n.126, 167–168
Grenberg, Jeanine, 63 n.9
Grenier, Jean, 121 n.61, 131
Goss, James, 126–127

Habermas, Jurgen, 75
Hannay, Alastair, 4–5 n.13
Hart, David Bentley, 135–136
Hefferman, George, 38 n.52
Hegel, G.W.F., 25, 29–30, 85–92, 108, 124–125,
    139–141, 152–154
Hegelianism, 12–13, 15–16 n.54, 87–90, 98–99
    n.113, 110–111, 141

Heidegger, Martin, 33–34, 90–92, 110–111 n.26,
    150–151
Heraclitus, 91–92 n.90, 116, 125
Hilderbrandt, Dietrich von, 75–76 n.49
Hinduism, Hindus, 121 n.61, 131
Historicism, 86–92, 110–111, 121
Hitler, Adolf, 84–86, 117, 161 n.192
Hursthouse, Rosalind, 114
Husserl, Edmund, 37–40, 48, 63, 73–74 n.43

Immortality, 32–33, 46–47, 78, 129, 144–146
Ishiguro, Kazuo, 123 n.69
Islam, 68–69, 122

James, William, 45–47
Jaspers, Karl, 28–34, 123–124
Jonas, Hans, 91–92
Judt, Tony, 156 n.170

Kaluza, Maciej, 1 n.3, 89–90
Kant, Immanuel, 12–13, 25–27, 63, 75 nn.47–48,
    91–92 n.90, 110
Kierkegaard, Soren
    As philosopher, 4–9
    Literary techniques, 1–8
    Pseudonymity, 3–19, 34–36, 65–66, 69, 100,
        148–149, 159, 167
    As religious thinker, 16–19
    On appropriation, 4–6, 153–154, 159
    Use of indirect communication, 4–6, 148–149
        n.152, 159
    On the stages of life, 4, 10–17, 65–66
    On the aesthetic, 10–20, 36–37, 54–55, 59–60,
        65–67, 86, 107–108, 132–133, 147–149, 167
    On the ethical, 10–21, 35–37, 60, 67, 101–102,
        132–133, 146–151
    On the religious, 10, 13–22, 34–37, 59–60, 67,
        86, 100–103
    On the self, 4, 12–13, 17–18, 82–83, 90,
        111–112, 167
    On knowledge, 23–30
    On scepticism, 24–28
    On Christianity, see Christianity
    On sin and guilt, 14–15, 36–37, 152–153, 159,
        165
Koestler, Arthur, 97
Kojeve, Alexandre, 89–90
Kolakowski, Leszek, 30–31 n.34, 39–40 n.57
Korsgaard, Christine, 75, 79–80

Lancellotti, Carlo, 86–87 n.80
Lannstrom, Anna, 114–115
Leiter, Brian, 82–83 n.71, 87–88 n.82
Lenin, Vladimir, 84–85 n.76

INDEX   179

Levinas, Emmanuel, 63–64
Lewis, C.S., 123 n.68
Lippitt, John, 10 n.33
Luther, Martin, 95, 143

MacIntyre, Alasdair, 30–31 n.34, 62 n.6,
   106–107, 112–113 n.27, 114, 160–161 n.188
McBride, Joseph, 7–8 n.25
McDowell, John, 112–113 n.27
McPherson, David, 79 n.52, 112–113 n.27, 115
   n.37, 116–117 n.43
Marx, Karl, 18, 70–71, 81–82, 85–88, 90–92,
   108–110, 154, 157
Marxism, 81–82, 85–88, 96–98, 102–103 n.120,
   110–111, 120–121
Martin du Gard, Roger, 145–146
Mediterranean, the, 97–98, 121–123, 162–163
Merleau-Ponty, Maurice, 39 nn.54–56, 150–151
Meursault (Camus character), 6–7, 18–19,
   46–47, 56–57, 103, 123, 145–146, 152
Midgely, Mary, 112–113 n.27
Mumma, Howard, 18–19 n.66
Murchland, Bernard, CSC, 156–157
Murdoch, Iris, 92–93 n.94, 112–113 n.27,
   127–128, 164 n.198
Mussolini, Benito, 84–85

Nagel, Thomas, 44, 142 n.131
Nazism, 61, 84–85, 110 n.21, 154
Nehamas, Alexander, 82–83 n.71
Nietzsche, Friedrich, 2–3, 18–20, 28–29, 55–56,
   81–92, 104–110, 114–115 n.35, 136–137,
   139–140, 144, 151, 154, 156–157
Nygren, Anders, 147–148 n.149

Parein, Brice, 29–30
Pattison, George, 4–5 n.13
Pfau, Thomas, 79 n.53
Piety, M.G., 25 n.5
Plato, 1, 29–30, 36–38, 62, 73–74, 79, 91,
   109–114, 117–120, 124–125, 136–138,
   147–148, 153–154 n.166
Plotinus, 119–121, 136–137 n.109, 137–138
   n.113
Phenomenology, 37–40, 63–65, 75, 99–100
Popper, Karl, 85–86, 102–103 n.120
Postmodernism, 82–83 n.71
Putnam, Hilary, 30–31 n.34

Rawls, John, 75
Rebellion (Revolt), 9, 12, 19–20, 23, 59–108,
   134–142, 167–168
Rebellion, Historical, 18–20, 71, 80–81, 134–135

Rebellion, Metaphysical, 9, 18–20, 56–57, 67–83,
   134–137, 139, 144, 148–149, 167–168
Religion, 18–21, 50, 68–71, 84–85, 101–103,
   128–135
Rhein, Philip, 151–152, 157
Ricoeur, Paul, 63–64 nn.15–16
Rieux, Dr. (Camus character), 6–7, 72–73,
   154–155
Rizzuto, Anthony, 56–57
Rorty, Richard, 47, 77–80
Rudd, Anthony, 10 n.33, 17–18 n.64, 27–28
   nn.17–18, 65–66 n.24, 74–75 nn.44–46,
   79–80 n.57, 115 n.37

Sacred, the, 69–71, 74–75, 83–84, 90, 101–102,
   106–107, 129–140, 167–168
Sartre, Jean-Paul, 1–3, 7–8 n.28, 18, 21, 24 n.4,
   30–31 n.36, 38–39, 43–44, 62–63, 64–65,
   80–99, 108–111, 113–114 n.31, 124–125,
   139, 154, 156, 158–159, 164–165
Scanlon, T.M., 75
Science, 3–4, 23–24, 26–27 n.15, 30–31 n.34,
   38–39, 42–43, 48–49, 76, 124–127
Schopenhauer, Arthur, 137–139
Scheler, Max, 75–76 n.49
Self-creation, 79–92, 99–100, 109–110, 123–124
Self-divinisation, 79–81, 155–156
Sextus Empiricus, 28 n.22
Shafer-Landau, Russ, 74–75 n.44
Sharpe, Matthew, 1–3, 20–21, 26–27, 113,
   126–127, 157–158
Shestov, Lev, 32–38, 82–83 n.72
Socrates, Socratic, 36–37, 117–118, 146–147
   n.147, 152–154, 159
Sokolowski, Robert, 38 n.51
Solomon, Robert, 156–158
Sophocles, 167–168
Spinoza, Baruch, 124–125
Sprintzen, David, 86–87, 93 n.95, 108 n.16
Srigley, Ronald, 1–2, 2–3 n.7, 7–8 n.25, 20–21,
   48–49, 69–70, 157, 163–164
Stalin, Josef, 85–86, 91–92 n.92, 93–98, 161
   n.192, 164–165
Stan, Leo, 2 n.5, 35–36 n.43
Stoicism, 74–75, 106
Strawson, Galen, 42–43 n.66
Street, Sharon, 76–77 n.50

Taylor, Charles, 28 n.23, 52–53
Todd, Olivier, 1, 121 n.61
Tragedy, 21 n.69, 86, 132–133, 137–142,
   146–147, 167–168
Trawny, Peter, 91–92 n.90
Turner, Jeffrey, 100 n.117

Van Gogh, Vincent, 137–138

Weil, Simone, 63–64 n.14, 70, 117–119, 120–121 n.60, 127–128, 149, 164
Whitehead, A.N., 127 n.79
Wietzke, Walter, 100 n.117
Williams, Bernard, 12, 30–31 n.34, 160–161 n.188

Wittgenstein, Ludwig, 1
Woelfel, James, 129–131

Young, Julian, 82–83 n.73, 92, 145–146 n.144

Zaretsky, Robert, 21 n.69
Zhu Xi, 39–43